IDIOT'S GUIDES.
AS EASY AS IT GETS!

Introductory
Accounting

by David H. Ringstrom, CPA, and Gail Perry, CPA, with Lisa A. Bucki

ALPHA

A member of Penguin Random House LLC

Publisher: Mike Sanders
Associate Publisher: Billy Fields
Managing Editor: Lori Cates Hand
Cover Designer: Lindsay Dobbs
Book Designer: William Thomas
Compositor: Ayanna Lacey
Proofreader: Michelle Melani
Indexer: Tonya Heard

First American Edition, 2016
Published in the United States by DK Publishing
6081 E. 82nd Street, Indianapolis, Indiana 46250

Copyright © 2016 Dorling Kindersley Limited
A Penguin Random House Company
16 17 18 19   10 9 8 7 6 5 4 3 2 1
001-289047-February2016

ISBN: 9781615648870
Library of Congress Catalog Card Number: 2015943281

Note: This publication contains the opinions and ideas of its author(s). It is intended to provide helpful and informative material on the subject matter covered. It is sold with the understanding that the author(s) and publisher are not engaged in rendering professional services in the book. If the reader requires personal assistance or advice, a competent professional should be consulted. The author(s) and publisher specifically disclaim any responsibility for any liability, loss, or risk, personal or otherwise, which is incurred as a consequence, directly or indirectly, of the use and application of any of the contents of this book.

Trademarks: All terms mentioned in this book that are known to be or are suspected of being trademarks or service marks have been appropriately capitalized. Alpha Books, DK, and Penguin Random House LLC cannot attest to the accuracy of this information. Use of a term in this book should not be regarded as affecting the validity of any trademark or service mark.

DK books are available at special discounts when purchased in bulk for sales promotions, premiums, fund-raising, or educational use. For details, contact: DK Publishing Special Markets, 345 Hudson Street, New York, New York 10014 or SpecialSales@dk.com.

Printed and bound in the United States of America

idiotsguides.com

Contents

Appendixes

Introduction

To use a sports analogy, accounting can be thought of as a way of keeping score within your business. Unlike a baseball game that results in a final score at the end, you're going to have multiple scores to keep track of in your business. For instance, how much cash do you have on hand? How much do your customers owe you? How much do you owe your vendors? How much have you spent on various aspects of your business? This scorekeeping is typically done on a calendar-month and calendar-year basis.

But now that much of accounting work is done with the help of a computer, you can easily keep score on a weekly or daily basis, or even in real time throughout the day.

In short, the main thing to remember is that accounting is what helps you learn about how your business is doing. How much information you want and how often you want it is up to you. This book helps you learn how to get the information (or the score, if you will).

In *Idiot's Guides: Introductory Accounting,* we teach you how to know if your business is meeting your expectations and how your understanding of the basic accounting procedures can make you more successful. You also learn about the tools and best practices that help you keep your accounting scorecard accurate and up to date.

With easy-to-understand, "plain English" language and helpful examples from a variety of accounting software programs (rather than recommend a specific program), we break down the sometimes-complicated fundamentals of accounting so you can ensure your books balance.

How This Book Is Organized

This book is divided into six parts, each dealing with a different aspect of accounting.

Part 1, Laying the Groundwork, leads off with key accounting terminology you'll encounter throughout the book. It also explains fundamental accounting concepts, such as how T accounts help you balance transactions and what types of transactions you'll perform as part of your ongoing accounting routine. Part 1 also walks you through what you need to know from an accounting perspective when you start your business. We look at choosing the best legal structure, handling the cash invested in the business; choosing an accounting method; and filing the right documentation with federal, state, and local authorities.

Part 2, Doing the Books, covers all the core activities you need to perform to set up your business's accounting system, including choosing accounting software, identifying account categories and setting up a chart of accounts, setting up for and tracking inventory, handling day-to-day transactions in your accounting software and online, working with the general ledger, and reconciling statements. Armed with the information in Part 2, you easily can run the day-to-day accounting activities for your business.

Part 3, Employee-Related Accounting, provides need-to-know information about employees and related accounting decisions and activities. We start by helping with decisions and steps with regard to any new team member you take on. From there, you learn about insurance and retirement plans, their impact on your business accounting, and the ins and outs of payroll taxes. This part should help you hire and manage employee compensation and taxes with confidence.

Part 4, Financial Reporting, looks at the various types of reports you should generate with your accounting software and how to use them. We show you reports that zero in on particular areas such as accounts receivable and accounts payable, as well as reports that focus on the big picture for the business: income statement, balance sheet, and statement of cash flow. A chapter also explores best security practices for your accounting information. By the end of Part 4, you'll understand how these reports help with business decision-making and communication with business stakeholders.

In **Part 5, Monthly, Quarterly, and Annual Activities,** you learn about and plan for activities you need to perform at specified times, either as business best practices or for regulatory and tax compliance reasons. You look at how and when to close the books and report employee and vendor tax information. Part 5 also covers the necessary personal tax returns and concludes with guidelines for keeping records for these and other accounting activities.

Part 6, Data Analysis and Forecasting, shows you how to use other software tools to supplement your accounting system. You discover how a spreadsheet program can help you perform activities not found in spreadsheets, starting with building a simple amortization schedule. Then we dive deeper into how a spreadsheet can help with budgeting and other forecasting.

Extras

Throughout this book, we offer four types of additional information, set apart in sidebars, to help enrich what you're learning. Here's what to look for:

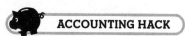

These sidebars share tips and tricks for more effective accounting.

Look here for further technical information or key ideas or practices to supplement what you're learning.

DEFINITION

Specialized accounting terms are italicized in the main part of the text and defined in these sidebars.

RED FLAG

When there's something discussed in the text that you might misunderstand, or some typical trap you might want to avoid, we highlight it in one of these sidebars.

Online Extras

As a bonus to this book, we've included additional tons of information on helpful accounting apps and software, key business forms, a small business tax and form calendar, and a handy accounting workbook online. Point your browser to idiotsguides.com/introductoryaccounting, and enjoy!

Acknowledgments

This book represents a culmination of knowledge I've accumulated over the course of my consulting career. As such, several people come to mind who have helped me along the way at critical junctures. I didn't initially plan to become a CPA, but Greg Chapin kept encouraging me until I prepared for and sat for the exam. Not long after, Stuart Vessels noticed me back on CompuServe in the mid-1990s, answering questions about Lotus 1-2-3, which led to my start as a freelance writer. Later, Chris Downing saw an article I wrote and invited me to teach Excel classes for a department of a local university. A critical milestone was when my co-author Gail Perry invited me to write for a website aimed at accountants. Writing for Gail ultimately led to the remarkable teaching career I enjoy today, as well as this book. I could write for days about the many people who have helped and encouraged me over the years, but first and foremost my wife, Erin, has stood beside me from the beginning. I also want to thank co-author Lisa Bucki for her significant contributions. Thank you to David Conley for checking our work and being a sounding board to me over the years. Finally, thank you to the team at Alpha Books, especially Lori Hand, who all have been so kind to this first-time author. —David Ringstrom

I've known and worked with co-author David Ringstrom for several years, and every collaboration we have had has resulted in a positive experience and outstanding results, so I am profoundly grateful to him for joining me on this project and taking the lead on so much of it. My association with Lisa Bucki dates way back to 1995 when I wrote my second book, *The Complete Idiot's Guide to Doing Your Income Taxes*. Lisa was my associate publisher and went out of her way to teach me the ropes of the book-writing business, and I'm so glad to have a chance to work with her again on this project. Thanks also to tech reviewer David Conley, managing editor Lori Hand, and all other parties who helped get this book into its final form. Finally, thank you to you readers, who have invested both time and money in this book. We wrote it for you. —Gail Perry

Special Thanks to the Technical Reviewer

Idiot's Guides: Introductory Accounting was reviewed by an expert who double-checked the accuracy of what's presented here to help us ensure learning accounting is as easy as it gets. Special thanks are extended to David Conley, CPA.

Laying the Groundwork

You can't really grow a successful business without having a handle on how the business is doing financially. Yet accounting can be a daunting topic for many business owners, who might find it too jargony and math- or rule-intensive. Even if you have the resources to hire a full-time book-keeper and consult with a CPA, you need to understand accounting concepts to ensure you can keep your company's accounting processes on track and your business financially healthy.

Part 1 guides you as you take your first steps into handling or managing the accounting for your business. In the following chapters, we teach you about basic accounting terminology and con-cepts and then review the basic accounting considerations at the point where you start your business, including selecting a structure for the business, choosing an accounting method, and handling all the paperwork needed to make the company official.

How Accounting Works

Every profession has its own seemingly cryptic vocabulary and ground rules, and accounting is no different. Almost every business owner needs to know the fundamentals of accounting in order to make sound business decisions, so in this chapter, we start by providing translations for the most important terms and concepts in accounting, laying the foundation for what you learn in later chapters.

In This Chapter

- Demystifying accounting terms and concepts
- Visualizing the accounting process with T accounts
- Examples of typical accounting transactions

Accounting Simplified

Accounting is a means of keeping score within your business, but unlike a lopsided baseball game, the numbers that represent the score for your business must balance.

A common formula that represents both elements is *assets – liabilities = equity*. As you'll read later in this book, assets are items your business owns, while liabilities are amounts you owe to others. What's left over is sometimes referred to as *capital, equity,* or the *net worth* of a business. Every transaction that affects your books affects the A – L = E formula. The components of this formula are represented on a report known as a balance sheet. Simply put, it's the scorecard for what you own, what you owe, and your financial stake in the business.

Here's another way to think of it: you might have a $100 bill in your pocket; that's an asset. You owe your friend $20 for lunch; that's a liability. So you have equity (capital) of $80. However, your brother owes you $10, so your total assets are $110 and your net equity is $90.

Accounting transactions themselves are broken down into a series of debits and credits. Don't panic if this sounds like a foreign language to you, as we'll be walking you through all the ins and outs, as well as sharing a helpful tool known as T accounts. T accounts help you visually break down an accounting transaction into the various components that affect your accounting records, or your books. Once you can fit the transaction into T account format, you're ready to record the transaction in your books.

We also provide an overview of some typical accounting transactions you'll encounter, with much more detail to follow later in the book.

Accounting Terminology and Concepts

The fundamental aspects of accounting, called principals, have been developed over a series of centuries. Any accounting work you do for your business is not solely for your own benefit. As you'll see later in the book, even if you're the sole owner of your business, you're far from the sole stakeholder. Lenders, tax agencies, customers, vendors, employees—all have an interest in your success.

Accounting conventions ensure everyone's books are kept in the same fashion. This enables governmental agencies to compare your books to similar businesses to decide if your financial results make sense. The structure also gives you a clear understanding of what your business owns, what it owes, and what capital it has that can be distributed to you or reinvested into your business.

There's a cause-and-effect aspect to accounting. If you buy pizza for a staff meeting, the cause is you've boosted employee morale, but the effect is you've reduced your cash on hand and recorded an expense on your books. It's important to understand that there are at least two sides to every accounting transaction. Your pizza purchase increased an expense and reduced your cash account.

It's not always one account goes up and another goes down, though. Let's say a customer pays you for a service. In this case, your cash account goes up and your sales go up as well.

Figuring it all out can feel bewildering at first, but as you gain an understanding of the structure of accounting, concepts that might feel like a constraint actually help you ensure you're correctly tracking the financial aspects of your business.

Books and Accounts

A big part of accounting is keeping a historical record of your transactions. Accountants often refer to this as the *books* for a business, a term left over from when those books were actual books. Today, the books typically appear on your computer screen.

Most of your accounting transactions record money changing hands between your business and other parties. Later we also discuss some noncash transactions that are important to your business.

The most basic element of accounting is *accounts*. Accounts are the various categories that describe the types of financial activity that exist in your business.

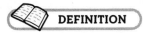 **DEFINITION**

In this context, **books** refers to a set of accounting records. And we'll get into the specifics of **accounts** later in this book, but for now, think of them as buckets in which you store the value of things you own or owe as well as things you've earned or spent money on.

Some accounts are for tracking what you own or are owed. For instance, a cash account reflects how much money you have in the bank. Other accounts reflect what you've earned or spent. If you're in the pet boarding business, for example, you might have one or more revenue accounts that keep track of the boarding fees your customers have paid you. You also might have multiple expense accounts to keep track of pet-related expenses such as pet food, waste disposal, and veterinarian fees. Each one of these items is a separate account. If you're in the catering business, you might have expense accounts for food, serving dishes, cookbooks, and so on.

Debits and Credits

Accounting uses a standard *double-entry system* in which the sum total of *debits* and *credits* balance each other. For example, writing a check to a supplier might result in several debits to different expense accounts and one credit to reduce the balance of your cash account. Every transaction you record to your accounting records has to balance.

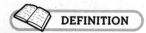

> **DEFINITION**
>
> A traditional accounting ledger has at least four columns: date, description, and two amount columns. This **double-entry system** requires that the entries or amounts in each column balance each other. **Debits** are amounts that appear in the left amount column and record changes in value. Depending on context, they might increase or decrease the value of an account. **Credits** also record changes in value and typically appear in the right column of an accounting ledger. Credits might also increase or decrease the value of an account. Beginning accounting students are often taught "Debits on the left; credits on the right."

Why the need for balance? Because every normal business transaction affects both the balance sheet and income statement. A cash sale, for example, increases Cash (a balance sheet account) and increases Sales (an income statement account) in equal amounts.

To help you wrap your head around this debits and credits concept, imagine you need some paperclips and a couple binders. You head over to the office supply store and purchase $10 worth of office supplies. Your Office Supplies account now has a value of $10, the amount you spent. To balance that $10, your Cash account now has a value of $10 less than whatever it was before you went to the store.

Assets and Liabilities

Much of the confusion people have with accounting can be attributed to their monthly bank statement. You'll see accounting transactions that debit your account for checks, ATM withdrawals, and fees along with credits that reflect deposits and transfers into your account. The problem comes in when, on your accounting records, you record the mirror image of these transactions.

Let's look at an example:

- You receive payment from a customer. In your accounting records, you debit (increase) your Cash account and credit (another increase) your Revenue account.

- You take the check to the bank to deposit it. Your banker credits your checking or savings account (an increase) and debits the bank's Cash account (another increase).

In your books, your Cash account is an *asset*. In your banker's books, that same account that contains your money is a *liability*. In other words, you're simply allowing the bank to hold your money temporarily; technically, the bank owes you that money.

 **DEFINITION**

From a financial accounting perspective, **assets** are items of value your business owns or is owed, such as cash, Accounts Receivable (unpaid customer invoices), inventory, vehicles, real estate, etc. A **liability** is an amount you owe to others. This could be unpaid bills (Accounts Payable), payroll taxes, sales tax you've collected and owe the state government, bank loans, mortgages, etc.

The source of so much confusion in your initial exposure to accounting is your bank reporting, "Here's what we did on our books," which is the exact mirror image of how you record transactions on your books for your business.

T Accounts

A T account isn't a type of account in your books, but rather a device you use for visualizing how to record an accounting transaction. You won't use T accounts very often, but they can come in handy.

As mentioned earlier, accounting primarily centers around two amount columns, debits on the left and credits on the right, and the sum of both columns has to match. If you're trying to figure out how to record a transaction, T accounts can help.

How T Accounts Work

To explain T accounts, let's first take a look at a simple example of how they work. Say you receive $100 as a payment from a customer. You increase Cash (it's a debit, by the way) by $100, and increase Revenue (a credit) by $100. Your T account for Cash shows $100 on the left in the debit column. (Cash is an asset, and increases to asset accounts are debits. We discuss this more later.)

Now you need a T account that balances this debit with a credit (right column). The T account for your Revenue shows $100 on the right. (Revenue accounts are increased with credits.) You've got $100 on the left and $100 on the right in your two T accounts, so they're in balance.

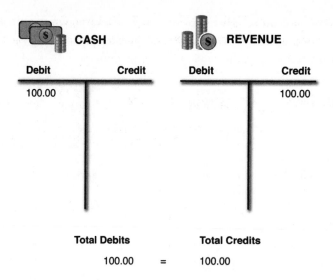

The $100 debit in the Cash T account balances the $100 credit in the Revenue T account.

Using T Accounts

Let's look at some more typical examples of how T accounts help you determine how to record a transaction, particularly when more than two accounts are involved. For purposes of these transactions, let's assume you're using accounting software and not writing down each transaction in a traditional ledger book. (See Chapter 3 for more information on accounting software options.)

Say you finance the purchase of a delivery truck for your business. This seemingly simple transaction touches multiple accounts on your books. Your truck costs $30,000, and you make a $5,000 down payment. When updating your books, you need to record that you used some of your cash, that you now own a truck, and that you also owe $25,000 on it. But what do you debit, and what do you credit? That's where T accounts cut through the confusion.

You need to record changes to three accounts:

- Your Cash account (in accounting vernacular, an asset account because we own the cash)

- A Vehicles account (another asset account because your business owns the truck)

- A Loan account (a liability account because your business owes the loan amount)

So you need three T accounts, Cash, Vehicles, and Truck Loan. On a blank piece of paper, draw your three T accounts, making them large enough you can write numbers on either side of the T.

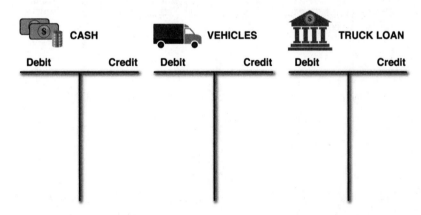

T accounts provide a framework you can use to break down an accounting transaction into its elements and ensure your debits and credits balance.

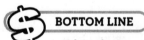 **BOTTOM LINE**

Taking the time to write out T accounts helps ensure you enter the transaction correctly in your accounting software. Remember that the sum of all amounts written on the left side of a T must balance with the amounts written on the right side of another T. Each T represents a separate account in your books or accounting software.

Now that you have your framework, you can begin to record the purchase. Debits (left-side entries) always increase asset accounts and reduce liability accounts, while credits (right-side entries) reduce asset accounts and increase liability accounts.

Here's how to record your transaction:

1. You wrote a check for $5,000, which reduced your Cash account. Write 5,000 in the right Credit column of the Cash T account.

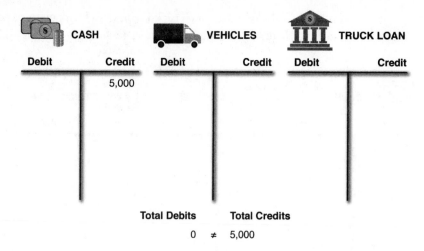

Increases to the Cash account go on the left side of the T; decreases go on the right.

2. Your business now owns a $30,000 delivery truck, which is an increase in assets. Write 30,000 in the left Debit column of the Vehicles T.

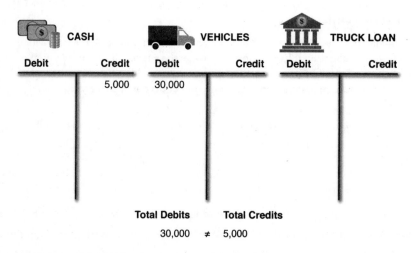

Increases to the Vehicles account go on the left side of the T; decreases go on the right.

3. You know the sum of your debits and credits must match at the end, but so far, you have a $30,000 debit and a $5,000 credit. You still need to record a $25,000 credit to get the transaction to balance. The last piece of your transaction is to record the $25,000 your business borrowed to purchase the truck. Enter that amount on the right side of the Truck Loan T.

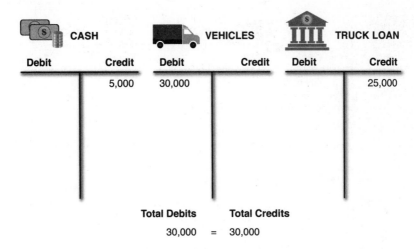

Increases to the Truck Loan account go on the right side of the T; decreases go on the left.

At this point, the sum of your debits and credits match. Remember, debits and credits aren't one-for-one. In this case, we have two credits and one debit, but in total, the three amounts balance.

Using T accounts, you've figured out where everything goes, so you can record this transaction in your accounting software.

Recording Your Transaction

Often your transactions are recorded when you fill out forms like invoices or bills, and your software puts those transaction amounts into the correct accounts.

You also can enter a transaction directly into the accounts through a journal entry. With a journal entry, you enter the amounts associated with a transaction directly into the accounts instead of using an entry form like an invoice. You likely won't have to enter journal entries very often into your accounting software. Most transactions are handled by other input screens, and many businesses let their outside accountants take care of any necessary journal entries.

But let's assume the bank withdrew $5,000 from your account as part of the loan closing process, so you don't have an actual check to record. You can record this transaction in your books in one of two ways, as a check or as a journal entry.

Check: Even if you don't physically write or print a check, you can still use the check screen in your accounting software to record a cash transaction. In this case, the transaction has two lines. You increase the Vehicles account by $30,000 and record the Truck Loan as a negative $25,000. The net $5,000 remaining reduces the Cash account because this transaction is a check.

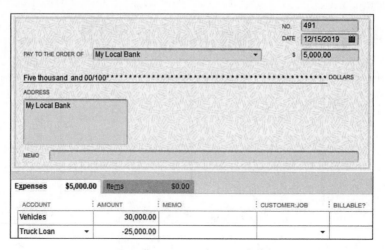

Recording a transaction as a check.

Journal entry: Alternatively, you can record a journal entry. Although it's not required, journal entries typically record changes in cash first, followed by changes in assets, liabilities, equity, income, and expenses, respectively.

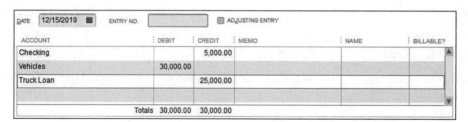

Recording a transaction as a journal entry.

ACCOUNTING HACK

Anything can be repaired in your accounting records, so don't overanalyze how to record transactions. If you're not sure exactly how to record something, take your best shot at it, and we'll show you how to clean it up later. It's far better to have the transaction recorded in some fashion in your books, even if it's temporarily not posted correctly. Don't put off logging transactions just because you're not sure how to do it. That could lead to much unnecessary grief and potentially cost your company money.

Typical Accounting Transactions

Throughout this chapter, we've mentioned debits and credits, but for most projects, you won't have to concern yourself with this level of detail. Most of the time when you perform accounting tasks, you're filling in blanks in the accounting software screens and letting it take care of the debiting and crediting.

Let's look at some sample transactions.

Checks

You'll have the option to handwrite checks when you pay your bills, or you can print checks directly onto blank check stock from your accounting software. No matter how you generate the payment, you'll record it as a check in your accounting software.

Let's assume the pet boarding business mentioned earlier has received a $1,000 shipment of dog food from a local vendor. Depending on how the business plans to use the food, the transaction might get entered one of two different ways:

As a check to record pet food expense: If the pet boarding business doesn't sell food to customers but only uses the food to feed pets in its care, this purchase is considered an operating expense. This means the purchase would reduce the Cash account by $1,000 and increase the Pet Food Expense account by $1,000.

As a check to record pet food that customers buy to take home: If the business plans to sell the food to its customers, the initial purchase isn't considered an expense, but rather a purchase of inventory. Remember, inventory is an asset, so the business has traded one asset, cash, for another asset, pet food to be sold at a profit. In this case, the purchase reduces the Cash account by $1,000 and increases the Pet Food Inventory account by $1,000. Later, when customers purchase the pet food, an invoice transaction increases the Cash account and increases the Revenue account.

Note that in addition to recording the sale and the application of the cash, something else is happening in the background. You've sold pet food, so you've reduced your Pet Food Inventory account. Your software reduces the Inventory account and increases a Cost of Goods Sold account. It automatically makes these transfers for you, so you can focus just on the sale itself and not worry about accounting for inventory.

Accounting is a unique discipline in that the intent of the business's use of the transaction often determines the category (account) used. In one case, it was operating expense, and in another, it was inventory.

Invoices

Depending on the nature of your business, you might provide goods or services to the customer in advance of receiving payment. In such situations, you'll record an invoice in your accounting software so you can keep track of the amounts due to you. These invoices can take a variety of forms, but let's look at a simple example.

Say your teenager provides lawn-mowing services for some of your neighbors. Your teen could try to collect payment each time he mows a yard, or he might invoice customers either after each mowing or perhaps in advance. In this case, the invoice transaction would look something like the following figure.

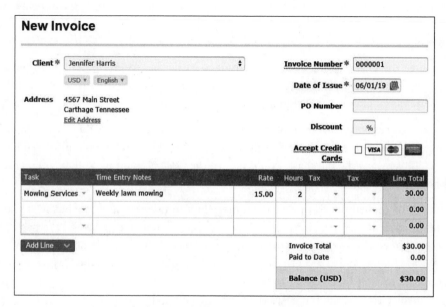

An invoice increases the revenue account, Mowing Services.

It's easy to see that Mowing Services, an income or revenue account, is being increased by $100. But behind the scenes, Accounts Receivable, an asset account, also is being increased by $100. If we were using T accounts to record this, increases in Accounts Receivable appear on the left side of the T, while increases in revenue appear on the right side of the Moving Services T.

At a later date, the customer will pay the invoice, which will result in a transaction to record the payment. This transaction will increase cash by $100 and reduce Accounts Receivable by $100.

BOTTOM LINE

Any amounts in an Accounts Receivable account should only reside there temporarily. Ideally, they'll be moved to cash when the invoice is paid.

Sales Receipts

Let's say your business is selling Popsicles from a cart. Customers pay you on the spot for their purchase, so there's no need to record an invoice and then a payment against it. Instead, you record a special type of transaction known as a sales receipt.

Sales of Popsicles affect your Cash account and your Income accounts. Other accounts can be affected as well, such as an Inventory or Cost of Sales account. However, the one account that *won't* be affected by a sales receipt is Accounts Receivable. Remember, Accounts Receivable is intended to be a holding bucket for unpaid transactions. By its very nature, a sales receipt implies that the purchase has been paid for on the spot.

Some transactions trigger a dual entry. The entry to lower inventory and the expense the cost of the Popsicle sold is an example of this. The selling of Inventory items almost always results in this dual-entry requirement, and both are required.

Credit Card Transactions

A good way to think of purchases you make with a credit card is as the inverse of a customer invoice. In this case, you're the customer of the credit card company, borrowing money today for a purchase you pay for later.

When you make a credit card purchase, you have an increase in a liability account. The offset of a credit card purchase could be many things:

- An expense, such as Telephone Expense for a cell phone bill or, returning to our pet boarding business, a Pet Food Expense.

- An asset account, such as Inventory, when you purchase inventory for your business with a credit card instead of writing a check.

- An insurance account, such as when you pay your monthly premium for a policy.

Record credit card transactions in much the same fashion as you write checks, but instead of reducing your bank account, you temporarily increase your credit card account in your books. When you pay the credit card, either in part or in full, you reduce both your Cash account and the credit card balance. You also might increase an Interest Expense account if interest has accrued on your unpaid balance.

 **ACCOUNTING HACK**

Create a separate account in your accounting records for each credit card you hold.

Recording Estimates and Sales Orders

Not every type of transaction actually affects your books. Let's say a customer is considering your services. The accounting software you use might enable you to create an estimate. This transaction looks very much like an invoice, and it might reference accounts on your chart of accounts. However, an estimate is simply a reference transaction and won't actually increase or decrease any accounts in your books.

When your customer agrees to the work, the accounting software allows you to convert the estimate into an invoice.

Invoices do affect your books, increasing your Accounts Receivable account and typically increasing one or more Income accounts.

Here's another example: assume your business sells parts for earthmoving equipment. A customer places an order for several teeth for his bulldozer, but you don't currently have them in stock. Some accounting software programs allow you to create sales orders, which are similar to estimates. The distinction is the word *order*.

With a sales order, you've a confirmed purchase you'll eventually deliver. But because you haven't provided the items in question yet, this isn't actually an invoice. Your accounting software enables to you ship all or part of the order, at which point an invoice is created for each segment of the order you deliver.

The Least You Need to Know

- Accounting can be thought of as a simple method of scorekeeping for your business.
- T accounts help you map out which accounts are debited and which are credited.
- The debits and credits created in various types of transactions you make always balance each other.
- Recording check, invoice, sales receipt, credit card transaction, estimate, and sales order transactions isn't difficult, and your accounting software handles much of the behind-the-scenes details.

Selecting Your Business Structure

Every business initially started out as an idea. From your local coffee shop to the "too-big-to-fail" Wall Street financial institutions, at some point, someone had the idea to launch that business. Just as everyone's life follows a different trajectory, every business follows a different path. Because a business is much more complicated, it needs some sort of structure.

When you see a flourishing business, you think about the product or service it produces, its location, and the people who work there. Rarely do you think or even care about whether the business is a corporation, partnership, proprietorship, or limited liability company (LLC). Nor do you care how the business is funded, who the stakeholders are, or who will take over if something happens to the owner.

In this chapter, we take a look at these and other behind-the-scenes aspects of starting a business from the ground up. It often falls on the business owner and the business's bookkeeper, accountant, and advisers to choose a business structure and create a business plan. These things should be done before you ever open your doors.

In This Chapter

- Deciding on a business structure
- Dealing with money
- Cash versus accrual basis accounting
- The importance of a tax ID number
- Crafting a business plan

Organizing Your Business

If you're starting a new business, one of the first decisions you'll make is choosing a business structure. You can choose from several legal structures for your business, as shown in the following table. Each has its pros and cons, and some entail more complexity and expense to establish than others. Also tied to this decision are important matters such as taxes, the ownership of assets, and the responsibility of liabilities. We offer some general information in this section but highly recommend you consult with legal and financial advisers before selecting the structure best for your business.

Comparing Business Structures

	Sole Proprietorship	Partnership	S Corporation	LLC	C Corporation
Legal paperwork	Minimal	Varies	Some	Some	Complex
Separate tax return	No	Yes	Yes	Yes (unless owned individually)	Yes
Liability protection	None	Varies	Full	Full	Full
Tax rate	Individual	Individual	Individual	Individual	Corporate

Note that this chart doesn't reflect issues relating to tax-exempt and nonprofit businesses.

 **ACCOUNTING HACK**

Before you engage paid advisers, look for free or low-cost resources such as the national nonprofit organization SCORE (score.org), supported by the U.S. Small Business Administration (SBA; sba.gov), which also offers guidance on launching a business. Many colleges and universities provide free or low-cost advice; sometimes students can use your business as a case study and share their findings with you. Many state and local governments offer economic development assistance, as do many nonprofit organizations. There's often no substitute for paid advice, but what you learn from free resources can help you invest in professional services more efficiently.

Sole Proprietorships

If you want to start a business flipping yard sale purchases on eBay, or if your teenage daughter begins a neighborhood babysitting service, or if your spouse starts moonlighting as a consultant, these informal ventures probably only require the most basic form of business structure, the *sole proprietorship.*

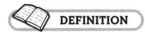 **DEFINITION**

> With a **sole proprietorship,** you are your business. You aren't a corporation, and your business doesn't exist without you. You can have employees, but you don't have partners or co-owners. If you decide to share ownership, you need a different type of business structure. In your sole proprietorship, you are personally and legally liable for every obligation of the business and for any damage caused by the business. (However, you can purchase insurance to protect yourself in the event of certain kinds of damage.)

You can treat your business as a sole proprietorship because you are the only owner and, at this point, your business doesn't have a formal legal structure. As we discuss in Chapter 19, you report all profit or loss from your business on Schedule C of your personal federal tax return, and the tax on your business income is calculated at your individual income tax rate. Typically, this business income passes right through to your state income tax return as well.

Sole proprietorships don't require any legal setup. In effect, you decide you're in business for yourself, and the business is born. Many businesses begin this way.

A sole proprietorship is fine for many businesses, but someday you might decide you want to make a change. Here are some reasons why you might want to consider using a different type of business structure beyond the sole proprietorship:

- You want to protect yourself from liabilities incurred by the business.

- You want to attract investors.

- You want to share ownership of the business.

- You want to keep your business and personal finances separate.

- You want to take advantage of a different tax structure.

 BOTTOM LINE

> Choosing the simplest form of a business by no means exempts you from much of the paperwork involved with other types of business structures. You might have to register your business with your secretary of state or with your state department if the products or services you offer are subject to sales tax. If you plan to hire employees, there's a whole host of paperwork related to that (see Chapter 12).

Partnerships

A *partnership* is typically a business owned by two or more individuals, and each owner is referred to as a partner. Some partnerships have different classes of partners, as in general partners and limited partners. General partners typically have full authority to make business decisions that affect the partnership and usually contribute significant funding for the partnership. By their nature, limited partners might not share in as much of the profits of the partnerships, but they also tend to have less liability should the business get sued. There must be at least one general partner in a partnership.

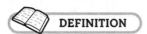 **DEFINITION**

From a business perspective, a **partnership** is a relationship between two or more individuals. Each person contributes money, assets, or talent to the venture and shares in the income or loss. Within a partnership, limited partners have less or no authority, while general partners are fully authorized to make decisions on behalf of other partners.

It's always best to have a legal agreement drawn up that defines each partner's rights and responsibilities. Let's say you and your best friend have always wanted to own a pet boarding business, and so you sell all your possessions and move to Maine to start your venture together. You might have more money available to invest in the venture, but your friend is a former veterinary technician, so you each bring a different type of value to the partnership.

Depending on the circumstances, you might agree to split everything 50/50 and equally contribute to the business and share in the profits. Or perhaps you both agree that you, as the primary benefactor, should get a 70 percent share of any profits, while your skilled but undercapitalized friend gets 30 percent. It's up to you and your partners to agree on an appropriate split of ownership and share of profit and losses. A partnership is unique in that the profits can be split one way (such as 70/30) while the ownership can be 50/50 (or any other agreed-upon percentage).

Typically, the partnership agreement is made in writing and is legally binding. Creditors can seek satisfaction of debts from the partners of a partnership, although there's some protection offered to limited partners. Usually, limited partners are liable only on business debts equal to share of ownership in the business. Partnership agreements can be arranged to fit many circumstances, but always be sure to seek legal counsel to ensure everyone's rights are being fairly represented.

Income and loss of the partnership are presented on tax form 1065: U.S. Return of Partnership Income and are then passed through to the partners via a Schedule K-1 for each partner. Each partner reports his or her share of the partnership income or loss (based on the split of ownership) on his or her individual income tax returns, and each partner is taxed at his or her individual income tax rate. Many states require a partnership tax return as well, with some taxing the partnership itself.

S Corporations

The term *S corporation* is a nod to the specific chapter in the U.S. Tax Code that permits organizing a business in this fashion.

An S corporation is a separate legal entity. Owners are called shareholders and own stock in the business, but the corporation is liable for its own debts, not shareholders. Shareholders are protected should the corporation fail. An S corporation can have up to 100 individual owners or shareholders (a husband and wife may count as a single shareholder) and may only have one class of stock. Each shareholder typically gets one vote per share of stock, but certain types of corporations can authorize multiple classes of stocks that provide different voting right levels on a per share basis.

Many small business owners adopt this type of structure for their business, not only for the liability protection but also for the tax benefits that come along with this choice.

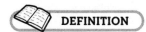 **DEFINITION**

An **S corporation** is the simplest structure for an incorporated business. Incorporating protects the owners from legal liability relating to the business and offers tax benefits. S corporations file state and federal income tax returns, but the corporations themselves pay no income tax at the federal level. Instead, the shareholders report the net income or loss from the business on their individual tax returns. Income is reported to the shareholders on a Schedule K-1, similar to a partnership.

There are limits to the types of expenses S corporation shareholders can deduct within the business, which makes the C corporation structure more attractive to some business owners. What's more, some states don't recognize S corporations and treat businesses like taxable C corporations instead. (More on C corporations later in this section.)

Limited Liability Companies

A *limited liability company* (*LLC*) is a hybrid of a partnership and an S corporation. The term *limited liability* is crucial here, because if you're an owner of an LLC, and someone decides to sue your business, they typically won't be able to sue you personally. The LLC structure protects your personal assets.

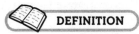 **DEFINITION**

A **limited liability company (LLC)** shares characteristics of both partnerships and S corporations. The LLC files a tax return each year to report its operations, but income or loss passes through to owners, known as members, who report it on their individual income tax returns.

LLCs share attributes of partnerships, as ownership structure, financial responsibility, and distribution of profits can be arranged in any fashion that suits the parties involved. Unlike corporations, which have formal officer roles such as president, secretary, treasurer, and so on, LLCs only have one equivalent: the managing member. This partner is authorized to act on behalf of the other LLC members, much like a general partner in a partnership.

Income or loss from the LLC is reported on the appropriate schedule (Schedule C, E, or F) of the individual owner's federal income tax return, if there is only one owner. If there are multiple owners of the LLC, the LLC must file a partnership tax return (federal Form 1065), which then passes the income or loss through to each of the owners via Schedule K-1 for reporting on their own income tax returns. As usual, states differ in the way they treat these entities for tax purposes, so check the specific rules in your state if this is the business structure you choose.

RED FLAG

Some states restrict the ownership options for an LLC, while others offer flexibility. Your state may or may not allow a single-owner LLC, two or more individuals, corporations, or even other LLCs to be owners of the LLC. Check the rules in your state before you make this choice. And again, seek professional advice from an attorney or tax professional when structuring your business.

Professional services firms such as engineers, doctors, accountants, and so on sometimes opt for a special version known as a professional limited liability company (PLLC).

C Corporations

A *C corporation* is a taxable entity on its own, one that stands alone in its responsibility to its creditors. Owners of a C corporation, which can number anywhere from a single person to hundreds, are shareholders who pay for the right to own part of the company. Debts of the C corporation belong to the corporation, and recourse is not permitted against the shareholders unless they've specifically agreed in writing to accept responsibility for corporation debt.

DEFINITION

A **C corporation** is an ownership structure for a business that's taxed separately from its owners. Owners are as shareholders, and profits are distributed as dividends or salaries. Dividends are subject to tax again when shareholders file their personal tax returns.

The C corporation files its own federal, state, and local income tax returns and pays its own taxes. Federal returns are filed on Form 1120, U.S. Corporation Income Tax Return. Income is passed through to the shareholders either in the form of dividends, which are taxed again at the shareholders' individual income tax rates, or as salaries, which are deducted by the company and personal income to the shareholder.

Some states require certain professionals to incorporate their business as a professional corporation (PC). If you are a service provider such as a lawyer, accountant, engineer, health-care professional, social worker, or veterinarian, check with your state for special rules that might apply to your business.

Tax-Exempt (Nonprofits)

The Internal Revenue Service (IRS) is authorized to approve 29 different types of nonprofit entities or *tax-exempt organizations*. Such organizations are exempt from state and federal income tax.

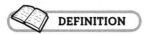 **DEFINITION**

> A **tax-exempt organization** is often referred to as a *nonprofit*. This doesn't mean the business doesn't make money, but rather that in general, the money it earns isn't subject to income tax.

The most common tax-exempt structure is the 501(c)(3) organization, often adopted by nonprofit organizations, which can be as small as a neighborhood advocacy group or as large as the American Red Cross. A 501(c)(3) organization must be organized and operated exclusively for one of these purposes:

- Charitable

- Religious

- Educational

- Scientific

- Literary

- Testing for public safety

- Fostering national or international amateur sports competition

- Preventing cruelty to children or animals

Other income not related to the primary purpose of the organization is subject to income tax.

Separate rules govern the other 28 types of tax-exempt entities. For instance, a 501(c)(3) organization files its taxes on federal Form 990, Return of Organization Exempt From Income Tax.

State rules also might vary, so be sure to check the tax rules within the states you operate your business. Keep in mind that being exempt from tax doesn't mean exempt from filing an annual tax return.

If you're interested in pursuing this type of business structure, you must apply and be approved for tax-exempt status with the IRS.

Your First Capital Infusion

Unless you're purely offering services, just about every business needs some seed money to get off the ground. Many small businesses rely on credit cards as an easy source of funding, but this can entail significant interest expense. You might be able to get family members to contribute money as a gift or perhaps in exchange for an ownership stake in your business. (For more information on funding from friends and family, check out the ebook available at 1x1Media.com.)

If your business is service-oriented, you simply can hang a shingle and announce that you're open for business. In this case, your startup capital is simply your time. However, if you want to have a social media presence, such as a website, you'll need money. For many people, that comes from their own pocket.

Separating Business from Personal

No matter what type of business entity you choose, always establish a separate financial structure for your business. This means a personal bank account for you and a separate business bank account for your business.

If your business is structured as a sole proprietorship, you don't necessarily have to open a business bank account, for which banks sometimes charge higher fees. Instead, establish a second personal account. Treat any fees related to the business account as tax-deductible expenses.

Any transactions related to your business, both deposits and withdrawals, should be written from the business bank account only. It's virtually impossible to maintain accurate accounting records if you're paying for household expenses from the same account you use to pay your employees. In some cases, you might need to pay for a business expense from your personal bank account. If you do, write a reimbursement check to yourself from your business account to cover it.

Separate credit card purchases in the same fashion. Expenses related to your business can offset income for income tax purposes, but it can quickly become difficult to differentiate personal expenses and business expenses when you put both on the same credit card. Further, the interest expense related to your business expenses is tax deductible, while interest related to household or personal expenses is not, so having a separate business credit card has extra benefits.

ACCOUNTING HACK

Although banks market "business" credit cards to small businesses, you can use any credit card you like, as long as you use it exclusively for business expenses. If you accidentally use your designated credit card for a personal expense, it's best to reimburse your business for the charge. Alternatively, as we discuss in Chapter 4, you might be able to record the purchase as an ownership distribution, but this depends on the legal structure you choose.

If your company is incorporated, paying for personal expenses from business accounts or credit cards can obviate the legal protection incorporation permits. The technical term for this is *piercing the corporate veil*, which means that if a disgruntled customer, employee, or other party chooses to sue your company, you as an individual can be held liable as well. By keeping business transactions separate, your accounting will be easier, and you'll have stronger protection against potential litigation.

Choosing an Accounting Method

One of the most important accounting principles is that of revenue and expense recognition.

In your personal life, whether you realize it or not, you operate on what's known as the *cash basis*. This means you don't count money as yours until you receive it, and you don't count money as spent until it actually leaves your hands. Some businesses use this same approach. However, because it often can take time for money to change hands, using *cash basis accounting* might not offer an accurate financial picture.

For instance, you could have $50,000 in your business bank account that's earmarked to pay $45,000 in bills. With cash basis accounting, the $45,000 in bills aren't reflected on your financial reports until you actually disburse the funds. This can give the mistaken impression that your business is well capitalized, when in reality, you could just be holding cash from a reimbursement for expenses.

On the flip slide, a customer might owe you $35,000 for a project, but your bank account only has a balance of $1,000. In this situation, it might appear that your business is teetering on *insolvency* when really, the check is in the mail and you just haven't received it yet.

Cash basis accounting operates in a vacuum in which no income or bills are reflected on the business's financial statements until the cash actually changes hands. This can result in wild swings in net income and other financial metrics from one accounting period to the next.

The alternative is *accrual basis accounting*. When a business uses accrual basis accounting, revenue is recognized as soon as it's earned. So if you send an invoice to a customer on 12/31/2019, it counts as income for tax year 2019 even though the customer won't pay it until tax year 2020.

Revenue that's been earned but can't yet be billed, or expenses that can't yet be paid, are placed on the books in the form of accruals, or special journal entries that serve as temporary place-holders for transactions. Accruals are reversed when the actual transactions take place.

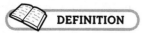 **DEFINITION**

Many businesses opt for **cash basis accounting,** which means they only report revenue they can deposit in the bank and expenses they've paid by cash or check. (For tax purposes, cash basis taxpayers can deduct business expenses paid via credit card even though the credit card company is paid in a subsequent year. This is an exception to the regular cash basis rules.) **Insolvency** is when you or your business are unable to pay your financial obligations. Insolvency is sometimes temporary in nature, such as when you need more time to raise cash, or can lead to bankruptcy. In **accrual basis account-ing,** a business recognizes income and expenses as soon as they're earned or incurred.

Deciding on a Tax Year End

It's common to think of the tax year as being the calendar year. After all, you file your individual income tax returns based on the prior calendar year. Businesses operate a bit differently, however. Businesses have more flexibility and can choose a date other than December 31 for the end of their tax year. One of the main reasons businesses elect to use a fiscal year end that differs from the calendar year is that they're too busy at the time when they normally would be closing their books and trying to file tax returns. Retailers with a busy holiday selling season often request a January year end for their fiscal year instead of December so all holiday sales will have been processed before the end of the fiscal year.

Your tax adviser can help you decide what would be the most advantageous year end for your business. If you want to change from calendar year to a business year ending in a different month, you need to explain your reasons and apply for approval from the IRS.

 **BOTTOM LINE**

You enter transactions into your accounting software the same way, no matter whether you choose cash or accrual basis accounting, and no matter your tax year. The distinction comes into play with your accounting software reports. Some accounting packages, such as QuickBooks, enable you to choose between cash and accrual when you generate reports; others, such as Sage 50 Accounting, require you to make a distinction when you first start using the software. You can generally specify a default fiscal year within your software as well.

Zoning/Business License

Depending on the nature of your business, you might have to request permission from your local government before you can launch it. This invariably results in some up-front fees and/or taxes. Some banks even refuse to open a business account for you unless you present a current business license. Others won't ask.

The rules truly vary from jurisdiction to jurisdiction, so be sure to do your research. Typically, a business license involves an annual tax that might be based on some combination of the type of industry, number of employees, and annual income. Expect up-front fees that could be in addition to the annual assessments that come with owning a business.

Your local government has a vested interest in your compliance with local zoning and business license rules, so it should be easy for you to find the rules and regulations on your local government's website. You might have to register your business with your Secretary of State's office, too.

Your Tax ID Number

Just as your Social Security number identifies you as an individual taxpayer, your business needs a similar tax identification number. If your business is a sole proprietorship, your tax ID number might be your Social Security number. However, you can and should apply for an employer ID number (EIN) using Form SS-4, Application for Employer Identification Number. The EIN for a business is often referred to as its tax ID.

If you provide services, such as legal representation or consulting, your clients might require you to provide Form W-9 detailing your business's personal identification information. This form is issued by the IRS and used as the basis to determine if the companies paying you need to issue a Form 1099 to you at the end of each calendar year to report the amount they've paid you for your services. Form 1099 also is filed with the IRS and compared to your or your business's tax return to ensure you're reporting all the income you've earned.

Your Business Plan

All the information we've discussed in this chapter relates to your business structure, but we haven't yet touched on something equally important, your business plan.

A business plan is like a map for your business in which you spell out your goals, define what success means for your business, and outline how you expect to achieve success. Creating a business plan forces you to define your expectations for your business. The more time you spend creating your plan, thinking through the opportunities available to you, and deciding what you want to achieve and quantifying how that can happen, the more successful your business is likely to be. Without a business plan as a guide, you're working day to day but not striving to meet any specific goals.

The entire team at your organization should know the plan for your business so everyone continually works toward the same goals. If you're preparing a formal, written business plan, it should be direct and simple but thorough. Be sure it includes the following:

- A description of your business, your objectives, your operations, your management team, your market, your competition, and what makes your company different and likely to succeed in the marketplace.

- A summary of the strategy and tactics that will enable you to reach your objectives, including marketing plans, pricing, and potential customers.

- A financial summary of prior activity and a future forecast, as well as information about how much money you will need to achieve your objectives, over what period of time, and how the funds will be obtained, used, and paid back.

 BOTTOM LINE

If you need to borrow money or attract investors to your business, they likely will require a business plan.

Just because your business plan is in writing doesn't mean it can't adapt as your business's circumstances change. In fact, it's healthy to review your plan occasionally and ensure it's still accurate.

The Least You Need to Know

- Your choice of a business entity impacts ownership, liabilities, and taxation of the company.
- Whether you use cash or accrual based accounting determines how your income and expenses are reported as well as how your business is taxed.
- Your business will have to register with some combination of federal, state, and local governmental agencies.
- A business plan provides direction for your business and is a necessity if you're looking for financial or investment support.

Doing the Books

You don't have to be a CPA to get up to speed on basic accounting. Today's easy-to-use accounting tools make managing the day-to-day books achievable for any business owner. With the right accounting software, proper setup for the basics within the system, an understanding of typical accounting transactions, and proper guidelines and procedures, you can be well on your way to getting a handle on your business bookkeeping, no matter what size your business.

Part 2 helps you get started from scratch. We start by discussing your options for accounting software and offer guidance on selecting the right program for your business. From there, we give you the steps for getting your system established, including setting up for your accounting method and establishing a chart of accounts to classify items for money spent and received and more. Then, we walk you through the key day-to-day activities for keeping the books, such as inventory management; handling transactions such as invoices, checks, and deposits; making online transactions; working with the general ledger; and finally, reconciling statements.

Choosing Accounting Software

You might be surprised to learn that modern accounting has roots that date to the late 1400s. Luca Pacioli, an Italian mathematician and Franciscan friar who lived from 1445 to 1517, is widely acknowledged as the father of accounting.

Fortunately, you don't have to—and shouldn't—use Pacioli's ancient accounting methods for maintaining your books. Even the smallest businesses should adopt some sort of modern accounting software, right from the start.

In This Chapter

- Why you need accounting software
- Comparing desktop and cloud-based software
- Looking at point-of-sale software
- Changing to different software
- Finding help when you get stuck

The Importance of Accounting Software

With the wide variety of easy-to-use accounting software available, there's no reason not to use it. Sure, it's entirely possible to maintain your books without the assistance of software, but it's also very possible you'll transpose two numbers, omit a transaction, or tally an invoice incorrectly when you're working without software. It's better to take advantage of the many ways accounting software can help you.

Prebuilt forms walk you through transactions such as invoices and check writing. The software handles all the behind-the-scenes entries for you, so you only have to handle each transaction once. This can be especially valuable in the sale of inventory items that can require two entries—one to record the sale and another to reduce the inventory and recognize the cost.

And with software, accounting statements and reports are just a few mouse clicks away. In addition, most programs enable you to drill down into reports. So if a number doesn't look quite right, you can investigate further, clicking your way into a series of reports to find the transaction screen where you originally entered the amount.

Although it might feel quick and easy to handwrite a check or invoice, this actually adds extra work because you have to then enter the data into your software. And if you don't do it right away, all that paper can accumulate into piles or easily get lost. Accounting software enables you to handle a transaction once, a key best practice for successfully maintaining accurate books.

What's more, the standard structure and methods built in to accounting software greatly simplify filing the various tax returns you'll learn about in Chapters 18 and 19.

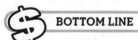

BOTTOM LINE

Every business of every size should have an accounting software program. There's simply no better way to keep tabs on your revenue and expenses. Plus, it's much harder to keep tabs on your bank balance if you don't have software to refer to.

Desktop Versus Cloud-Based Software

Traditionally, accounting software had to be physically installed on your computer from a floppy disk or CD. When new versions were released, often on an annual basis, you had to purchase the new version and reinstall or update your software. Early on, it was often worthwhile to purchase the updated versions to gain new functionality.

These days, however, desktop accounting software has matured to the point that software vendors have to stretch to come up with new features that warrant purchasing an upgrade. So although a company such as Intuit, which makes QuickBooks, might issue a new software version each year, not all customers purchase the upgrade—and some might let years go by before paying for a newer version.

As a result of fewer purchases and upgrades, software vendors began supplementing their reduced cash flow by offering recurring services, such as payroll processing, credit card processing, and other add-ons. A condition to subscribing to such ancillary services is that you had to upgrade your software at least every 3 years. If you failed to upgrade, you might lose access to certain services, such as payroll processing.

In more recent years, software vendors have found a better model for delivering accounting software—via the cloud. Software that resides solely online is known as *cloud-based software*. You access the software via the internet, usually using a web browser. This type of software makes it easy for you to access your books and enter transactions from just about anywhere. The trade-off is that cloud-based accounting packages aren't nearly as mature as their desktop-based brethren, so working in the cloud often means settling for less functionality.

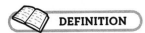 **DEFINITION**

> **Cloud-based software** is housed on remote servers so users access the software online.

The rise of cloud-based accounting software has been a boon to software developers, as the subscription model for cloud-based accounting software ensures a reliable and monthly revenue stream. Fulfillment is easier as well because manufacturers don't have to create physical CDs of their product that must be boxed and shipped.

We think it's fair to say that over time, desktop-based accounting software will go the way of the traditional hand-written accounting ledger, but we're still a number of years away from that eventuality. However, what's good for software vendors isn't necessarily good for accounting software customers.

When you purchase a desktop-based program, you're buying a license to use that software on a single computer. If you have multiple users who need to access your books, you must purchase a license for each user. Most desktop accounting programs don't expire after a period of time if you don't upgrade, or at least you won't be directly cut off. Instead, access to certain services is discontinued after 3 years, as mentioned earlier.

Depending on the software you buy, you might only have to purchase the software license, or you might be required to subscribe to a support plan. Pricing for support plans varies widely but commonly costs around 20 percent of the license amount. You might be able to opt out of the support plan and continue using the software, although you then wouldn't be able to call the software company for help if you had a problem. Regardless, with desktop software, you're able to establish as many sets of books as you want at no additional cost.

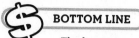

BOTTOM LINE

The least expensive desktop-based accounting software usually starts around $200. Cloud-based programs have monthly subscription fees that often start around $10 to $15 per month.

With cloud-based accounting software, you have ongoing monthly fees for each set of books you need to maintain. You also might have fees for other services such as payroll processing, credit card processing, and so on.

Historically, the screens within your desktop accounting software only changed when you installed a new version. However, QuickBooks in particular is starting to add and remove features during the year through regular software updates. Conversely, the screens within cloud-based programs can and do change, often without notice. New features are added, and old features may be dropped. All of this is beyond your control because you're signing into a central version of the software.

Common Desktop Accounting Packages

Many long-time desktop accounting programs have been purchased by larger software vendors and discontinued. For instance, Sage is planning to discontinue DacEasy, with support ending as of September 2016. As time goes by, fewer and fewer options for desktop-based software are available, but we'll cover some current options here. Most of these programs are only available on Windows-based computers. We'll note which ones are available for Mac computers.

Quicken

We're going to be specific here about suggesting Quicken (quicken.com) as an accounting software—as you'll see, only two versions of Quicken qualify as such. Quicken itself is a personal finance program that's well suited to managing records for your personal or household finances. Typically, using Quicken to manage the books for a business is like trying to fit a square peg into a round hole. With that said, two versions of Quicken can be suitable for the smallest of businesses. These two versions are only available for Windows and cannot be used on a Mac:

Quicken Home and Business: This hybrid version of Quicken enables you to manage your personal finances and a very small business at the same time. The accounting features are limited, and in some cases rudimentary, but it's a starting point, particularly if you're already using Quicken. In fact, current Quicken users can simply unlock the business features by paying a small fee. Once your business grows to the point that you need more features, it's an easy transition to QuickBooks Pro.

Quicken Rental Property Manager: The collapse and subsequent resurgence of the housing market has spawned a large number of owner-investor landlords. If you own rental property, you might find Quicken Rental Property Manager a suitable accounting program for managing your portfolio.

QuickBooks Pro

QuickBooks Pro (quickbooks.intuit.com) is the base model of the QuickBooks family of desktop-based accounting products. Designed to offer basic accounting features for new businesses, it allows up to three users to work simultaneously within the software.

QuickBooks is easy to get up and running with, and in some cases, Intuit has gone to great lengths to remove as many vestiges of accounting as possible. This can be helpful for nonaccountants, but sometimes the simplicity means certain tasks you could carry out with ease in other accounting programs become difficult in QuickBooks.

As shown in the following example, QuickBooks's simple flowchart interface makes it easy to jump right to the task you need to carry out. You'll typically need to look pretty hard to find any mention of debits and credits in QuickBooks.

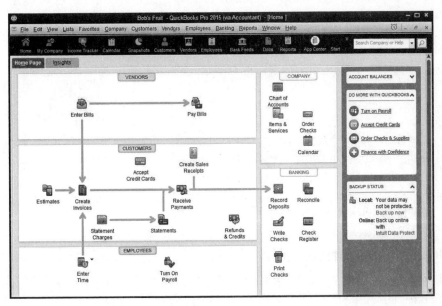

QuickBooks Pro offers an accounting flowchart that makes it easy to follow the trail of transactions.

Mac users can purchase QuickBooks for Mac that's very equivalent to QuickBooks Pro for Windows.

QuickBooks Premier

The QuickBooks Premier line offers additional functionality beyond the Pro level, including the ability to have up to five simultaneous users working in the software and an expanded slate of reports.

You also can use the generic version that's designed to apply to almost any business or choose an industry-specific version, such as Contractor, Non-Profit, Retail, Manufacturing and Wholesale, Professional Services, or Accountant. The industry-specific versions turn on additional reports and features that apply to those industries, some of which aren't available in the Pro version.

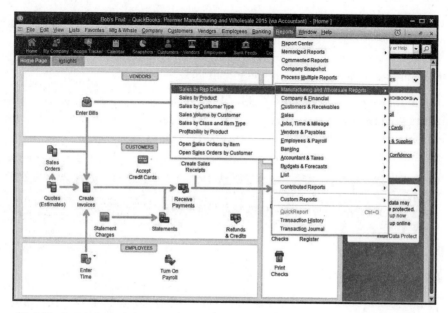

QuickBooks Premier includes industry-specific versions, such as this one for manufacturing and wholesale businesses.

The Premier version is not available for Mac computers.

QuickBooks Enterprise

As your business grows, it's easy to reach the upper limits of what QuickBooks Pro and Premier have to offer. For example, those versions restrict you to a total of 14,500 customers, vendors, and employees, and each list is limited to a total of 10,500 names. Similarly, you'll be held to 14,500 inventory items, which can pose a problem for some businesses.

Fortunately, QuickBooks Enterprise (enterprisesuite.intuit.com) provides an easy transition to a more robust accounting package. QuickBooks Enterprise allows between 1 and 30 simultaneous users, with lists for up to 100,000 items each. You also can benefit from advanced features such as expanded inventory tracking and costing capabilities and custom financial reporting by way of the QuickBooks Statement Writer that integrates with Microsoft Excel.

QuickBooks Enterprise shares the same look and feel as the Pro and Premier versions, but within the menus, you'll find commands and options that aren't offered in those versions.

One limitation of QuickBooks Pro and Premier is that you can only have open one set of books at a time. If you need to enter transactions in another set of books, often referred to as a company inside most accounting programs, you have to close the first company and open the second. QuickBooks Enterprise (and most of the Sage 50 product line, discussed next) allows you to open two companies or sets of books simultaneously.

Enterprise is not available for Mac computers.

 **RED FLAG**

If you want to move from one version of QuickBooks to another, you simply purchase the requisite license(s), open your software in the new version, and go through a one-time conversion process to migrate your data to the new format. Unfortunately, there's no path backward. So if you upgrade from QuickBooks Pro to Premier, you can't go back to using Pro unless you start all over again. Premier costs more than Pro, so you'll be locked in to purchasing Premier upgrades in the future. The same goes for Enterprise.

Sage 50

Sage 50 (sage50.com), formerly known as Peachtree Software, actually beat QuickBooks to market in 1982. Sage 50 hews fairly closely to the definition of traditional accounting software. There's an informal monthly closing process by which you physically switch the software to a new accounting period. You can go back in time to previous accounting periods, to an extent.

Sage 50 allows you to access two fiscal years concurrently and switch to any month within those years. At the end of the second year, you need to close the fiscal year, which then allows you read-only access to accounting periods in the year you closed. You won't be able to enter new transactions in that time frame.

Sage 50 is typically best suited for users who have an accounting background. Although the software offers some ease of use aspects for nonaccountants, the concepts of changing accounting periods and closing fiscal years isn't something users of QuickBooks, for example, have to think about.

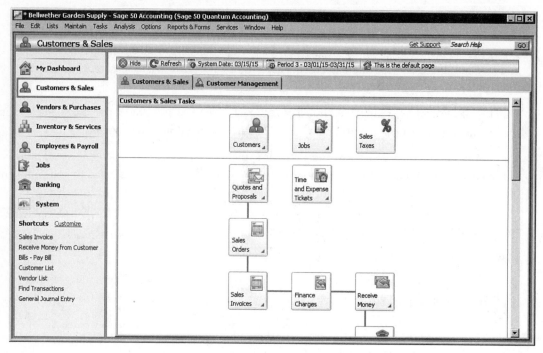

Sage 50 offers a flowchart-based interface in addition to traditional drop-down menus.

Similar to QuickBooks, Sage 50 offers three product levels:

Sage 50 Pro Accounting: The functionality in this version closely parallels QuickBooks Pro; however, this is a single-user product. Only one user has access to the accounting records.

Sage 50 Premier Accounting: This version is similar to QuickBooks Premier, but it allows up to four users at a time. The software offers expanded capabilities beyond QuickBooks Pro, such as being able to open more than one set of books at a time.

Sage 50 Quantum Accounting: This version competes with QuickBooks Enterprise, and it allows you to have up to 40 licensed users at once. This goes beyond the 30-user limitation of QuickBooks Enterprise.

Accountant Edition: This software is designed for professional accountants and bookkeepers who maintain or review books for multiple clients. It also provides access to industry-specific features, such as the unique construction or manufacturing software, without requiring users to install multiple versions.

Sage 50 is only available to Windows users, not Mac.

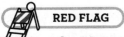
RED FLAG

In recent years, Sage 50 has been tinkering with the licensing of its desktop-based products. For a time, you couldn't purchase a perpetual license to the software and instead had to rent it on a subscription basis. Sage has backed away from the enforced subscriptions, and you can now purchase perpetual licenses again or use it on a subscription basis. Read the fine print carefully to ensure that when you purchase this software you get the license you're expecting.

Mid-Range to Enterprise Accounting Software

We've written this book primarily for introductory accounting software users, so the programs we mention specifically are well suited for entry-level users. As your business grows, however, you might reach a point where the top-tier versions of programs such as QuickBooks Enterprise or Sage 50 Quantum are insufficient for your business' needs.

At that point, you'll need something beyond the basics, both with software functionality and pricing. The accounting programs we cover in this chapter are typically priced from $200 to less than $10,000. Mid-range accounting packages such as Intacct, Microsoft Dynamics, Sage 100, and so on generally run tens of thousands of dollars for the software licenses, plus you generally need the expertise of a consulting firm to implement the software.

Common Cloud Accounting Programs

At first glance, cloud-based accounting systems seem like the way to go. Sure, these programs have benefits for end users, but if you've worked with desktop-based accounting software programs at all, you'll find the cloud-based versions markedly different.

The following sections review some of the more popular cloud-based accounting programs. You can generally access these programs on any internet-enabled device—PC, Mac, smartphone, or tablet.

QuickBooks Online

QuickBooks Online (qbo.intuit.com) is cloud-based accounting software that's offered on a subscription basis. As of this writing, QuickBooks Online is available in three versions, with three different price points:

Simple Start: This basic version enables you to track income and expenses, create estimates and invoices, and sync your bank account with your accounting records. It's best suited for business owners who have little or no accounting experience and few transactions to process.

Essentials: This middle-tier version provides all the functionality of QuickBooks Simple Start but adds the capability to pay bills online along with an expanded group of reports. Reporting is meager in the Simple Start version.

Plus: Plus has all the features of Essentials plus the capability to track inventory and prepare and print 1099s. Creating purchase orders, entering billable hours for a customer, using classes (departments), and accounting by location (branch offices, etc.) are other Plus features.

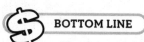

BOTTOM LINE

You can migrate between the desktop and cloud-based versions of QuickBooks with relative ease. So if you'd like to give cloud-based accounting a try and you're already using QuickBooks, it's a simple process to move from your desktop to the cloud.

An important distinction about QuickBooks Online: you can easily upgrade from Simple Start to Essentials, or Essentials to Plus, but once you move to a given tier, you can't downgrade. The only way to move from the Plus version to the Essentials plan is to cancel your Plus subscription and start over with the Simple Start or Essentials plan. This catches many QuickBooks Online users by surprise; other users are frustrated because a key feature such as generating 1099s can cost an additional $150 a year if you don't need any of the other Plus features.

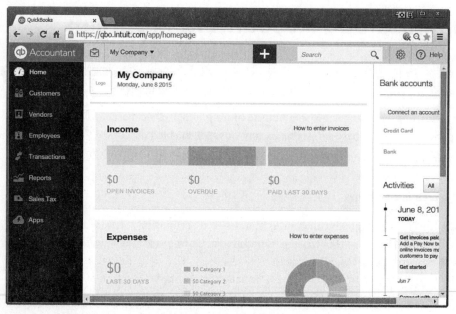

You can access cloud-based accounting programs such as QuickBooks Online online.

Xero

One of the main companies going head-to-head with QuickBooks Online is New Zealand–based Xero (pronounced *zero*). Xero (xero.com/us) first launched in 2006 and was designed to be cloud-based. It shares similar functionality to QuickBooks Online, and it even offers a free conversion service from QuickBooks to Xero. It's designed to appeal to all types of small businesses.

Some of Xero's key features include connectivity with banks around the globe and automatic reconciliation features; inventory tracking; dashboards that show at a glance how your company is doing; and of course, the cloud capability that enables you to view and work on your accounting records online. Xero partners with more than 400 add-on products that enable you to customize your accounting experience to fit your business or your clients' business.

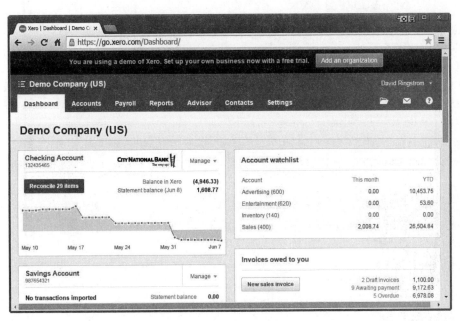

Xero offers a company dashboard where you can keep tabs on key metrics for your business.

FreshBooks

FreshBooks (freshbooks.com) started as cloud-based software designed for professionals who bill by the hour or project to send invoices. It's since grown into a full-fledged cloud-based accounting software. Ideal FreshBooks users are freelancers, consultants, or micro businesses that utilize contractors. The program includes automatic bank feeds, expense management tools, time tracking, and document sharing.

ACCOUNTING HACK

You don't have to make any irretrievable decisions when settling on an accounting package. Each program we discuss here either offers a free trial, money-back refund period, or dummy demonstration company you can play around with before you purchase. To determine if an accounting package offers a free demonstration version, do a web search for "online demo" and the name of the software you're interested in. In some cases, such as with Xero or FreshBooks, you must sign up for a free trial.

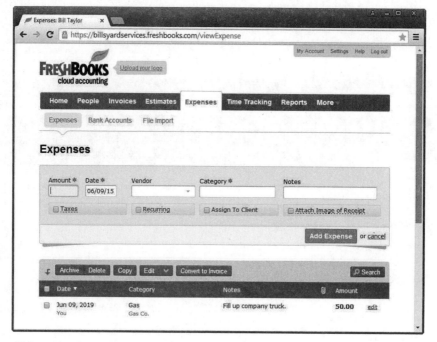

Click a tab at the top of FreshBooks to select your next activity, such as entering business expenses.

Point-of-Sale Software

Most of the time, when you make a purchase in a store, you benefit from point of sale (POS). These types of programs allow retail businesses such as stores and restaurants to manage sales, inventory, and sometimes payroll all in one place.

Small business owners who frequent trade shows at various locations across the country or globe might find POS software useful. If you're a very small business owner or run a mobile business, some of the apps you can use on your mobile device to accept credit cards might be more suitable. Larger businesses and establishments such as retail stores or restaurants typically require a more advanced solution.

Because POS is a specialized need, we'll only discuss two of the many options available.

QuickBooks Point of Sale

QuickBooks Point of Sale (quickbooks.intuit.com/point-of-sale) is an accounting program geared toward retail establishments that require a cash drawer and other hardware such as scanners and receipt printers. This software requires a PC and is a supplement to, and not a replacement of, the QuickBooks desktop program.

Revel Systems POS

As more and more businesses become mobile, chances are you'll soon pay for a purchase on a tablet-based POS solution, if you haven't already. The market leader in this area is Revel Systems POS (revelsystems.com). With this setup, you reduce paperwork by having customers sign for credit card purchases on-screen and opt to get their receipt by text or email.

A testament to the success of this platform is that Intuit, the maker of QuickBooks, has licensed Revel Systems POS as a cloud-based solution to integrate with QuickBooks Online. In this case, the tablet computer takes the place of a PC or Mac that other platforms require.

Changing Software

Don't obsess too much about which accounting software you should start with. As long as you choose a major brand, you'll be able to easily migrate to another platform if you find that you need to at some point. As we've noted, many of the major programs have built-in conversion tools that let you move from one program to another.

Let's say you start with QuickBooks Online, but discover that you need features or functionality offered only in the desktop versions of QuickBooks. Within QuickBooks Online, you can request an export of all your accounting records for use with QuickBooks Desktop. Keep in mind that this is an either/or proposition. You can't use QuickBooks Online and QuickBooks Desktop simultaneously. The platforms are distinct and you can maintain your books in only one platform. But let's say you start with QuickBooks Desktop and then decide you'd rather use Sage 50. The latter has a built-in QuickBooks conversion tool that makes moving easy.

Many cloud-based programs also let you to covert from another cloud-based platform or from your desktop-based software. Keep in mind, though, that in some cases, not every bit of activity from your old accounting software will be migrated to the new accounting program. Carefully check or do a test run on a software conversion before you finalize your move to a new platform.

If you want to move from one accounting program to another, the start of a new fiscal year is a good time to convert. You might have to enter the ending balances from your trial balance (a report we discuss in Chapter 7 as the starting point for your books).

If you're migrating from a desktop-based accounting software, you can keep the old software installed on your computer as long as you like to reference old transactions. If you cancel a cloud-based service, you'll still have read-only access to your old accounting records for a period of time that varies by service provider.

Getting Help with Your Accounting Software

You'll never be completely on your own when it comes to accounting software. Many entry-level programs such as QuickBooks and Sage 50 offer tips that pop up throughout the software while you work. The vendors' websites typically feature elaborate support sections, and numerous user communities are online where accounting software users help each other.

In addition, many software companies have certification programs accountants and bookkeepers can take to become certified users of the accounting software and then offer personalized assistance with your accounting software.

If you don't have the budget for professional assistance, many universities and colleges have business development resources where accounting students can help you with software planning and implementation at little or no cost. If you currently use an outside accountant, he or she might be a member of the Intuit network and can offer you a 50 percent discount off the regular monthly fee for assistance.

The Least You Need to Know

- You should use accounting software, even for a very small business.
- A variety of desktop and cloud-based accounting systems are available, geared for businesses of all sizes and types.
- You have to pay a license fee for desktop software, but you get the capability to set up multiple users and companies.
- You pay a subscription fee for cloud-based systems, typically one per company.
- Point-of-sale programs let retailers integrate inventory management and other functions with accounting systems.
- It's typically fairly straightforward to migrate from one system to another, although once you upgrade to a more robust or complex system, it's often impossible to downgrade.

Managing Your Accounts

In this chapter, we discuss the foundation of your books—the chart of accounts. As mentioned in Chapter 1, accounts can be thought of as various buckets in which you categorize the money-related activities of your business. The chart of accounts lists the specific buckets for your business.

But before we get to the chart of accounts, let's review the general conventions you need to follow for defining accounts. You'll see that for the most part, you'll want and need to tailor your chart of accounts to suit your personal preferences and the needs of your business.

Then we show you how to set up your chart of accounts in your accounting software and share two key reports you should view to ensure your accounts balance.

In This Chapter

- Categorizing your financial activity by account
- Balance sheet accounts: Assets, Liabilities, and Equity
- Income statement accounts: Revenue, Cost of Goods Sold, Expenses, and Other Revenue/Expense
- Customizing your chart of accounts
- Ensuring balance

Account Categories

Accounting involves grouping transactions into buckets so you can keep track of what you own and owe, as well as what you've earned and spent. Your accounting software includes a feature known as the *chart of accounts* that enables you to organize your activities so your reports are meaningful to you.

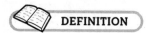 **DEFINITION**

> The **chart of accounts** lists all the accounts used for categorizing the money-related aspects of your business.

Let's take a look at the most common types of accounts found on a chart of accounts by overall category. As you read through the following sections, think about how you might want to adjust these accounts and add others to suit the needs of your business.

Assets

The Assets section of the chart of accounts is comprised of what your business owns. The mix of asset accounts for the smallest of businesses includes at least Cash and probably also Accounts Receivable. Other businesses may have one or more Inventory accounts, along with perhaps Equipment, Real Estate, Investments (both in stocks and bonds as well as ownership stakes in other businesses), and Prepaid Expenses.

Typical asset accounts include the following:

Cash: Your business typically has at least one bank account. You might simply name this account Checking, or perhaps if you do business with more than one bank, include the name of the bank on the account or maybe the last 4 digits of the account number. Your accounting software might refer to these as Cash accounts or Bank accounts.

Accounts Receivable: This type of asset account has special significance within your accounting software. The current balance of this account reflects the amounts customers owe you for goods or services your business has provided.

Inventory: We discuss the concept of inventory extensively in Chapter 5.

Prepaid Expenses: Some businesses create accounts that specifically identify the type of prepaid expense, such as Prepaid Insurance, Prepaid Rent, and so on. No matter what you call it, this type of account allows you to record monies that will become expenses in future months.

QuickBooks Online uses the term Bank *account, but other programs might use* Cash *account.*

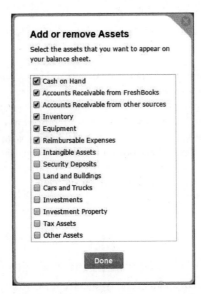

Accounts Receivable is an account type within your chart of accounts, as shown in this FreshBooks example.

Advances to Employees: From time to time, you might loan money to an employee that's to be paid back at a later date. An Advances to Employees account helps you maintain a record of such advances to help ensure the amounts do get repaid.

Advances to Owners: As an owner, you might occasionally need to borrow money from your company that you intend to pay back. Any amounts you're borrowing from your business short-term should go in an Advances to Owners account. Alternatively, as you'll see in the "Equity" section later in this chapter, it's possible to make distributions to yourself that represent a permanent transfer of funds.

Asset accounts typically have debit balances. Increases to asset accounts are recorded as debits, while credits are used to record decreases.

Although you pay for an expensive asset all at once, such as buying a car or a computer, on your books, you'll recognize the expense for such assets slowly over time through depreciation. When you enter depreciation expense on your books, the amount is offset with a credit to the Accumulated Depreciation account. This account shows the amount of the asset's cost that's been expensed over time, called the *accumulated depreciation*. Because this "asset" account carries a credit balance, it's called a *contra-asset account*.

In effect, Accumulated Depreciation is a negative balance account because it offsets the corresponding asset account. If you acquire an asset that has value but no physical substance, such as a patent or a trademark, that asset is called an *intangible asset* and is expensed over time with *amortization expense* instead of depreciation. The contra-asset account, Accumulated Amortization, records how much of the intangible asset has been expensed (the *accumulated amortization*).

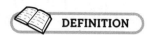 **DEFINITION**

Accumulated depreciation refers to the amount of an asset's cost that's been expensed over time. **Intangible assets** can't be seen or felt but have value to your business. Examples include patents, trademarks, franchises, and goodwill. (If you pay more than fair market value for another business, the difference between the market value and the purchase price is recorded as an asset referred to as *goodwill* and amortized over time.) **Accumulated amortization** is the amount of the asset that's been expensed. Both Accumulated Depreciation and Accumulated Amortization are **contra-asset accounts,** or accounts that offset a corresponding asset account.

Liabilities

It's conceivable that a small business using cash basis accounting won't have any liability accounts. Most businesses at least have an Accounts Payable account, which represents any money you owe to vendors. You'll need to create a separate account for each party and/or loan.

Here are the typical liability accounts you might have:

Accounts Payable: This catchall account is used to record ongoing bills your business incurs without having to establish a separate liability account for each vendor.

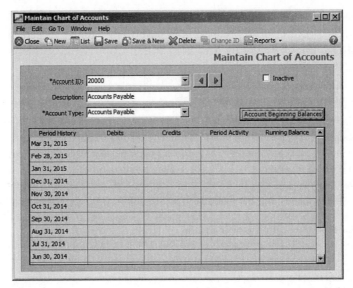

Accounts Payable is an account type within your chart of accounts, as shown in this Sage 50 example.

Federal Payroll Taxes: As we discuss in Chapter 12, if you have even one employee, your business is responsible for a dizzying number of taxes. At a minimum, you'll want at least one account to track payroll taxes, but you might want to separate payroll tax liabilities into two or more accounts. For example, you might want a Federal Withholding account where you can temporarily store income tax withheld along with Social Security and Medicare taxes, and a separate Federal Unemployment Tax account so you can keep track of what amounts you owe for each type of tax.

State Payroll Taxes: We discuss state payroll taxes more in Chapter 12, but if you have at least one employee, you'll be responsible for submitting unemployment taxes to your state as well. Most states levy an income tax, which means you might need to establish a State Income Tax Withholding account that parallels your federal accounts. You might have local payroll taxes, too.

Sales Tax Payable: In Chapter 18, we discuss sales taxes, which many but not all businesses are subject to. If yours is, you'll need a Sales Tax Payable account. As with all taxes you collect on the government's behalf, you're only temporarily holding the money before you remit to the agency responsible for the given tax, so always be sure to record sales tax as a liability. It would be improper to count sales tax as revenue when you collect it and log it as an expense when you pay it. This tax simply passes through your business but isn't part of your income stream.

Loans: Lines of credit, car loans, equipment loans, mortgages, and so on should each have a separate account in your chart of accounts. Liabilities should be tracked at a very detailed level.

Liability accounts typically have credit balances. This means that transactions that increase a liability credit the account, while a reduction or payoff of a liability is recorded as a debit with an offsetting credit to cash.

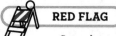

RED FLAG

Some businesses hold customers' money for a period of time, such as in the case of deposits or retainers. Such funds must be tracked as a liability until you've earned the money and can count it as revenue. Businesses such as law offices are required to establish separate bank accounts to keep from commingling retainer funds. Commingling is a situation in which you combine your money with someone else's, which can make it hard to distinguish whose money is whose. It also greatly raises the odds that you spend someone else's deposit and are unable to pay back the money should the transaction get cancelled.

Equity

You'll have a variety of equity accounts on your chart of accounts. Some accounts track the amount of money you and any co-owners, partners, or shareholders have invested in the company. Others track the amount of *distributions* from the company.

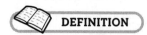

DEFINITION

Owners can take money out of a business in a variety of ways. As we discuss in Chapter 9, you might receive a paycheck from your business, which is subject to payroll taxes. Profits from the business shared above and beyond paychecks are called **distributions.** These reduce the overall equity in a business because money is being taken out. It's important to note that paying yourself distributions results in different income tax treatment than payroll, and distributions must be posted to an equity account and not an expense account. In other cases, distributions can be considered a return of capital, meaning a return of the money they previously invested in the business.

Here are the types of equity accounts you might need to set up (your accounting software might set up these for you):

Retained Earnings: Every business has a Retained Earnings account. As noted later in Chapter 14, at the beginning of a new year, the Revenue, Cost of Goods Sold, and Expense accounts all start out with a zero balance. This doesn't mean the prior year's activity simply vanishes, but rather that your accounting software moves the activity from those accounts into a retained earnings account. This account serves as a bucket for the accumulated income or loss of your business over the years.

Capital Contributions: If you invest money into your business, that's often considered a contribution or investment. This distinction is important because this isn't revenue from the business, but rather funding being provided by one or more owners so the business can operate. Each owner or partner should have his or her own Capital Contributions Account, or Capital Account.

Distributions: As discussed earlier, owners can take money out of the business in a few ways. Each owner should have his or her own separate Distributions account, or Withdrawal account. Partnerships may have accounts referred to as Draw accounts to record funds paid to owners.

The natural state of most equity accounts is a credit balance, but there are exceptions to this rule. Any transaction that increases the equity in a business, such as capital contributions, is recorded as a credit, while any reductions in equity, such as distributions, are recorded as debits.

Revenue

Your revenue accounts should reflect the combination of goods and services offered by your business. You have a wide range of latitude here; you can have a single, catch-all Revenue account where you post all your income-related transactions, or you could create individual revenue accounts for money derived from different types of services or even specific clients. For example, an auto mechanic might create revenue accounts to track brake jobs separately from engine replacements, with other accounts for oil changes and perhaps scheduled maintenance.

There's an art to establishing revenue accounts. If you get too detailed, your financial reports will be fragmented and your transactions will be harder to post. However, by striking the right balance of individual revenue accounts, you can compare one period to the next to see how much revenue is being derived from various sources.

Revenue transactions are typically recorded as credits, but you might have a revenue account you use to record discounts granted to customers. Discounts are typically considered a reduction in revenue, as opposed to an expense, and should be recorded as debits.

Cost of Goods Sold

Depending on the nature of your business, you may or may not have any Cost of Goods Sold accounts. These accounts represent the expenses directly related to selling or producing goods and services. For instance, as you learn in Chapter 5, when you sell an inventory item, your accounting software automatically records a transaction that reduces the value of your Inventory account and increases a Cost of Goods Sold account. The Cost of Goods Sold account includes the cost of materials that go into creating your product, as well as any freight costs and the labor costs directly associated with making it.

In some cases, the IRS requires an allocation of your indirect costs to be added to your year-end Inventory amount. Generally speaking, your tax preparer can make this entry at the close of your business year. Indirect costs can include, but are not limited to, administrative salaries, utilities, security, and other costs that cannot be directly traced to a specific product, yet the product cannot be created unless the business spends money on these costs.

Indirect costs differ from overhead, which are general expenses of the business that cannot be attributed to manufacturing goods. This is another cost you'll need to track. (More on this in the upcoming "Expenses" section.)

Cost of Goods Sold (or Direct Costs in some software) is a key element in determining your business's *gross profit*. Costs of goods sold are an offset to your revenue, so such transactions are recorded as debits.

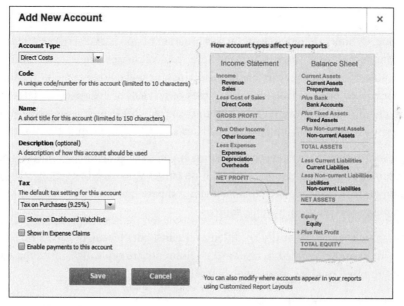

Xero uses the term Direct Costs *in lieu of* Costs of Goods Sold, *but the account serves the same purpose.*

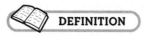 **DEFINITION**

The revenue from a business minus the cost of goods sold is often referred to as the **gross profit** (or *gross margin* or *gross income*).

Expenses

A business's expenses are typically overhead expenses not directly attributable to selling goods and services. For example, you might have to pay rent on office space, budget for monthly internet access, and purchase advertising to market your business. You should have a separate account for every overall expense.

We could write a whole book on classifying expenses, but in short, expenses are costs your business incurs that aren't related to purchasing assets or producing goods and services. Such expenses are often referred to as *overhead* or *operating costs*. As the saying goes, it takes money to make money, so you'll incur costs you wouldn't bear if you didn't own a business.

Expenses are usually recorded as debits.

Other Accounts

The broad categories of revenue and expenses are designed to capture the income and outflows that relate directly to operating your business.

But you sometimes might have ancillary income that isn't directly related to operating your business, and you'll need an account for each type you receive. Examples include Interest Earned on Investments, Referral Fees, Affiliate Commissions, and Vendor Compensation for properly submitting sales tax returns.

Including such items in your revenue can distort your gross profit and gross margin calculations, so if these amounts are meaningful, it's best to put them into special accounts or one overall Other Revenues account.

You also might have expenses that aren't directly related to operating your business, such as tax penalties or parking tickets, which can be put into an Other Expenses account.

Managing a Chart of Accounts

Now that you've learned more about accounts overall, let's go over the mechanics of working with your chart of accounts in your accounting software.

One of the first actions you'll take when you start using accounting software is to set up a chart of accounts. Most likely, your accounting software gives you a jump-start on this task by asking you to choose what industry your business is in. A realtor's chart of accounts looks much different from one for a veterinarian, for example, because each type of business has its own unique mix of revenue sources and expense types. You don't have to live with the chart of accounts your accounting software builds for you, but it can be a good starting point you can shape and bend to suit your needs.

Each accounting program offers a different user interface and menu structures. Within desktop accounting programs you'll likely find the chart of accounts command on a Lists or Maintain menu. Cloud-based accounting programs might offer a dedicated Accounts menu, a Settings button, or perhaps an icon shaped like a gear. You might find a variation on the *term chart of accounts,* such as *account list* or *accounts,* within the software.

Depending on what software you use, you might have to assign account numbers along with account names. Or you might be able to use account names only.

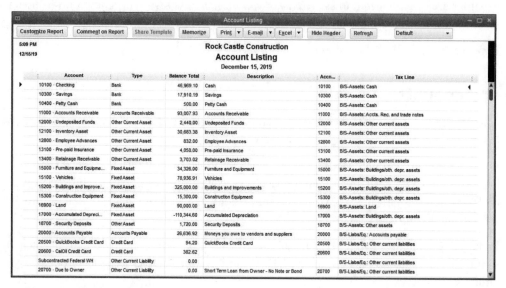

Most accounting programs let you generate a chart of accounts report, like this QuickBooks Desktop example.

Making Everything Balance

The sum of all of your accounts must net out to 0, because as we noted in Chapter 1, accounting is a system of balances, not only individual account balances, but a balancing of debits and credits. Your accounting software will generate at least two reports that must net out to 0: the general ledger and the trial balance. (We discuss these reports in Chapters 7 and 17, respectively.)

Trial Balance

As shown in the following figure, the trial balance report serves as an overall listing of your account balances. The report has three or four columns, depending on how you've configured your accounting software:

Account number: The first column lists account numbers if you've chosen to use them in your chart of accounts.

Account name: The trial balance lists every account on your chart of accounts. Depending on your accounting software, accounts that have a 0 balance may or may not appear on this report.

Debits: The amounts for any account with a debit balance appear in this column. Keep in mind that even an account that typically has a credit balance can appear in the Debits column if you've posted transactions that result in a debit balance.

Credits: This final column shows the amounts of any accounts that have credit balances. As with debits, it's not necessarily unusual for an expense account to have a credit balance. For instance, an overcharge from one year might be refunded in a subsequent year.

The term *trial balance* dates to the early days of double-entry accounting when this report would be used to determine if the sum of all debits equaled the sum of all credits. Typically, your accounting software reports total debits and total credits at the bottom of the respective columns. These numbers in no way reflect any meaningful measure of your business other than confirming that your books do indeed balance.

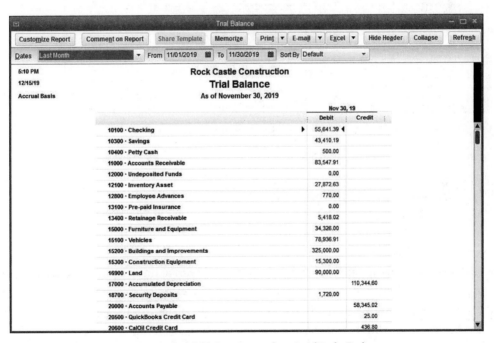

An excerpt of a trial balance report from QuickBooks Desktop.

General Ledger

We discuss the general ledger more in Chapter 7, but in essence, this report provides a detailed accounting of every transaction in your books. Any event that triggers an exchange of money within your business is recorded within the general ledger.

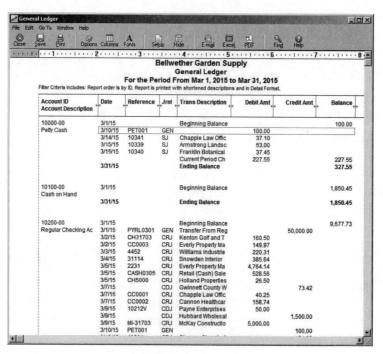

A general ledger report from Sage 50.

The Least You Need to Know

- The balance sheet accounts are made up of Assets, Liabilities, and Equity. The total of your assets always equals the sum of your liabilities plus equity.

- The income statement accounts are your Revenue and Expense accounts. The difference between your revenue and expenses equals your net income (or loss).

- Your accounting software might provide a basic chart of accounts you can customize with the accounts needed for your business.

- When your accounts are in balance, all your credits should equal all your debits.

Accounting for Inventory

Businesses come in all shapes and sizes and offer a variety of products and services for sale. When a business creates and sells a physical product, it generally keeps a stock of that product on hand as inventory. A business also might house a supply of raw materials for creating finished inventory. You might resell products you don't physically stock on-site, or you might need to standardize prices and descriptions for service items. The inventory feature in your accounting software can track all this and more.

In this chapter, we discuss some of the risks and benefits of maintaining inventory. We also offer a breakdown of the various types of inventory items you might be tracking in your business, how the tracking generally works, and how this might impact your financial statements. From there, we move on to the various methods you can use to value your inventory and discuss when and how to perform a physical count of inventory and report on it. And along the way, we explain how your accounting software gives you a huge hand in managing inventory.

In This Chapter

- What inventory is and why we care about accounting for it
- Different types of inventory items
- Methods of valuing inventory
- Counting your physical inventory
- Inventory reporting

The Importance of Tracking and Valuing Inventory

Physical inventory often poses a high degree of risk for small businesses. Let's say you sell chicken feed to farmers. You have to forecast the amount of feed you need to stock so you don't run out and lose sales. When the feed arrives, you have to store it someplace dry, clean, and secure from rodents and other pests. You have to be sure to sell your oldest bags of feed first so you don't get stuck with spoiled product. And you must stay aware of your competitors' pricing practices so they don't undercut your prices and leave you with inventory you can't sell.

Depending on your business, you also might have the stress of borrowing money to fund your inventory. For instance, new car dealers often don't actually own all the cars on their lot. Rather, they use a mechanism called floor plan financing to borrow money to keep a certain number of cars at the dealership. The longer a new car stays on the lot, the more interest the dealer has to pay on that car. This added cost raises the stakes of maintaining certain types of inventory.

Physical inventory clearly has special requirements: items must be stored, counted, valued, and sometimes financed. Your inventory might be perishable or have an extraordinarily long shelf life, such as metal parts for earthmoving equipment. You might have high-value items you need to track by serial number, or your inventory could be less specific, like piles of cypress mulch you'll measure imprecisely.

Your inventory might consist of physical items never directly in your possession. In effect, you're able to leverage someone else's warehousing and inventory system to offer products to your customers. This approach is often referred to as drop-shipping. Paradoxically, inventory also can serve as an effective means to sell and track services.

Even if your business sells intangible services, the inventory feature in your accounting software can help you streamline accounting tasks. Later in the chapter, we describe how service-based businesses can use a special type of inventory item to simplify data entry and also track sales.

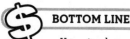 **BOTTOM LINE**

Knowing how much inventory to keep can be tricky. You want to have enough to fulfill customer requests and maintain an on-hand stock in your showroom so potential buyers can see what you offer. But you don't want to keep excess inventory that can spoil, nor do you want to spend a lot of money on slow-moving products. The physical inventory counts we discuss later in the chapter enable you to keep tabs on how much inventory is in stock. Over time, your experience can guide you on how much inventory you can afford and how to keep it turning at an appropriate pace.

Inventory Item Types and Setup

If your accounting software offers inventory tracking, you might have a large number of item-type options to choose from when identifying your inventory. The level of control and flexibility you have with regard to tracking your inventory items varies based on your software. In this section, we look at the most common types of inventory-related software issues you'll encounter along with a summary of other related software features. (We cover how to purchase and sell inventory items in Chapter 6.)

Unfortunately, we can't provide specific guidance on where to start adding inventory items within your accounting software because almost every program seems to take a different approach. With that said, desktop-based accounting programs often have a Lists or Maintain menu across the top in which you can find Inventory commands. Within cloud-based accounting programs, you might have to look for a Settings command (sometimes represented by a gear-shape icon). Once you find the inventory section of your software, actually adding new items should be intuitive from there.

Stock Items

Stock items are physical goods you keep on hand for sale to customers. Depending on your industry, these could be cans of green beans you take out of the case and put on a shelf or manufactured goods you assemble from raw materials. Your customers might purchase items from a retail location you own, or you might ship everything to your customers. Whatever your product, you'll need to keep track of the physical count of these items and very likely take certain items off your books occasionally due to *shrinkage.* The wording your accounting software uses can vary; for instance, Xero uses the term *tracked items,* while QuickBooks Online allows you to *track the quantity on hand.*

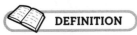 **DEFINITION**

Ideally, you'll sell 100 percent of the inventory items you purchase. However, sometimes unfortunate things happen to inventory. Items break, get stolen or misplaced, or any of a number of things. The term **shrinkage** refers to these events and the reduction of your stock.

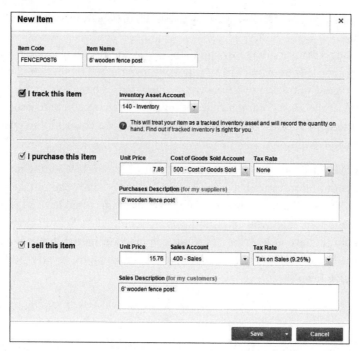

Your accounting software keeps track of the number of stock items you have on hand and notifies you if you try to sell beyond the quantity you have.

Nonstock Items

Nonstock items are the physical goods you sell that are typically never in your possession, or perhaps you house them only temporarily. Often referred to as drop-shipments, you place an order for these items through your supplier who then ships the products directly to your customer.

Your accounting software won't keep track of any quantities on hand for nonstock items. You can run reports that track the amount of these items you've sold, but they won't affect the Inventory account on your balance sheet because you never actually take possession of the physical goods. Your Inventory account only reflects items you keep on hand or store elsewhere but maintain ownership of.

For instance, you might sell bottles of rare wine that a distributor ships on your behalf. This contrasts with bottles of wine you purchase and cellar in a special facility. The latter would be considered stock items you carry on your balance sheet.

Let's say you purchase a bottle of wine for $10 and sell it to your customer for $25. You'll invoice your customer for $25, pay your vendor $10, and pocket a profit of $15, and the vendor will ship the wine directly to your customer (assuming customer's state permits sales of alcohol by mail).

Assemblies

Assemblies are best thought of as a collection of goods and/or services that go together to make one inventory item that's sold as a unit. For example, a manufactured product might be comprised of four individual parts and two labor processes to put together those parts. When you create an assembly, you assign a name to the item and then assemble a list of two or more other inventory items (the individual parts for the assembly, which you previously purchased and added into inventory in your accounting software).

In turn, when you sell the assembly, your accounting software takes the individual items out of stock and records the cost of both the parts and labor. One sales price applies to the entire package that comprises the assembly.

Assemblies are typically considered an advanced feature within accounting software, so you might need to choose a desktop-based program to use this feature. The following figure shows an assembly screen from Sage 50. Notice that the active tab is referred to as the Bill of Materials.

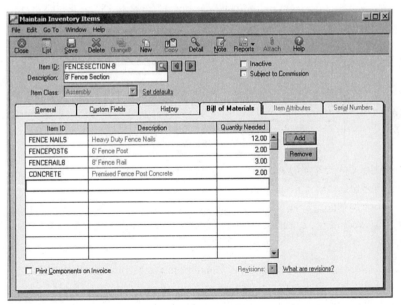

Assemblies enable you to sell combinations of inventory items and/or services as a single item.

RED FLAG

Assemblies allow you to sell multiple items at once. However, when you create the assembly items, you might need to carry out a "build" step in your accounting software. Building an assembly lowers the on-hand quantity of the individual stock items so you don't inadvertently try to sell them twice. Physical inventory, which we discuss later in this chapter, can be trickier if certain items on your shelves are earmarked for assemblies you haven't sold yet. Depending on your business and your software, you also might have the option to "unbuild" assemblies, which restores the on-hand quantities for the individual items that were formerly part of the assembly.

Service Items

Within the context of an accounting program, service items represent services you provide to others. There's nothing physical to keep count of, but service items can provide a helpful tracking mechanism if you offer two or more types of services. For example, as writers, we offer multiple services at different price points. In our accounting software, we might have service items ranging from Consulting Services, to Freelance Writing, to Technical Editing, all with different prices and descriptions.

Service items help ensure you price services consistently and provide consistent descriptions on your invoices. The following example shows the window in QuickBooks Online you'd use to establish a service.

Service items simplify the invoicing process by enabling you to use consistent descriptions on invoices.

Special-Use Items

Some accounting programs use the inventory feature for more than just tracking products. For instance, in the desktop versions of QuickBooks, you can add a variety of items, as shown in the following figure. Each of these allows you to streamline some aspect of your invoicing process. In this example, Other Charge allows you to add an ad hoc charge to an invoice. The Discount item lets you calculate discounts on an invoice.

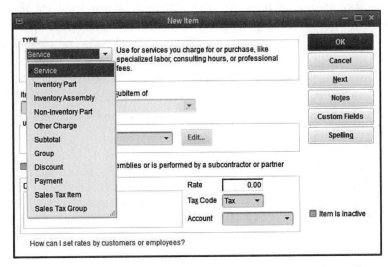

The desktop versions of QuickBooks offer the capability to establish other charges, discounts, subtotals, and special-use items.

ACCOUNTING HACK

You might want to be able to offer special pricing to specific customers. Instead of keeping this information in your head to recall when you create an invoice, your accounting software might allow you to establish price levels. These let you provide automatic discounts to customers when you record invoices. Price levels are typically set at a global level, meaning you'll establish discounts of, say, 10 percent, 15 percent, 20 percent, etc. and then assign the respective price levels to specific customers.

Physical Inventory Valuation Methods

When you purchase inventory, you exchange one asset, cash, for another asset, inventory, which you hope to convert to cash again by ideally selling at a higher price than what you paid.

The inventory items or assemblies you sell could rise or fall in value. For instance, if you sell sand and gravel, the price most likely won't change very often. If you sell freshly baked bread, the value of your inventory can drop to 0 within a day or two as the bread becomes stale. A jeweler buying gold for necklaces can pay a different price for an ounce of gold every day—and sometimes even within a given day. Multiply these complexities by dozens, hundreds, or thousands of products, and you can see how critical accounting software can be for tracking your inventory.

You'll need to keep track of not only how many items you have on hand, but also the current value of the items. Further, when you sell an item from your inventory, the portion of your inventory cost relating to the item you sell is recorded as an expense on your books. When you first purchase inventory, the cost is recorded as an asset, but as you sell items, the cost of the items sold appears as an expense on your profit and loss or income statement. As you might expect, there can be some nuance involved in determining exactly how much to treat as an expense when you've bought various items at different times and at different prices. In accounting terms, these nuances are referred to as *costing methods*.

 **DEFINITION**

Costing methods are used in your accounting software to determine the amount you should record as an expense when you sell an item. You don't have to use the same costing method for every item in your inventory, but you might find your inventory reports confusing or misleading if you mix and match costing methods for the same type of inventory items.

Depending on which accounting software you use, you might be able to choose from up to four different inventory valuation methods. When you purchase inventory, it stays on your books at the price you paid for it. By "on your books," we mean the amount you see on your balance sheet in your Inventory account. The amount in the Inventory account reflects the sum of your total current inventory on hand. Your accounting software enables you to run inventory valuation reports that reflect the underlying detail on an item-by-item basis.

You shouldn't take inventory costing methods lightly, as your choice of method can not only affect the bottom line of your income statement, but also impact the amount of income taxes you pay. With that said, you should follow the *matching principle* when making this determination, as it affects an expense on your income statement known as *cost of goods sold* (*COGS*). Your accounting software typically allows you to mix and match costing methods item by item, but the Internal Revenue Service (IRS) expects you to choose one costing method and use it across the board. Exceptions to this rule are permitted on a case-by-case basis if you're able to document a valid business purpose.

Cohen & Cohen Agency

AMERICAN INCOME LIFE
insurance company
323-938-7663 · www.ailla.com

Cash	Vehicle	Truck loan
5,000	30,000	25,000

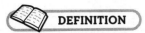 **DEFINITION**

The **matching principle** of accounting strives to match revenues and expenses. So when you report the sales price of an item you sell, you also should report the price you paid, to the extent possible. Both the sales price and the commensurate price you paid should flow through your profit and loss statement. The price you paid for inventory is known as **cost of goods sold** (**COGS**). When you sell an item from your inventory, your accounting software reduces the cost value inventory on your balance sheet and records an expense in the Cost of Goods Sold section of your income statement.

In the following sections, we look at four costing methods you can choose from and share information to help you decide which one applies best to your inventory situation. Be sure to make your selection of a valuation method and note it in your accounting software before inputting your actual inventory amounts.

Average Cost

As you might have already gathered, the concept of tracking costs for inventory items can be confusing. Many accounting programs try to simplify this by only offering a single inventory valuation method known as *average cost*. When you sell an item, the software looks at the average cost of all the items you've purchased and uses that as the cost of goods sold. This eliminates fluctuations in your cost of goods sold because each item you sell is expensed at roughly the same amount.

If your inventory items were all purchased at approximately the same price, the average cost method represents a reasonably fair value for your inventory items. If the prices fluctuated significantly, this method wouldn't be very accurate.

First in, First Out

If your accounting software permits it, first in, first out (FIFO) often gives the best representation of your cost of goods sold. In this case, the price for the oldest items in your inventory is applied to sales of inventory items first. You sometimes goof up your local grocer's definition of FIFO when you grab a gallon of milk from the back that has a later expiration date instead of taking a gallon from the front.

FIFO is particularly well suited to perishable goods. You want to sell the items you purchased first—for example, a gallon of milk—before you sell anything you've purchased more recently.

Last in, First Out

Last in, first out (LIFO) is often used in industries where prices are typically fluctuating upward, so your cost of goods sold reflects the current cost of items being sold. LIFO is also sometimes used for bulk items where a new load is dumped on top of whatever is still in the bin. In these cases, you're actually selling the last items first, so LIFO is appropriate.

The following figure provides a table of example inventory purchases and shows how the average, FIFO, and LIFO costing methods vary based on the example purchase data. In particular, this example illustrates how LIFO results in the highest inventory cost.

Purchases	Quantity	Price	Total Cost
4/1	100	49.75	4,975.00
4/4	150	42.57	6,385.50
4/9	75	52.18	3,913.50
4/16	200	48.19	9,638.00
4/22	175	54.18	9,481.50
Totals	700		34,393.50

$49.13
Average Cost
$34,393.50 divided
by 700

$49.75
FIFO Cost
Uses first purchase
cost from 4/1

$54.18
LIFO Cost
Uses last purchase
cost from 4/22

The amount applied to cost of goods sold can vary widely based on your choice of costing method.

Specific Identification

When you sell an item using specific costing, your accounting software uses the actual cost you paid for that specific item as the cost of goods sold. Specific identification also is used for items for which you track individual serial numbers.

The higher the cost you pay for an item, the more important it is to ensure the cost is directly associated with the sale, per the matching principle discussed earlier. Charging the wrong cost of goods sold to a high-value item can unnecessarily fluctuate your cost of goods sold and result in misstatements within your financial reports.

For this reason, most accounting software geared at small businesses doesn't offer this costing method as an option. It's usually only used for selling high-value items, such as expensive watches or jewelry.

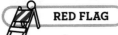

RED FLAG

As soon as you click Save to add a new inventory item to your accounting software, you can't change its costing method. If you need to change it, you have to create a new item, transfer the balances by way of inventory adjustments, and potentially create fictional transactions to provide the proper costing history. If you decide to change your inventory valuation method, you need to notify and get permission from the IRS by filing form 3115, Application for Change in Accounting Method, after the first day of the year you're making the change. Most inventory valuation change requests are approved, but special rules apply if you use LIFO. Work with a tax adviser if you use LIFO.

Keeping Count

There's definitely an art to effectively managing inventory. You don't want your inventory level to be too large or too small, but rather just right. Keeping your inventory too low can save money on inventory costs, but it could result in lost sales. Buying too much inventory not only drives up costs, but also can result in items you can't sell due to changes in the marketplace, spoiled inventory, damage, or myriad other problems.

Reordering

Rather than manage inventory based on gut feelings, use your accounting software to make inventory purchasing decisions based on actual sales data. Your software might enable you to specify a minimum stock level, so, ideally, you can keep a certain number of items on hand at all times and never miss sales opportunities because you were out of stock.

As we discuss in the reporting section of this chapter, you also might be able to run a report that lets you know which items you're getting low on and should consider ordering. For example, your accounting software might offer a report like the Inventory Stock Status report from the desktop versions of QuickBooks shown in the following figure.

Although most of the accounting programs we discuss in this book don't offer inventory optimization features, you might be able to purchase or subscribe to an inventory management program that can fill the gap. For instance, TradeGecko (tradegecko.com) connects with QuickBooks Online, Xero, and other cloud-based programs. On the desktop front, QuickBooks users who need enhanced inventory tracking and analytics often turn to Fishbowl (fishbowlinventory.com).

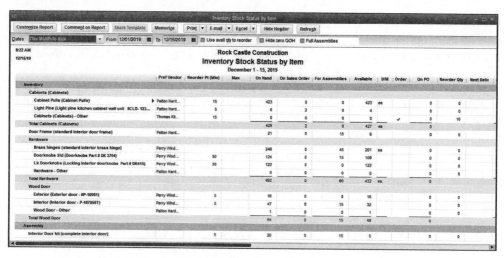

Your accounting software might offer reports that notify you when it's time to reorder stock.

Taxes, Accounting, and Inventory

The physical inventory count we describe in the next section is used to back up the amount of inventory you report on your year-end financial statements and the amount of inventory you report on your income tax return. Your accounting software can maintain a perpetual count of the inventory you started with minus the items you've sold, but it can't determine spoilage, obsolescence, or shrinkage—only your physical count can do that. To ensure accuracy in your financial reporting, it's necessary to perform periodic inventory counts.

Physical Inventory Count

Occasionally you need to perform a count of the physical items you have in stock. Your accounting software maintains a perpetual inventory count as it tracks the items you buy and sell so you can keep a general sense of what you have. But you still need to verify that what your accounting software reports actually matches what physical inventory you have.

As you'll see in the upcoming inventory reporting section of this chapter, your accounting software enables you to print a report or worksheet that lists all your inventory item types, with blanks for filling in the physical count. This report shouldn't contain the quantities on hand, because knowing how much of something you should have can sometimes inadvertently prejudice the person performing the inventory count.

Here are the two types of inventory counts:

Periodic inventory count: During a periodic inventory count, you perform a physical count of every item you have on hand so you can reconcile what's in your warehouse with what your accounting software reports in. Depending on the nature of the items and their value, you might perform this inventory annually or even daily.

Cycle count: For some businesses, it might be cost-prohibitive or too disruptive to do a physical count of all inventory items at once. In such situations, businesses often rely on a method called *cycle counting,* wherein a rotating subset of the inventory on hand is counted.

Inventory Adjustments

You'll sometimes need to make adjustments to your inventory due to situations such as loss, spoilage, or obsolescence. For example, you might find that you only have 8 purple propeller hats instead of the 10 you thought you had. You can use an inventory adjustment command to change the quantity of items on hand.

Although most of the accounting programs we discuss in this book don't offer inventory optimization features, you might be able to purchase or subscribe to an inventory management program that can fill the gap. TradeGecko (tradegecko.com) connects with QuickBooks Online, Xero, and other cloud-based programs. On the desktop front, QuickBooks users who need enhanced inventory tracking and analytics often turn to Fishbowl (fishbowlinventory.com).

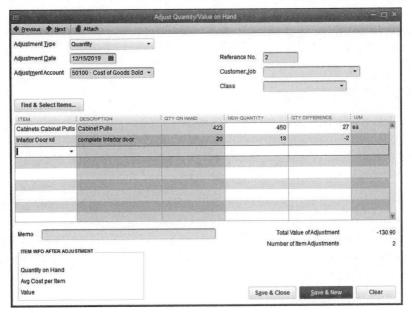

When changing the quantity of items on hand, use your software's inventory adjustment feature.

You also might be able to record changes in value, should you find that the price of an item has changed substantially since you first purchased it.

If you consistently make large adjustments to your inventory, it's a good idea to research the reasons why. You might find indications of employee theft, more spoilage than you anticipated, or even evidence of unrecorded sales.

Reporting

Your accounting software enables you to generate a surprising number of reports that allow you to analyze your inventory activities. In this section, we review which reports to look for and how to use them.

Inventory Valuation Report

A key report you'll want to view frequently is the Inventory Valuation report. The actual name of the report might vary based on the accounting software you use, but the purpose of this report is to document the detail of the Inventory account balance on your balance sheet.

Rock Castle Construction
Inventory Valuation Summary
As of December 15, 2019

	On Hand	U/M	Avg Cost	Asset Value	% of Tot Asset	Sales Price	Retail Value	% of Tot Retail
Cabinet Pulls (Cabinet Pulls)	423	ea	2.56	1,082.60	3.5%	0.00	0.00	0.0%
Light Pine (Light pine kitchen cabinet wall unit #CLD-123...	6		1,500.00	9,000.00	29.3%	1,799.00	10,794.00	44.1%
Cabinets (Cabinets) - Other	0		0.00	0.00	0.0%	0.00	0.00	0.0%
Total Cabinets (Cabinets)	429	ea		10,082.60	32.9%		10,794.00	44.1%
Door Frame (standard interior door frame)	21		12.00	252.00	0.8%	0.00	0.00	0.0%
Hardware								
Brass hinges (standard interior brass hinge)	246	ea	3.00	738.00	2.4%	0.00	0.00	0.0%
Doorknobs Std (Doorknobs Part # DK 3704)	124		26.91	3,337.16	10.9%	30.00	3,720.00	15.2%
Lk Doorknobs (Locking interior doorknobs Part # DK415)	122		35.27	4,302.35	14.0%	38.00	4,636.00	19.0%
Hardware - Other	0		0.00	0.00	0.0%	0.00	0.00	0.0%
Total Hardware	492	ea		8,377.51	27.3%		8,356.00	34.2%
Wood Door								
Exterior (Exterior door - #P-10981)	16		308.51	4,936.10	16.1%	120.00	1,920.00	7.9%
Interior (Interior door - P-187065T)	47		69.90	3,285.17	10.7%	72.00	3,384.00	13.8%
Wood Door - Other	1		1,750.00	1,750.00	5.7%	0.00	0.00	0.0%
Total Wood Door	64			9,971.27	32.5%		5,304.00	21.7%
Total Inventory	1,006	ea		28,683.38	93.5%		24,454.00	100.0%
Assembly								
Interior Door kit (complete Interior door)	20		100.00	2,000.00	6.5%	0.00	0.00	0.0%
Total Assembly	20			2,000.00	6.5%		0.00	0.0%
TOTAL	1,026	ea		30,683.38	100.0%		24,454.00	100.0%

The total asset value calculated at the bottom of the Inventory Valuation report should always match the Inventory amount that appears on your balance sheet.

Sales by Item

This report details the sales quantities for each particular item. It shows sales of all your inventory items, not just stock items, so it's a great way to track the popularity of the various products and services you sell. You can use this information to set minimum stock levels so you don't inadvertently run out of popular items. You also can use this report to determine which items aren't selling so you can jump-start sales through promotions or perhaps price cuts.

Items Sold to Customers

This report details the products and services each customer has purchased. You might find this report useful for identifying customers who haven't purchased recently or helpful in suggesting to current customers other, complementary products you offer. You can run this report for two or more separate periods to try to identify customer purchasing trends.

Physical Inventory List Report

Print the Physical Inventory List report before a physical inventory count, and use it as the worksheet for recording the count. It provides a list of your inventory items with space for recording the quantity of each item on hand.

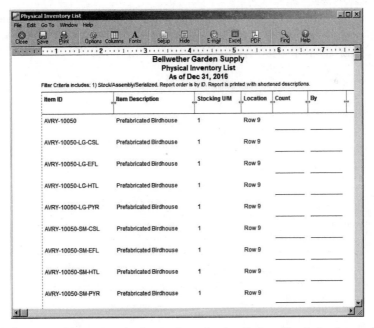

The Physical Inventory List report omits the quantity on hand to eliminate bias during the counting process.

Be sure to keep copies of completed inventory reports as documentation for the IRS. It pays special attention to inventories because some taxpayers try to defer or evade income taxes by manipulating inventory values. Clean and accurate count sheets with initials are your best defense from an IRS query about your inventory.

The Least You Need to Know

- The stock of the items you sell represent your inventory, and the value of your inventory appears on your balance sheet.
- Accounting software aides you in keeping track of how much inventory you have on hand by adjusting your inventory balances with every sale you make.
- Inventory can be classified as stock items, nonstock items, assemblies, service items, and special-use items.
- The method you use for valuing your inventory plays a role in how your inventory appears on your balance sheet as well as how your cost of sales is calculated. Methods include average cost, FIFO, LIFO, and specific identification.
- You might lose inventory through damage and other issues, so it's important to physically count inventory periodically and make inventory adjustments in your accounting software.
- Inventory reports in your accounting software can show your inventory value, sales by item, and sales by customer, as well as provide a handy worksheet for a physical inventory count.

Doing Business Day to Day

In Chapter 1, we provided an overview of typical accounting transactions; in this chapter, we look at those in more depth. We describe the most common types of accounting transactions you'll perform in your accounting software. The frequency with which you'll carry out any of these transactions depends on the nature of your business, and you might not need to carry out every type of transaction. In some cases, we describe more than one way to carry out the same transaction. In doing so, we try to show you the most efficient means for your situation.

You might be surprised to find that there are actually a couple different ways to record customer-related transactions in your books. We explain why and when you might choose each. We also discuss paying suppliers and vendors, with special emphasis on purchasing inventory. We touch on payroll, too, because the steps can vary among accounting programs.

In This Chapter

- Recording and accounting for sources of revenue
- Recording and paying your bills
- Recording and managing inventory levels
- Recording and managing payroll

Recording Sales

Unless you happen to run a foundation tasked with spending down a billionaire's wealth, sales are going to be a critical part of your business operation. We don't mean sales in the sense of 50 PERCENT OFF! EVERYTHING MUST GO! posters. Rather, accountants use the word *sales* as an all-encompassing term for revenue a business generates. *Revenue* refers to money your business earns from selling goods and/or providing services.

Depending on your business, you might get paid on the spot by your customer, or you might have to submit an invoice and wait to receive payment. You'll record transactions where you have immediate payment as sales receipts; otherwise, you'll record an invoice and keep track of your customers individually.

Customer Records

Your accounting software should offer some leeway on when you add new customers to your accounting records. A Customers button or menu should appear prominently within your software. This typically allows you to access a list of customers, and you'll be able to easily add new customers as needed. As shown in the following figure, the new customer window in your software allows you to add a variety of information about your customers, including payment terms, which we discuss in Chapter 13.

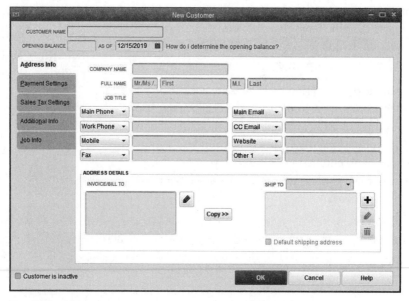

Most fields within a new customer record are optional and can be completed at your discretion.

However, you don't always have to go to this area of your software to create a customer-related transaction. As you'll see later in this chapter, if you attempt to create a transaction using an ID or customer name that doesn't yet exist in your records, your accounting software will ask if you want to create a new customer.

ACCOUNTING HACK

Your accounting software requires you to create a unique identifier for each customer. One way to make your accounting easier is to use as much of a customer's name as fits in the ID field. Customer IDs may be limited to 20 characters or fewer, so you might have to use letter and number combinations, such as BBB001 instead of spelling out Bob's Big Bonanza.

Sales Receipts

This type of transaction allows you to directly record sales to your cash account and revenue account in one step. As shown in the following figure, a sales receipt looks much like an invoice but is used to record immediate payments.

Some programs, such as the desktop version of QuickBooks, provide a dedicated Sales Receipt screen, while others, such as Sage 50, offers a Receive Money window that serves double-duty, meaning you can apply payments against invoices and record sales receipt activity in a single transaction if you want.

With regard to sales receipt transactions, if you perform consulting services, a customer may occasionally surprise you by offering to write you a check when you leave for the day. In this situation, there's no need to record an invoice and then apply payment against it—you already have the money in hand.

Sales receipts also provide an easy way to post a summary of your day's sales, such as when you use a point-of-sale software that operates separately from your accounting software to handle customer interactions.

If your business is strictly cash-based, such as a hot dog cart, you can record one sales receipt per day to post your sales.

If your business accepts credit cards, you might need to use one or more journal entries to record transactions for a given day's sales. For example, you'll likely take any cash and checks to the bank all at once while you could receive separate deposits for American Express, Discover, and Visa/MasterCard transactions.

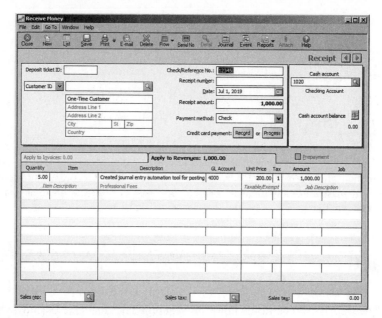

Receive Money in Sage 50 is the equivalent of Sales Receipt in other accounting programs.

Depending on which accounting software you use, you might have to create a customer record for every sales receipt transaction. So if someone only needs something from your business one time, you still have to add them to your customer list. However, you don't necessarily need to fill in all the fields in the new customer record. Completing the customer ID and customer name should suffice, although your accounting software might prompt you for additional required fields. If you use Sage 50, you can skip over the Customer ID field in the Receive Money window and complete the Name field instead. This eliminates the need to set up a customer for a one-time transaction.

Many businesses have a mix of regular customers who purchase on a recurring basis, and one-time buyers who may or may not purchase again. Setting up a general customer ID such as "Walk-In Customer" enables you to record the one-time buyer but still be able to use the many sales analysis reports that come with the accounting software.

The details of completing a sales receipt are similar to creating an invoice, which we cover next.

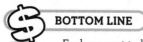

BOTTOM LINE

Each amount to be deposited in your bank account from a given day's sales should be recorded on a separate sales receipt or journal entry. When you reconcile your bank account (more on this in Chapter 8), you want to be able to clear each amount individually. For instance, your Visa/MasterCard sales for the 29th of the month might deposit to your account on the 30th, while the American Express deposit might not appear in your account until the 1st. Listing each separately helps you keep better track.

Invoices

Many businesses are unwitting lenders, delivering goods or services to a customer before payment is rendered. In these situations, you'll record an invoice to note the amount due.

When you post an invoice to your books, typically your accounts receivable account is increased by the amount of the invoice, as are one or more revenue accounts.

You can include many items on an invoice, but usually there's some upper limit. For instance, Sage 50 limits invoices to 160 lines. The first time you create an invoice, your accounting software will require you to create a customer. This is an action you can carry out on the fly in your software. Simply type a customer name in the invoice screen, and respond to the on-screen prompts.

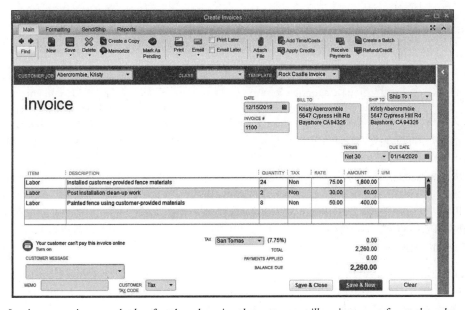

Invoice transactions record sales of goods and services that customers will remit payment for at a later date.

RED FLAG

Your accounting software might offer a Quick Add feature, similar to what's offered in the desktop versions of QuickBooks. This is designed to be a convenience, allowing you to create a customer ID without leaving the transaction screen. The downside is you might not have the opportunity to fill in the customer's address and/or email. If you mail printed copies of your invoices, you might not notice a missing address until after you've generated the paper invoice.

Accounting program transaction windows are typically separated into three unlabeled sections: header information at the top, line item details in the middle, and total information at the bottom.

For invoices, the header section includes information about your customer, the transaction date, a due date, and payment terms. Depending on the software you use, you might be able to turn other header fields on or off, such as Ship Via to indicate a shipping method, Purchase Order Number if your customer requires you to reference their customer number, and possibly a Sales Rep field if you have commissioned salespeople.

Within the line item section, you'll detail the products or services being sold to your customer. Some accounting programs, such as the desktop versions of QuickBooks, only allow you to add items to your invoice that appear on your inventory item list. Note that in this case, services you sell have to be categorized as inventory items as well.

 RED FLAG

Tread carefully if your accounting software doesn't require you to choose an item ID for each line item. As mentioned in Chapter 5, inventory items of all types can streamline your invoicing process. More importantly, you must choose item IDs for inventory items you sell so your accounting software can post the requisite cost of goods sold entries and adjust the quantity for each item you have on hand. Further, if you don't have to choose an inventory item, you need to pay attention to the general ledger accounts the transactions are posted to. This is an area that can cause problems in your general ledger and financial statements, such as those we discuss in Chapter 7.

If you sell physical goods that you keep in stock, be sure to record sales as soon as possible so your software inventory records are always up to date. You don't want to deflate a customer's expectations, and possibly lose sales, when you can't deliver a requested item because you were behind on paperwork.

In other cases, you might want to reserve inventory items on a customer's behalf so you can ship them as soon as you receive them. To do so, you'll use a transaction similar to an invoice known as a *sales order,* which we talk more about later in this chapter.

Receiving Payment

You might end up receiving payments from customers in a variety of ways. Depending on your business, your customers might pay in cash for the most part, write checks at the time of delivery, or mail in checks. Some might be able to pay you electronically through ACH transactions, and others might pay by credit card. No matter the method, you'll follow the same approach in your accounting software.

Although the exact name of the command varies by program, you'll have the equivalent of the Receive Payment window shown in the following figure. Within this window, you'll choose a customer and get a list of their outstanding invoices. If a customer is paying a bill in full, you'll usually be able to check a box to enter the full invoice amount, or you can type in the actual amount paid. The header section of this window enables you to specify a payment method if you want to track the different ways customers pay their invoices.

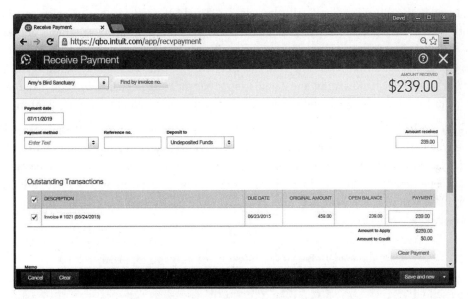

Most accounting programs offer a Receive Payment screen; in Xero, you must select an existing invoice and post the payment at the bottom of the screen.

Customers who pay by credit card might complicate your accounting somewhat. Credit card processing generally results in fees that are usually a small percentage of the transaction (typically 2 to 4 percent) and sometimes an additional per-transaction fee of perhaps 30 to 50 cents. Financial institutions take two approaches for posting these amounts to your bank account.

Some deposit the full transaction amount and then deduct the transaction fees in one lump sum per month. In this case, you can mark the invoice as paid in the same fashion you would for a check.

Others post a deposit that's the net of the transaction fees. In these situations, you need to mark the invoice as paid in full, but also record a discount that reflects the credit card transaction fee so the net amount is reflected in your bank account and your accounting records.

Making Bank Deposits

When you record payments from customers, don't panic if you don't immediately see the amounts in your Cash account within your accounting software. Some programs establish a special asset account, referred to as Undeposited Funds. This allows you to aggregate two or more customer payments into a single transaction that will post to your bank account. Doing so makes reconciling your bank account, which we discuss in Chapter 8, much easier.

As shown in the following figure, the deposit feature within your accounting software offers another unexpected opportunity. Tucked away within many accounting programs' deposit screen you'll find the capability to print deposit tickets. To use this feature, you do have to purchase preprinted deposit forms, but in the end, this can save you time and money because you won't have to spend time handwriting and calculating totals for bank deposits, and you avoid potential fees your bank may charge for submitting deposits with an incorrect total at the bottom.

It's also possible that you can deposit checks without even going to the bank. Businesses with large volumes of checks can rent check scanners that enable you to zip through sending batches of checks to the bank. Your bank might also offer an app that enables you to use a mobile device to take a picture of the front and back of checks you want to deposit. Such services are primarily offered through personal bank accounts as of this writing, but your bank might offer it for commercial accounts as well.

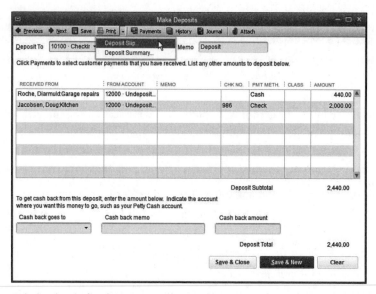

Printing deposit slips from your accounting software saves time versus handwriting and ensures your records match the bank's records.

Sales Orders

Your accounting program might offer the ability to generate sales orders for customers. As we discuss in Chapter 7, these are nonposting transactions that won't affect your general ledger or financial statements. However, sales orders can be a powerful inventory management tool.

You create sales orders in a similar fashion to sales receipts and invoices; the transaction form looks almost identical. The distinction is that sales orders offer several inventory management features invoices don't, including the following:

- Your accounting software likely enables you to print a pick list report that tells you which items to pull from inventory.

- Certain inventory reports show you the quantity on sales orders for given items. This helps you stay on top of backorders and determine if you need to seek an alternate source for in-demand products.

- You might be able to configure your accounting software to include items on sales orders when reporting the quantity on hand. This can prevent you from overselling products.

- Your accounting program might let you automatically generate a purchase order for inventory items with insufficient stock. (We discuss purchase orders later in this chapter.)

Another benefit of sales orders is that you can convert all or part of the sales order to an invoice. When you do so, any inventory items are taken out of stock, as opposed to potentially being earmarked. After you ship all the items on the sales order, your accounting software marks the sales order as closed, but you also have the option to do so whenever a partial shipment is suitable or when the order is canceled.

Customer Retainers and Deposits

Some businesses accept or require retainers or deposits before starting work. These also might be referred to as prepayments. No matter the verbiage, you'll have to do a little bit of work in your accounting software to accommodate these types of transactions.

You can record these on either an invoice or a sales receipt, but take care to record these transactions carefully. Depending on your software, you might be required to establish an ID for Prepayment, Retainer, or Deposit; or you might be able to leave that field blank and choose a liability account instead.

Once the work is completed and you're doing the final billing, you'll need to apply the prepayment against the invoice. It's at this point that the money shifts on your books from a liability to revenue earned.

The specific means by which you apply the prepayment varies based on your accounting software. Typically you'll add a line item at the end of the invoice and enter the amount of the prepayment you're applying as a negative amount posted to the liability account.

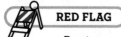

> **RED FLAG**
>
> Retainers or deposits customers pay to you aren't necessarily your money yet and should be recorded on your books as a liability. You could treat a nonrefundable retainer or deposit as income on your books, but be sure you have a signed agreement with your customer for this. Further, if you prematurely record a deposit or retainer as income, you might end up paying income taxes on the money prematurely. It gets more complicated if you have to refund the customer's money for some reason. Conversely, if you don't apply a prepayment properly when invoicing, you might leave a phantom liability on your books and unnecessarily pay income taxes on nonexisting income.

Other Invoicing-Related Transactions

Sometimes a customer might want to return an item or request a discount on services not rendered to their satisfaction. In these cases, your accounting software enables you to prepare a credit memo. The exact procedures and capabilities vary based on your specific accounting software, but generally, credit memos enable you to return inventory items to stock and provide discounts for services. You might be able to apply the credit memo directly against an open invoice, or you might have to match the credit memo and invoice together manually, as we discuss in Chapter 13.

Depending on the nature of your business and your accounting software, you might have the option of issuing progress billing invoices. This is typically an advanced option you'll need to enable or search for in specific programs, but it enables you to generate multiple invoices for a project based on the percentage complete or other milestones.

Another option you might have is preparing *estimates*. An estimate is similar to a sales order, but it won't earmark inventory. Be sure to include language on estimates that allows you to reserve the right to change the estimate, and mention that if there are changes, you'll contact the customer for approval before performing any work beyond the costs shown on the original estimate.

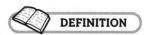

> **DEFINITION**
>
> An **estimate,** sometimes referred to as a quote, is a proposal or bid for a job wherein you set out how much you think it will cost the purchaser based on particular circumstances.

Programs that offer estimating capabilities enable you to convert an estimate to a sales order or invoice without retyping it, which can be a big timesaver. Entering estimates in your accounting software can be a helpful tracking mechanism, and you'll have the option to delete or mark the estimate as closed should your customer fail to approve.

Paying Bills

You'll likely spend more time than you care to paying bills for your business. The process of entering and paying bills is very similar to how you enter customer invoices, so we won't go into as much detail here. Your accounting software permits you to process bills in the style that suits you.

You can enter bills as you receive them and then process payment all at once, such as on Fridays or on the third Tuesday of every month. Look for a command labeled Enter Bills, Receive Items, or perhaps Purchases/Receive Inventory. (We discuss the nuances of bills for physical inventory items later in this chapter.) Bills you enter in this fashion appear on your Aged Payables report (more on that in Chapter 13).

A separate command along the lines of Pay Bills enables you print checks for multiple bills at once based on selections you make. This functions in a similar fashion to the Make Deposits command discussed previously.

Or you can simply write checks for bills when you're ready to pay them. If you pay a bill on the spot, it's unnecessary to enter a bill transaction first. Just write the check directly, using a form such as Write Checks or Spend Money.

Your accounting software may allow you to pay your bills electronically. If so, you'll process payments as described, but instead of printing checks, you'll send the transactions to your bank, which will print and mail checks or send electronic payments.

If your software doesn't allow you to send transactions directly, or requires fees for such services, you probably can initiate electronic bill payments through your bank's website. You'll enter these payments in your accounting software in the same fashion you would a paper check, but you won't need to print an actual document. You simply make up a check number or use the word *Online* if your software requires the check number field to be completed.

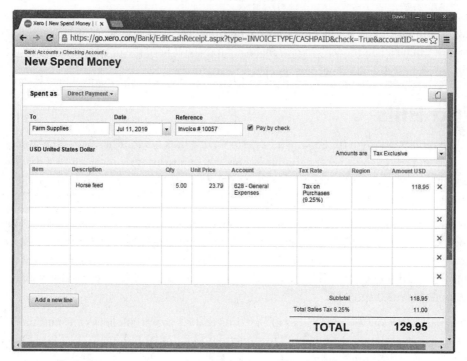

Most accounting programs have a Write Checks screen; Xero calls it Spend Money.

 **ACCOUNTING HACK**

Some small businesses hand-write checks when issuing payments. This results in extra work because handwritten checks must be entered into the accounting software and then an envelope must be addressed for the payee. Every accounting program allows you to print checks directly. So once you sign the check, you can send it in a window envelope. You can purchase computer checks from your bank, from your software provider, or through third-party check printing services.

Credit Card Purchases

A business credit card can simplify your accounting because instead of writing multiple checks to various vendors, you simply write one check per month to the credit card issuer.

You might have as many as three ways to record credit card transactions in your books. Your accounting software might allow you to automatically download credit card charges to your books. Or you might have a dedicated credit card transaction entry screen. What's more, you might have to enter your credit card statement manually as a bill. Each line of the bill transaction represents a line item on your credit card statement. You can lump together multiple similar charges if your statement is particularly lengthy.

No matter how you get the transactions in your books, be sure to reconcile your credit card statement monthly, as discussed in Chapter 8.

RED FLAG

The IRS expects you to issue a Form 1099 to many of your vendors at the end of each calendar year and can penalize you for noncompliance. Right now you're not required to issue 1099s to incorporated businesses, but Congress has contemplated making businesses issue 1099s to every vendor, not just those that operate as partnerships and sole proprietorships. It's best to require all your vendors to give you a W-9, Request for Taxpayer Identification Number and Certification. Add the tax ID number to your vendor records, and specify in your software if the vendor should receive a 1099.

Purchasing Inventory

Take special precautions when purchasing inventory for your business.

You can pay for inventory a variety of ways—cash, check, online payment, or credit card. When recording inventory transactions, your software likely has a special Receive Inventory transaction screen. It's important to use this window so you accurately receive the purchase of your inventory, which isn't immediately an expense to your business but rather an asset purchase (more on this in Chapter 5). Your inventory reports will automatically reflect the new quantities on hand as well as the cost that you paid.

Don't try to shortcut the data-entry process by entering a quantity of 1 and a lump sum amount. Take the time to enter the details of each individual inventory item. It's possible that your accounting software can streamline part of this process for you if it offers a purchase order feature.

Purchase Orders

Purchase orders are a special type of accounting transaction that won't directly affect your books. You don't have to use purchase orders in your business, but there are several benefits to doing so if your accounting software offers the functionality.

A version of an Open Purchase Orders report enables you to track orders you've placed with vendors. This can be a useful cash-management tool that allows you to forecast upcoming cash flow requirements.

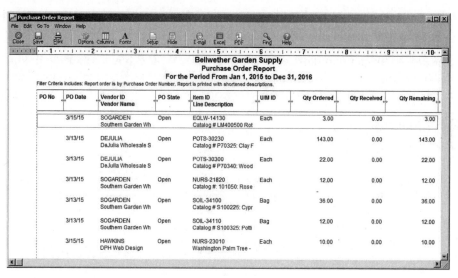

Purchase orders provide a means for tracking orders you've placed with vendors and suppliers.

As noted in Chapter 5, you can specify minimum order quantities for inventory items you keep in stock. Your accounting software might enable you to automatically generate purchase orders for items you need to order, which can help avoid unexpected inventory shortfalls.

Regardless of how you create a purchase order—by hand or automatically through your software—your inventory reports reflect the quantities you have on order. This is a vital inventory management tool that can help you avoid double- or triple-ordering products that have a long shipment time.

Keep in mind, though, you don't need to enter a purchase order for every inventory item you buy. For instance, you might run down the street and write a check for items you purchase from a competitor or wholesaler. In such cases, when you enter the check in your books, you'll be able to specify the inventory items you purchased as you write the check.

Purchase orders are best suited for situations when there'll be a time delay between when you order and actually receive inventory items.

Processing Payroll

We devote a couple chapters later to setting up payroll and managing payroll taxes (see Chapters 12 and 18). The complexities and deadlines involved encourage many business owners to outsource payroll processing to third-party providers, but you certainly can use most accounting programs to process payroll in-house.

Cloud-based accounting programs often require a higher monthly subscription fee. Desktop-based programs often require an annual payroll service fee in addition to the cost of the software.

We give you an overview of setting up employees in Chapter 9. Once your employees are in the system, you'll use transaction windows such as what's shown in the following figure to enter the number of hours worked during the pay period for hourly employees, or to confirm the pay amount for salaried employees. You might have to fill out additional fields to record vacation time and/or reimbursements, which we discuss in Chapter 11.

Depending on the capabilities of your software and the associated level of service you purchase, you might be able to pay employees by direct deposit. This typically involves sending the payroll transactions 3 banking days in advance of when you want to have the amounts deposited in your employees' accounts.

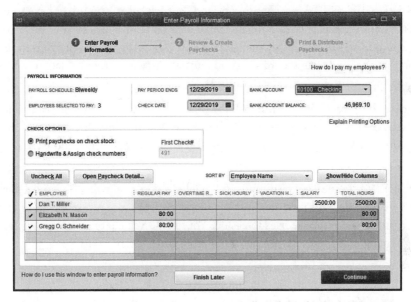

Accounting programs that offer payroll processing typically include a batch processing option that streamlines payday-related tasks.

You'll also have the option to print paper checks. Although you can handwrite payroll checks, computer checks save you time and provides your employees a paystub that documents their earnings and withholdings both for a given pay period and the year to date.

Voiding Checks

Your accounting software offers a feature by which you can void a check, which reverses the effects of the original transaction. Your cash balance will go up by the amount of the check, and the other side of the transaction will be reversed.

You might be inclined to simply delete checks, but voiding leaves an easy-to-find audit trail in your books, particularly if you've printed or handwritten the check. As for the physical check, if you keep it in your paper records, write VOID in large block letters across the face of the check. Or destroy the check by shredding it or tearing it up. Just be sure it can't be inadvertently cashed.

Exercise caution when voiding checks, as the transaction date you choose for voiding the check could impact your financial statements and, in turn, tax returns for a prior year. Checks should typically be voided as of today's date, but some accounting programs won't give you a choice and may backdate a void to a prior accounting period. In such cases, you might have to use adjusting journal entries (see Chapter 7) to mitigate the impact on your books so your prior period amounts aren't affected. In short, you'd enter one journal entry as of the date of the void to reverse its impact on that date and then record a second journal entry as of today's date to update your cash account and the corresponding offset or offsets.

If you choose to process your payroll in-house, be especially cautious when you void an unclaimed payroll check. Some accounting programs post the void in a prior year or quarter (based on the check date), which can cause payroll reports, W-2 forms, and payroll tax returns to differ from your books.

If a check gets lost in the mail or disappears somehow, you might want to issue a stop-payment order with your bank. This instructs your financial institution to refuse payment on the check should it turn up and someone tries to cash it. Your bank will charge a fee for this service, and the stop payment order will expire after a period of time.

The Least You Need to Know

- Tracking your revenue and recording it properly ensures you stay on top of cash coming into your company.
- Your accounting software enables you to record bills as they arrive so you don't run the risk of missing a payment due date.
- Inventory control features in your accounting software enable you to maintain proper levels of inventory.
- You can choose to process payroll in-house by way of your accounting software, or outsource payroll to a service provider.

Tackling the General Ledger

The essence of your accounting records, or your books, is a report known as the *general ledger*. This comprehensive report records every transaction that affects your accounting records.

As you'll see in this chapter, most but not all transactions you enter into your accounting software are recorded in the general ledger. Your accounting software takes care of most of the work for you as you prepare invoices for customers, issue paychecks to employees, and pay bills to vendors. However, you'll need to use a special transaction type known as a *general journal entry* to record certain activities that affect your books or to correct misposted entries.

In This Chapter

- Why the general ledger matters
- Understanding general ledger transactions
- Working with misplaced transactions
- Recording noncash and nonposting transactions
- When you shouldn't change your general ledger

The Importance of the General Ledger

At first, your general ledger might feel a bit overwhelming, because depending on the number of transactions you have in a given month, the report can easily run dozens or even hundreds of pages. The report is always arranged in the order of your chart of accounts, which we discussed in Chapter 4, and includes all of your accounts that have activity. You might not see accounts that have a 0 balance or haven't ever had any transactions posted to them; this varies by accounting software.

Each account reflects the following information:

- Account number (if you choose to use account numbers within your software)

- Account name

- Beginning account balance

- Transaction type, such as invoice, bill, payment, check, journal entry, and so on

- Customer, vendor, or employee name, when applicable

- Transaction date

- Descriptive information, such as a memo or item description (Your accounting software might automatically provide this when you enter the transaction, or you can add it manually.)

- Some accounting programs include a column that shows you the other side of a given transaction; -SPLIT- in this column signifies that the transaction affected three or more general ledger accounts instead of just two (The desktop and online versions of QuickBooks show this, but not all programs do.)

- Debit and credit columns (remember: debit = left, credit = right)

- Ending account balance

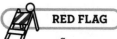 **RED FLAG**

Some accounting programs go to great lengths to simplify accounting procedures and reports—sometimes too far. For example, Xero's General Ledger report doesn't include any transaction activity and is actually what most accountants would call a trial balance report, which we discuss in Chapter 17. If the general ledger in your software doesn't provide as much detail as we describe here, look for an alternative, such as the Account Transactions report in Xero.

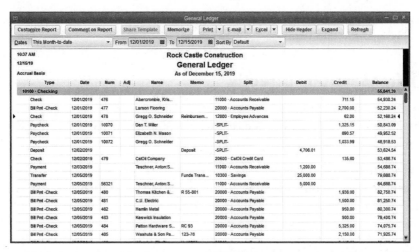

This general ledger report from the desktop version of QuickBooks is pretty typical of what you'll see in other programs.

Typically, your accounting software lets you see the detail of any general ledger entry when you click or double-click it. For example, if the amount you see in the ledger originated with a check you wrote, you can click on the amount and the actual check will open. The transaction activity will identify a customer, vendor, or employee, if applicable, along with any descriptive text you entered when you recorded the transaction.

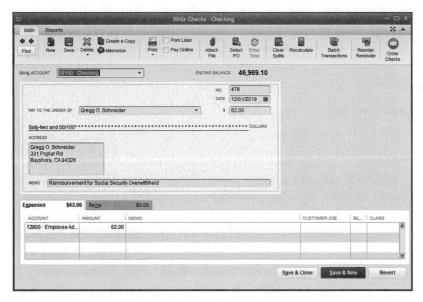

In QuickBooks desktop, double-clicking the check issued to Gregg O. Schneider in the preceding figure shows the actual transaction where the check was written.

By having both the general ledger entry and the full transaction detail, you have two different means to make corrections to misposted transactions.

Updating Transactions Directly

Let's say you find a mistake in your books where a transaction is in the wrong account. In many cases, you can simply click or double-click the transaction amount to display the original document window and make your corrections.

Be careful when changing dollar amounts of transactions if you've already reconciled the bank or credit card account for that period. Modifying a cleared transaction can throw your previous reconciliation out of balance, which will carry forward to your current reconciliations. (We discuss reconciliations in detail in Chapter 8.)

However, you're not stuck if you encounter a transaction you can't fix directly, thanks to general journal entries.

Adjusting Journal Entries

You can use an adjusting journal entry to correct account balances in your books. This is a standard operating procedure.

Such transactions are typically dated as of the last day of a month, but you can use any date in the month if necessary. At the very least, you or your accountant will make journal entries at the end of the year to properly close the books (as discussed in Chapter 17). Typical year-end journal entry adjustments include recording depreciation (addressed later in this chapter and in Chapter 17). Your accounting software automatically generates a hidden journal entry that zeroes out your income statement.

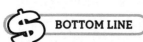 **BOTTOM LINE**

> At the end of each fiscal year, all your revenue, cost of goods sold, and expense accounts reset to 0. It might be disconcerting to see beginning balances for your assets, liabilities, and equity at the start of the new year but not the other types of accounts. This is to be expected, as your income statement starts over at 0 at the beginning of a new year, while your balance sheet accounts carry their balances forward perpetually.

In addition to year-end journal entries, there may be times when an adjusting journal entry is required to correct an error or affect a necessary change. For example, if you paid for insurance expense for the year and recorded a prepared asset (debit) of $1,200 reflecting the entire insurance payment, then each month you're going to make a journal entry to reduce (credit) the prepaid asset by $100 and expense (debit) that month's share of the insurance cost.

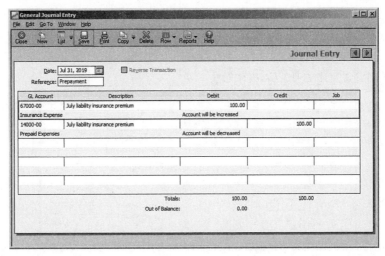

This Sage 50 transaction moves $100 from Prepaid Expenses to Insurance Expense for the month of July.

ACCOUNTING HACK

If you have more than one bank account, you might sometimes need to record a transfer of funds between the accounts. Some accounting programs have a Transfer command that allows you to easily record the movement of funds. However, in any accounting software, you can always use a journal entry to post the transfer. You'll debit the cash account receiving the funds and credit the account the funds come out of. Take the time to document the reason for the transfer within the journal entry so you can remember later when reconciling your bank account or reviewing your general ledger.

You might discover that transactions were entered incorrectly into your books. Maybe inventory items were set up incorrectly, which can in turn affect how revenue, cost of goods sold, or inventory amounts are recorded in your books. As covered in Chapter 5, when selling physical goods, you must specify general ledger accounts that indicate where to post the sale of an item, the item cost for the item, and your inventory account on your balance sheet. It's all too easy to inadvertently choose the wrong accounts when setting up an item.

Let's say you use the same general ledger account for both the Cost of Goods Sold and Inventory account fields. As you sell items, your accounting software posts a debit and a credit to the very same account, resulting in a 0 impact in your books. Normally when you sell items, cost of goods sold should increase and inventory should decrease. Some cloud-based programs, such as QuickBooks Online and Xero, prevent you from making such a mistake, but many desktop programs don't have such built-in protections.

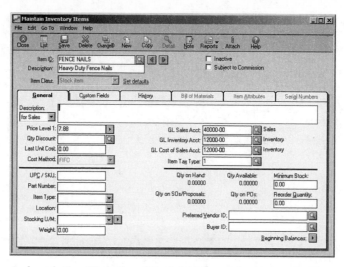

*As shown in Sage 50, the Cost of Goods Sold Account for this item should not
be Inventory but rather an expense account.*

Maybe dozens or even hundreds of invoices were posted incorrectly in this fashion. Because
your accounting software automatically posts inventory-related transactions in the background,
correcting such mistakes isn't as easy as you might hope. Fortunately, accounting rules allow you
to correct mistakes. To do so, you'll record a journal entry in your books to adjust the account
balances in question to their actual amounts, as shown in the following figure.

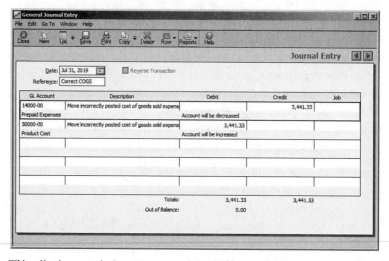

*This adjusting entry in Sage 50 moves activity double-posted to Inventory to the Cost of
Goods Sold account, which corrects both accounts.*

RED FLAG

Remember, the sum of the debits for every journal entry you record must match the sum of the credits. We've seen numerous accounting software users attempt to create what's referred to as a *one-sided journal entry,* in which they want to force one account to be a certain amount without affecting any other accounts. You can't do this in your accounting software. When you touch one account with a journal entry, you have to ensure you also touch at least one other account for balance.

As you can see, there's a lot to accounting and entering transactions. You don't want to allow just anyone to enter journal entries—only knowledgeable users well versed in accounting should do so. Likewise, you shouldn't allow your employees to simply double-click and change the original entry because the traceability (sometimes called the audit trail) is gone forever. The proper use of a journal entry documents why the transaction is being changed. If you're ever unsure about a journal entry, consult an accountant or your tax adviser.

Your accounting software gives you several ways to determine if any journal entries have been added, and in some cases by whom:

General Journal Entry transaction window: Your accounting software might provide an on-screen list of recent journal entries when you go to add a new entry. This can help you avoid inadvertently recording the same entry twice.

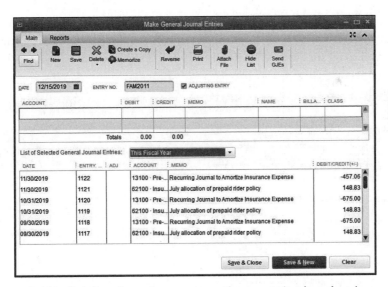

QuickBooks desktop always gives you an easy glance at previous journal entries.

General Journal report: This report, if available in your accounting software, is simply a list of all journal entries recorded in your books during a specific timeframe. In cloud-based programs such as QuickBooks Online and Xero this is considered an advanced report.

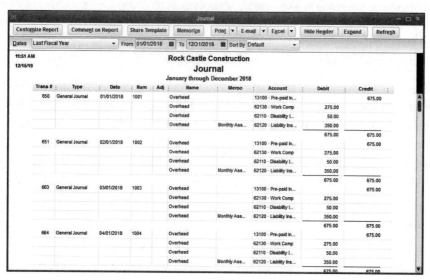

In QuickBooks desktop, you can filter the Journal report to show only journal transactions.

Audit Trail report: Most accounting programs offer a report that records the date, time, username, and details of all new and changed transactions in your books. This can be helpful when you need to figure out why a certain entry is in your books or who put it there.

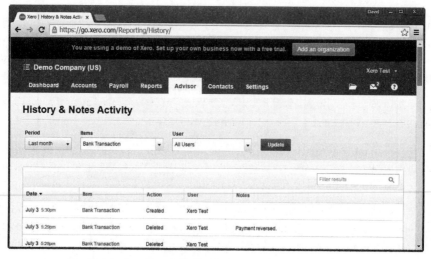

Xero's equivalent of an Audit Trail report is called History and Notes.

Prior Year Adjustments

Sometimes you might find mistakes in your books that were made last year or even earlier. For example, maybe you incorrectly posted an amount to an expense account that actually belongs in a balance sheet account. In such cases, you can't post the correction directly to the expense account, because doing so distorts your current year financial statements. Also, the change should have affected prior year books, so correcting entries in prior years that affect revenue, cost of goods sold, or expense accounts must use your Retained Earnings account as the offset instead.

A typical example of a prior period adjustment is a journal entry to correct an error in depreciation. Suppose you miscalculated the depreciation on a new piece of equipment—you should have taken an extra $500 in depreciation expense—but your books for the year are already closed (as discussed in Chapter 17).

A journal entry to depreciation expense is inappropriate at this point because the error is on last year's expense, not this year's, and last year's income and expenses have already been zeroed out and combined with your retained earnings account on your balance sheet. You need to make a prior period adjustment.

Instead of debiting depreciation expense for the $500, you'll debit retained earnings. The offsetting credit goes to accumulated depreciation because that account isn't closed out at the end of the year.

Note that you'll also have to make this change on your tax return for last year. If you've already filed the return, you might need to amend it to make the correction. At least make a note in your tax file so there's a record of the additional deduction.

Finding Misplaced Transactions

Your eyes might glaze over when looking at your full general ledger. That's understandable. To gain more insight from the general ledger, including finding misplaced transactions, consider modifying the report options within your general ledger to only view selected accounts. This can help sharpen your focus.

Or export the report to a spreadsheet, such as Microsoft Excel. In Chapter 22, we discuss using the Filter feature to collapse a report based on specified criteria.

You also could print the report and make notes with a pen and highlighter. You might use a significant amount of paper, but the change of venue from your screen to a printed page can help make issues in your general ledger easier to spot.

Another option is using the transaction search feature in your accounting software. Desktop-based programs often have a Find command on the Edit menu. Cloud-based programs may have a magnifying glass icon you can click to display a search window.

Finally, some accounting programs, such as the desktop version of QuickBooks, offer centralized screens for customers, vendors, employees, and inventory. These allow you to quickly scan through transactions posted for a specific customer or a particular amount.

Noncash Transactions

Your accounting software provides easy-to-use transaction screens for any activity that records money going into or out of your business. However, there are certain transactions you only can post in the form of journal entries.

For example, IRS Publication 946 explains in great detail how to depreciate property. The journal entry itself is simple enough: you'll debit a Depreciation Expense account and credit an Accumulated Depreciation account. What isn't necessarily simple is determining the amount of depreciation to record.

Many small businesses outsource depreciation calculations to their accountant or tax adviser, but some programs, such as Xero, have a built-in feature for calculating depreciation and posting the amounts to your books. Other programs get you part of the way there. QuickBooks, for example, allows you to create a list of fixed assets, but you must use either the Accountant or Enterprise version to calculate depreciation and automatically record the corresponding journal entries.

Alternatively, income tax programs like TurboTax, TaxAct, or H&R Block may allow you to perform the calculations, but you'll most likely have to enter the transactions in your books manually. This can lead to a circular situation in which you can't complete your tax return until you calculate depreciation in the tax software, post the entries in your books, and update your financial results in the tax software again.

Many small business owners question the need to depreciate assets because doing so doesn't have any effect on the operation of the business. Unfortunately, some amount of paper shuffling is endemic to accounting. The aforementioned Publication 946 has 114 pages of guidance on depreciation alone. What's more, your business might need to maintain two sets of depreciation schedules—one for book purposes and a second for tax purposes. Accounting rules require you to record depreciation for your books, but there can be tax advantages involved in maintaining a second set of depreciation schedules.

The U.S. Tax Code spans thousands of pages, so clearly we can't get very deep into many tax aspects in this book. With that said, a knowledgeable tax adviser likely can save you much more than you pay him or her in fees on your income tax bill—and provide the peace of mind of knowing your books are compliant with both IRS and general accounting rules.

ACCOUNTING HACK

In some cases, you can record depreciation for an asset all in one year, often referred to as Section 179 depreciation. Under certain circumstances, the IRS enables you to take a current year tax deduction for the entire purchase price of equipment and software you use in your business instead of spreading the cost over several years. As of this writing, most small businesses can deduct up to $25,000 of equipment and software that's placed in service by the end of the year. But exceptions abound, so consult your tax adviser for current Section 179 limits. Journal entries to record Section 179 depreciation debit Depreciation Expense for up to the permissible limit and credit Accumulated Depreciation by the same amount.

Nonposting Transactions

You may have heard an accountant or bookkeeper state they "posted a transaction to the books." This simply means they recorded the transaction in the accounting software. However, there are three types of transactions you won't ever see posted in your general ledger: estimates or quotes, sales orders, and purchase orders. Each of these is a placeholder transaction that eventually leads to activity on your books.

As mentioned in Chapter 6, you might prepare an estimate for a customer who's considering your products or services. No money changes hands as the result of this request for pricing, so you won't see the estimate listed in your general ledger. When the customer approves the estimate, your accounting software likely allows you to convert the estimate to either an invoice or a sales order.

Invoices appear immediately in your general ledger, but sales orders are simply a request for you to deliver products or services. Again, no money has changed hands yet. Once you fulfill all or part of the sales order, you'll create an invoice that will then appear on your books.

Purchase orders work in the same fashion, except in this case, you've placed a request with a vendor for products or services that haven't yet been fulfilled.

Your accounting software enables you run a report that shows open estimates, sales orders, and purchase orders. You can use these reports to stay abreast of pending transactions awaiting action.

When *Not* to Use Journal Entries

You might be thinking journal entries are the magic cure for anything that ails your books. Journal entries do make it easy to make corrections on your books, but you can compromise your books by using journal entries in the wrong situations.

Here are a few instances when you shouldn't use journal entries:

In Chapter 13, we show you the correct way to write off invoices that customers cannot or will not pay. Instead of journal entries, you use credit memos to offset these invoices so your Accounts Receivable balance always matches your balance sheet account.

Similarly, we show how to use vendor credit memos in Chapter 13 to write off bills from vendors that you've either entered twice or purposefully won't be paying. Using a journal entry to force your Accounts Payable balance down can result in your balance sheet not reconciling with your Aged Payables report.

You periodically might need to write off inventory that's spoiled, been damaged, or gotten lost. We referred to this as shrinkage in Chapter 5, where we also showed you the proper method for adjusting your inventory balance. Be sure to use the inventory adjustment feature offered in your software; journal entries cannot record changes in quantity on hand in your inventory records.

If you use your accounting software to process payroll, as we discuss in Chapter 9, always use payroll transactions to record adjustments to an employee's paycheck. Your accounting software only takes actual payroll transactions into account when you generate payroll tax returns and reports, as we discuss in Chapter 18. Adjustments that you make by way of journal entries can result in misstatements on your payroll tax returns.

The Least You Need to Know

- The general ledger houses every single financial transaction that occurs in your business.

- Adjusting journal entries are used to enter certain noncash transactions and correct errors in the general ledger.

- Prior period adjustments are used to correct errors and make changes that affect accounting years that have already been closed.

- Your accounting software offers multiple ways for you to find misplaced transactions.

- Certain transactions such as sales orders, purchase orders, and estimates never post to the general ledger.

- You should not use journal entries for transactions such as invoice and inventory write-offs; however, journal entries are the only way to post noncash entries such as depreciation and amortization.

Reconciling Bank and Credit Card Statements

Reconciling your bank and credit card accounts are some of the most important accounting activities you can perform. And you really can't reconcile too frequently. You might be surprised how often you can discover transactions—that you haven't even posted to your accounting records yet—that have affected your bank account already. Keeping a close eye on your bank accounts is one of the best ways to head off fraud or at least minimize the effects of fraudulent activity (more on this in Chapter 15).

In this chapter, you learn the ins and outs of reconciliation. We discuss how frequently you need to reconcile your accounts (more often than you think!) and explain how to prepare for reconciliation. You get an overview of how to reconcile in the leading accounting programs, as well as deal with automatic reconciliation features, when available. The chapter wraps up with information on reconciling credit card accounts, identifying when you've transposed digits in entries, and what to do if you simply can't get an account to reconcile.

In This Chapter

- Why you should reconcile
- Reconciliation step by step
- Working with automatic reconciliation
- Reconciling a credit card account
- Tracking down transpositions
- When an account won't reconcile

It's Not Just for Month-End

Reconciling helps you ensure your accounting records agree with your account records from your bank or financial service provider. A business can have several different types of financial accounts. Virtually every business has a checking account, but some also have business savings accounts. Many have business credit cards as well as accounts for other financial services such as PayPal.

Although your accounting software might give you the impression that reconciling your bank account is a once-a-month activity, it's not out of the question to reconcile your bank account weekly or even daily if you have access to your account information online.

When you reconcile a bank account, you're ensuring that any transactions that have posted to your bank account also appear in your accounting records. Further, this allows you to confirm that any transactions in your books that haven't cleared the bank yet are recent enough you'll know whether or not to stop payment on a check and reissue it. By reconciling your bank account periodically during the month, you can avoid unpleasant surprises, such as an overdraft fee when you handwrite a check you forget to log into your books, or purchases you make with a business debit card and forgot to post.

Yet another reason to do frequent reconciliations is that, in the event of a bank error, the law favors your bank. If money is debited from your account in error, you have 60 days to protest; however, if the bank makes an error in crediting your account, it has years to correct it.

Reconcile often, and you can catch errors immediately.

Preparing and Reconciling

Successfully reconciling a bank or credit card statement requires attention to detail, so try to choose a quiet time of day. You'll simply find yourself frustrated, and likely waste your time, if you try to reconcile your account amidst many distractions. However, if distractions are a perpetual state of your existence, don't defer reconciling your bank account for very long.

You'll typically only need two things to get started reconciling: your bank statement and access to your accounting software.

Your bank probably mails a paper copy of your statement to you monthly. Different banks use different cutoff dates for sending statements. Some send them near the first of a month for the preceding month, while others might use a mid-month cutoff date. You don't have to wait for the paper statement, though, if your bank offers access to your statements online.

ACCOUNTING HACK

We strongly encourage you to use the electronic statement as your main source of information and use the paper copy as a reminder in case time slips by without you reconciling your account.

Your bank might offer a template you can use to reconcile your account on the back or last page of your paper statement. Many banks have dropped this format in the interest of saving paper, but it's possible your bank still provides it.

Why Reconcile?

Your bank balance isn't necessarily a good measure of how much cash your business has on hand. Your accounting records usually provide a better measure, but they still might not reflect reality.

Several things can cause differences between your book balance and your bank balance. (In this context, by "book" balance, we mean the balance of your checking account, for example, as shown in your accounting software. By "bank" balance, we mean the amount the bank shows is in your bank account at a particular time.) Maybe you wrote one or more checks that have been taken out of your book balance but haven't yet cleared your bank, or you posted one or more deposits to your books, but the bank hasn't yet posted the deposits to your bank account. It could be that you made one or more bank deposits without first entering the amounts into your books. Maybe you handwrote a check and entered the amount of the check incorrectly in your books, you entered a transaction more than once, or someone you've authorized to make ACH withdrawals from your bank account posted a transaction you need to record in your books.

In rare instances, your bank may clear a check for an amount that's different from what you wrote or printed on the check. Or it could have assessed one or more fees you haven't yet reflected in your books.

Whatever the reason, you need to restore the balance.

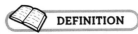

DEFINITION

The abbreviation **ACH** stands for Automated Clearing House, an electronic network most banks are part of. These electronic transactions may be ACH withdrawals or deposits and allow money to be moved around the banking system without any paper. You generally must grant explicit permission for someone to add or remove funds from your account in this fashion. If you have authorized your internet provider to take its monthly fee from your bank account automatically, that's an ACH transaction.

Reconciling at a Glance

Reconciliation ensures that your books agree with what the bank shows as your current balance. Here's how to reconcile your accounts, in a nutshell:

- You'll mark transactions that match both on your bank statement and in your books as cleared.

- Transactions that don't yet appear on your bank statement are still in transit, and so you'll leave those on your books as uncleared.

- If you find transactions that appear in both places but with amounts that don't match, you'll make corrections in your accounting software to bring your books up to date. However, banks are not infallible, so if you find an error in your bank statement, it might be best to temporarily change your books to reflect the erroneous amount while you investigate the issue with your banker.

Starting a Reconciliation

Let's go through an example reconciliation using QuickBooks desktop so you can learn what to look for when reconciling your bank account. Accounting programs vary, but typically a reconciliation command appears on a Banking or Tasks menu. In the case of QuickBooks, we'll choose Banking and then Reconcile. At this point, a Begin Reconciliation screen appears. It prompts you to select or enter several pieces of information:

Account: If you have multiple accounts, select the account to reconcile from the drop-down list. (You often can select an account before opening this dialog box.)

Statement date: This is the date from your statement. Use today's date if you're reconciling to your online bank statement.

Ending balance: On a paper bank or credit card statement, this is simply listed as your ending balance. Online banking statements or current activity reporting may show several balances:

Current Balance: This is the number you should reconcile to. It's the net amount in your bank account at the present time.

Collected Balance: When you deposit a check into your account, your bank sometimes grants you immediate access to the funds, even though the check hasn't cleared yet. Even paper checks often clear instantaneously upon deposit, but sometimes transactions may take time to fully clear.

Available Balance: If you wanted to go to the bank and empty your bank account, you'd only be able to withdraw up to the available balance amount, which at certain points might be less than the Current Balance amount.

Service charges: Include any service charges or interest that may have posted to your account since you last reconciled.

Date range: Access to a list of transactions since you last reconciled. This might be a paper statement if you reconcile once a month. If you view your bank statement online, typically you can filter the transactions shown on screen to a specific date range. Limiting what you see to only the transactions you need to focus on can speed up the reconciliation process.

With that information, you'll complete the corresponding fields in your accounting software.

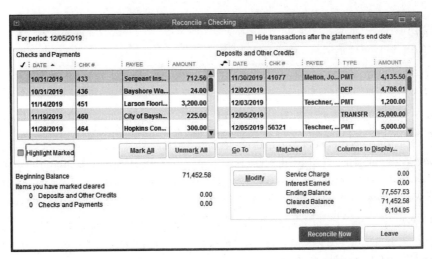

At a minimum, when reconciling, select an account, specify a statement date, and note an ending balance.

Once you've completed the initial fields, click Continue (in QuickBooks; your software might have a different option) to view the actual reconciliation screen.

A reconciliation screen lets you mark the items that have cleared your bank or credit card account.

Keep in mind we're using QuickBooks desktop to show you examples of a reconciliation screen, so the actual screens in your accounting software might look different. However, no matter what software tool you use, you'll still need this basic information.

Clearing Transactions

A typical reconciliation screen shows all uncleared transactions. In the case of the desktop versions of QuickBooks, this information is divided into two sets of columns: Checks and Payments and Deposits and Other Credits. Your accounting software might take a different approach. Sage 50, for example, shows all transactions in a single list.

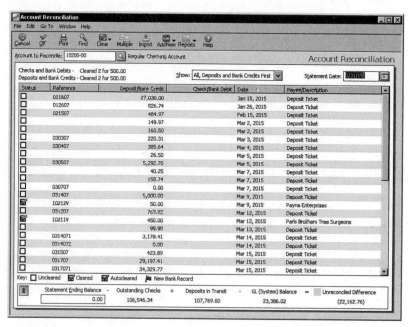

Sage 50 presents a single list of transactions. Your specific software might show two columns.

No matter what software you're using, a difference amount appears on-screen. This represents the current difference between the ending account balance shown in your books as of the statement date and what your bank reflects as your current balance. The goal of reconciling is to work this difference number down to 0. The difference amount changes every time you mark a transaction as cleared, so don't panic if the difference appears to fluctuate. Just remember your ultimate goal here is to get the difference down to 0.

To get started, choose the first transaction on your bank statement and then find the corresponding transaction on the reconciliation screen. When you find it, click the Clear column, which might be called Clear or be represented by a checkmark. Repeat this process for each transaction on your bank statement. Remember, you're making your books agree with the bank, so transactions that appear on your books but not on the bank statement simply haven't cleared yet or could be an error.

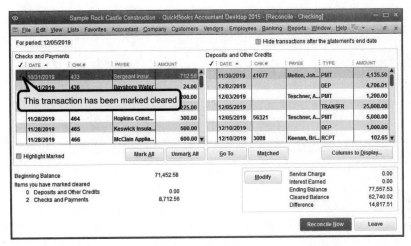

Your accounting software shows an indicator such as a checkmark, a checkbox, or sometimes the letter C to indicate transactions you've cleared.

Making Corrections

If you find an error, such as a check that cleared for a different amount than what you have listed on your books, simply double-click on the transaction in the reconciliation screen. Your accounting software should show you the original transaction, as shown in the next example.

There, you can modify any aspects of the transaction, such as amount, date, payee, and so on, and click the Save button to close the transaction. The revised transaction will appear in your reconciliation screen, which you can then mark as cleared.

As part of the reconciliation process, you might discover transactions that have cleared the bank but aren't yet on your books. Common situations include the following:

- Checks you scheduled for online payment through your bank or wrote by hand but forgot to enter into your accounting software.

- Fees assessed by your bank, such as for submitting a deposit ticket that doesn't match the total of the accompanying checks.

- ACH withdrawals from a service provider.

- ACH deposits made by customers you haven't yet posted to your books.

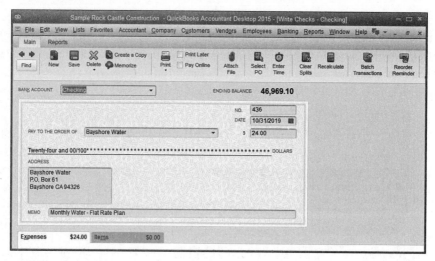

When needed, double-click a transaction within the Reconciliation screen to make corrections.

You can correct any of these situations without leaving the reconciliation screen. To do so, simply use the menu in your accounting software to initiate a new check, deposit, or journal entry as needed to record the missing transaction. When you close the transaction window, you should be returned to your account reconciliation window.

In some cases, the software might inform you that you'll need to save the reconciliation as is in order to add a new transaction. Simply accept that option, and when you return to the reconciliation window, you'll be able to pick up where you left off.

Tips for Successful Reconciliations

One of the biggest challenges of reconciling a bank account, particularly one with lots of transactions, is combating the "blur." As you compare the many numbers and columns on your statement to the reconciliation window, it won't take much for your eyes to glaze over.

To help with this, most modern accounting programs allow you to sort columns within reconciliation windows. Simply click a column heading, such as Amount, to sort the transactions in ascending amount order (smallest to largest). Click the column heading a second time to sort in descending order (largest to smallest). Every column within the reconciliation window should be clickable and, therefore, sortable. Click the Date column to return items to Date order.

If your reconciliation takes several screens to view, you might be able to zero in on an out-of-balance amount by sorting on the dollar amount column. You often can sort by payee or check/reference number as well.

All the scrolling and clicking involved with reconciling a bank account can quickly become tedious. You'll likely be relegated to using your mouse with cloud-based programs such as QuickBooks Online, but there's an easier way in desktop-based accounting software. Within the reconciliation window, you can use the up or down arrow keys on your keyboard to navigate the list and then tap the spacebar on your keyboard to toggle between marking an item cleared or uncleared.

Finally, as much as you might hope to, you won't always be able to finish your reconciliation in a single sitting. Anticipating this, your accounting software lets you save your work in progress. Depending on the software, you might see a Leave or Finish Later button. If you don't see a button like this, simply close the reconciliation window and a prompt should appear asking if you want to save your work.

Automated Reconciliations

Depending on the accounting software you use, you might be able to have your software automatically reconcile your bank account for you. Once you grant permission for your software to connect to your bank account over the internet, at your request, it can synchronize transactions from your bank account with your accounting records, automatically clearing any matches.

Anything that doesn't match is left on-screen for you to decide how to handle.

Unmatched transactions could be items that cleared your bank account before you entered them into your accounting software. Or, maybe you inadvertently entered the same transaction more than once in your accounting software. If this happens, you can simply delete or void the duplicate transaction.

Cloud-based accounting packages may allow you to reconcile your statement on your mobile device, although this can be a tedious exercise unless you have both a large screen and a paper copy of your statement.

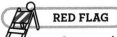 **RED FLAG**

Automated bank reconciliation can feel like being liberated from a tedious task, but there's much value in being forced to sift through your transactions. By clearing each transaction individually, you can easily notice any amounts that seem out of scale for your business. And if you take a hands-off approach to reconciling your bank account, you might miss fee increases or changes in recurring charges that over time can eat away at your bottom line.

Reconciling Credit Card Statements

By this point, we hope you can see the importance of reconciling your bank account. Reconciling credit card statements is equally important because recurring charges can slowly erode your line of credit. (Plus, these should be reflected as expenses on your books.) For the most part, the process of reconciling your credit card statements is the same as for your bank accounts.

However, we do want to point out one difference. When you're reconciling your bank statement, ideally your bank balance is always above 0, so you enter positive numbers. However, if you're reconciling to a non-0 balance on your credit card statement, such as $5,000, in some programs, you'll enter 5,000, but in others you might need to enter −5,000.

QuickBooks, for example, enables you to enter the balance as you see it on your bank statement. Other programs more suited to users with an accounting background, like Sage 50, expect you to enter the balance as a credit amount, hence the minus sign in front of the number.

Remember, your financial statements are only as accurate as the work you put into them, which means a sizeable amount of your financial activity could be left off your books if you don't reconcile your credit card statements. Further, your income tax bill could be higher than necessary at the end of the year if you've neglected to reflect every expense incurred by your business.

Identifying Transpositions

The goal of reconciliation is to get that unreconciled difference down to 0. However, you might find that you can't get the unreconciled difference down to 0 and you're off by an inexplicable amount. Fortunately, accountants and bookkeepers have long relied on a trusty technique: divide the discrepancy by 9. If the discrepancy divides evenly by 9, then most likely you've transposed two digits because the difference between numbers with transposed digits is always divisible by 9.

For example, you meant to enter $45.54 but you inadvertently posted it as $45.45. The difference between $45.54 and $45.45 is 9 cents, which is evenly divisible by 9. This could cause a 9 cent unreconciled difference.

Once you suspect a transposition, you have to track it down. That requires you to double-check the amount of each transaction. We share one way of doing this in the next section.

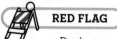 **RED FLAG**

Don't assume you can skip reconciling accounts that don't have much activity. If you have a business savings account where you squirrel away money for a rainy day, be sure to reconcile it at least once a month, even if you haven't touched the account for a while. The odds of recovering money unexpectedly taken from your account drop precipitously with each passing day.

When You Can't Reconcile

One of the best favors you can do yourself is knowing when to take a break, and that's especially true when you're working on a computer. Transactions on a reconciliation screen can blur together so easily, you might not be able to see the obvious solution right in front of you.

Remember, reconciliation isn't something that has to be performed in a single sitting. Most accounting software offers a Postpone or Leave Reconciliation option so you can exit and save your work for later. Many times, when you come back the next day with fresh eyes, that missing transaction or transposed amount jumps right out at you.

However, if you have a particular reconciliation you just can't seem to clear up on-screen, it's time to go old school.

Print your bank statement, reset all the transactions in your accounting software to uncleared, and work through your bank statement, putting a checkmark next to each item you clear on-screen. It can be a slow and laborious process, but it's a proven way to find the discrepancy in your reconciliation.

From time to time, the issue causing you to be unable to reconcile your account could be lurking in a prior month. Before you start reconciling your current month's bank statement, run a report for the previous month to ensure the reconciled difference is still 0. In some cases, you might have to work your way back several months. If you modify a previously cleared transaction, such as to fix an accounting error, it can turn uncleared. This can cause a domino effect on all subsequent accounting periods.

If all else fails, simply start over. If you haven't saved the reconciliation yet, click the Cancel button or leave the window and choose No when asked if you want to save your work. If you've saved your work already, unmark any transactions you've cleared and start over from the top. The answer is always there, somewhere between your bank statement and your books, so it's a matter of getting the proper perspective so you can see any issues that have been eluding you.

Your paper-based bank statement contains information that can help as well. You'll notice that the reconciliation window in your accounting software shows totals of cleared Deposits and Withdrawals. The terminology might vary, but there should be a section on your screen that lists this information. Compare this to the Total Deposits and Total Withdrawals listed on your bank statement. In some cases, you might have to add two or more amounts together, such as Checks and Other Withdrawals, to get to Total Withdrawals. In any case, if you can't reconcile and you find that at least the Total Deposits shown on the screen matches your bank statement, you know the remaining difference is somewhere among the checks and withdrawals.

Successful reconciliations are a process of elimination, and anything you can do to limit the scope of your scrutiny will help you finish the reconciliation faster.

Reconciling your accounts is one of the most important accounting activities you can carry out. Not only does reconciling help you keep a close eye on your cash balance, it also ensures that your financial statements present an accurate picture of your business. It's easy to forget to post recurring charges, such as health insurance premiums, that charge automatically to a credit card. Reconciling your credit card statements helps ensure all your expenses are listed in your books. Plus it helps you avoid overlimit fees, rejected credit card charges, and other problems that can arise from an account left unattended from periodic financial scrutiny.

The Least You Need to Know

- Reconciling helps you ensure that your accounting records agree with your account records from your financial service provider and should be performed monthly, at the least.

- After you gather your statement and transaction records, you can step through the reconciliation process in your accounting software and correct any discrepancies.

- Reconciling your credit card account helps you clear errors and note any fee changes that may erode your business's bottom line.

- If a reconciliation discrepancy divides evenly by 9, then most likely you've transposed two numbers in a transaction.

- You can resolve a discrepancy by starting over and comparing each transaction. Comparing Total Deposits and Total Withdrawals between your bank statement and the software reconciliation window can help you narrow down where the discrepancy might be.

PART 3

Employee-Related Accounting

Adding employees to your business can be both thrilling and intimidating. The good news is that you've got enough demand for your company's product or service to justify expanding the team. The bad news is that not only do you need to cover that person's salary, benefits, and employment taxes out of the business revenue now, but you also need to handle all the related accounting decisions, forms, and filings.

In this part, we help you manage employment issues, from bigger-picture decisions down to nitty-gritty tasks. First, you learn what you need to do for an initial hire, including whether you should classify a job as an independent contractor or employee, what governmental forms to complete, and how to compensate the person (and yourself as business owner). Then we take a look at what benefits you might consider or be legally required to provide for your employees and business, plus their impact on your accounting. Various types of insurance for employees, various types of insurance for the business, and different flavors of retirement plans are included. We wrap up Part 3 by leading you through employment taxes, emphasizing the importance of meeting deadlines so you avoid penalties.

Setting Up New Team Members

Not every business has employees. Sometimes a business is organized to simply own property or hold an ownership stake in other companies. Many businesses, though, have at least one employee.

In Chapter 2, we discussed different business structures. If you operate your business as a sole proprietorship, you are a de facto owner who, in some ways, is treated as if you're an employee of your business. However, the other types of businesses may or may not have employees. As you'll see in this chapter, you might be required to classify yourself as an employee. In Chapter 4, we discussed the concept of paying distributions to yourself; beyond that, the Internal Revenue Service (IRS) does require corporate officers to pay themselves a reasonable salary.

You also have to determine whether your "hires" are employees or independent contractors, file the correct paperwork to establish employment, meet the requirements for paying hourly wages and salaries, and choose a method for processing payroll. This chapter walks you through the essentials of all these employment issues.

In This Chapter

- When to treat yourself as an employee
- Employees versus independent contractors
- Forms for new employees
- Paying hourly and salaried workers and owners
- Processing payroll

Are You an Employee?

If you're an officer in a corporation you own, you might be required to treat yourself as an employee. The IRS provides specific guidance to help with making this determination in Publication 15-A Employer's Supplemental Tax Guide. In short, if you take an active role in the day-to-day operations of a corporation, at least a portion of your compensation must be paid to you in the form of payroll.

As noted in Chapter 4, owners of a corporation may elect to pay themselves distributions. However, distributions from a S corporation are often exempt from the payroll taxes (more on this in Chapter 12), so owners tend to want to minimize this tax. Dividends disbursed from a C corporation are taxable to the owner.

The IRS only provides vague guidance that owners must pay themselves a "reasonable salary." We say vague guidance because the IRS reserves the right to make its own determination if you've been underpaying yourself. A tax professional can help you determine an appropriate pay level for your industry, or you might be able to find resource material online or at your local public library. You can be subject to additional taxes, as well as interest and penalties, if the IRS inspects your records and finds that you've been substantially underpaying yourself.

The Difference Between Employees and Independent Contractors

Now, should your team members be considered employees or vendors? Having employees triggers a number of payroll taxes (more on this in Chapter 12), some of which are borne solely by the business. As such, business owners sometimes try to classify new hires as contractors, which shifts the burden of those taxes to the contractor instead of the business. Further, employees are often entitled to benefits and reimbursements (see Chapter 11), whereas contractors are not.

The IRS lists three specific criteria for determining whether someone is an employee:

Behavioral control: Factors such as set work hours, specific work locations, required meetings, and whether or not work can be performed by a substitute without issue all contribute to whether a worker is considered an employee or independent contractor. The more control the employer has over the behavior of the worker, the more likely the worker is classified as an employee.

Financial control: Another primary determining factor is whether required equipment and supplies are provided to the worker, or if the worker is responsible for supplying them. The latter tends to suggest the worker is an independent contractor. Other factors include whether customers pay the worker directly, whether expenses are reimbursed, and the worker's responsibility for economic loss or financial risk.

Relationship type: A primary test of employment is if the worker performs services for only your firm or provides services for yours and other firms as well. A worker who performer services for multiple companies is more likely to be classified as an independent contractor. Further tests include whether the worker is entitled to paid vacation, holidays, or sick pay—all of which equate to employee benefits—and whether the relationship can be terminated without liability or penalty, which is more likely to describe an independent contractor.

Keep in mind that as an employer, you really don't have a choice regarding this classification unless there's a very gray area. If these guidelines point to a clear definition of either an employee or an independent contractor, that's the classification you must use.

However, if the lines between employee and independent contractor are fuzzy, consider other issues when making a decision as to how to classify workers. Aside from the obvious benefit of not having to withhold and pay payroll taxes if your workers are independent contractors, here are some additional issues to consider when determining classification of workers:

- Employees are subject to wage guidelines, including minimum wage and overtime laws.

- Employees must be covered by workers' compensation insurance, paid for by the employer, as well as unemployment tax.

- Employees are entitled to benefits based on the company's benefit structure.

- Employees have the right to vote to unionize.

- Employees are often subject to right-to-work laws that allow employers to terminate them without cause, whereas independent contractors are under contract and the employer might not have the right to choose which contractors are doing the work.

- Independent contractors decide how and when they're going to do the job and what they're going to charge.

- Independent contractors are not necessarily covered by workers' compensation insurance, but that might not alleviate the employer's liability if the worker is hurt on the job. Your workers' compensation carrier might require you to report amounts paid to independent contractors, which will increase the premium you pay.

- Employees who are paid any amount of wages during a calendar year must be issued Form W-2 (see Chapter 18). Conversely, you must issue Form 1099 to report compensation paid to independent contractors in the amount of $600 or more per calendar year.

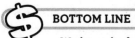

BOTTOM LINE

Workers who feel they've been inappropriately classified as independent contractors can file Form SS-8, Determination of Worker Status for Purposes of Federal Employment Taxes and Income Tax Withholding with the IRS. This document requests information about the working relationship so the IRS can launch an investigation. However, employers may also elect to file Form SS-8 on a preemptive basis to avoid unexpected tax penalties for making an inappropriate determination regarding a worker.

New Hire Paperwork

Hiring a new employee can be an exciting time for your business, but it also can be a lot of paperwork. Although we can't provide specific guidance for every situation, we can provide an overview of the types of rules and regulations with which you might be expected to comply.

As we noted in Chapter 2, your business must register for an employer identification number (EIN) with the IRS if you have any employees. You also will be required to register with one or more regulatory agencies within your state government and possibly your local government.

Federal Paperwork

Employers are required to hire only individuals who are legally entitled to work in the United States. This obviously includes all U.S. citizens, but also foreign citizens who have proper authorization, commonly referred to as a Green Card.

U.S. Citizenship and Immigration Services operates a system known as E-Verify employers can use to determine the eligibility of job applicants. Presently, E-Verify is optional for many employers, although participation can be mandatory for employers that perform work for the federal government. Further, certain states require either all or most employers to participate in the E-Verify system. Visit uscis.gov/e-verify to register for and utilize the E-Verify system.

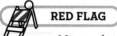

RED FLAG

Many websites masquerade as free or paid services that will purportedly get you up to speed on complying with government regulations. As a general rule, federal government websites usually end in .gov. Tread carefully when seeking online guidance on federal and state regulations so you don't inadvertently expose yourself or your employees to identify fraud or unnecessary fees.

Other than the E-Verify system, the federal government doesn't require any formal notification that you've hired a new employee. However, you will want to request the following documents from every new hire:

Form I-9, Employment Eligibility Verification: Individuals use this form to verify they can legally work in the United States. It provides the information you need to provide to the aforementioned E-Verify system.

Form W-4, Employee's Withholding Allowance Certificate: This form allows employees to either document, in limited cases, that they are exempt from federal income tax withholding, or document the number of exemptions they want to claim for withholding purposes. Each exemption reduces the basis for which an employee's federal income tax withholding is calculated but does not affect Social Security or Medicare withholding. This form also documents an employee's Social Security number, which you need to file Form W-2, Wage and Tax Statement, at the end of each calendar year when reporting each employee's wages and state and federal withholding taxes.

ACCOUNTING HACK

To help new employees determine how many exemptions to claim, direct them to the online withholding calculator available at irs.gov/Individuals/ IRS-Withholding-Calculator.

Beyond these two forms, the federal government won't take any other initial interest when you first hire new employees.

State Paperwork

Your state takes interest in new hires from two perspectives:

New hire reporting: In 1996, Congress enacted the Personal Responsibility and Work Opportunity Reconciliation Act, which requires employers in all 50 states to report new hires, re-hires, and temporary employees. In part, this program helps enforce child-support compliance and helps detect citizens who attempt to collect public assistance or unemployment insurance and paychecks at the same time. An internet search with your state's name and the phrase "new hire" helps you locate the official website for your state's new-hire directory.

Federal law requires you to report new hires within 20 days of their hire date, but your state might set an even shorter timeframe. Check your state's specific procedures and timeframe.

Withholding allowances: States with an income tax typically have their own version of the federal Form W-4. Most employees will want the same number of withholdings for both state and federal purposes, but you should provide the state form when applicable.

Local Paperwork

In certain situations, your new hires might have to register for a permit from your local municipality, which could mean city, county, or township. For instance, in Georgia, the city of Atlanta requires professionals in the medical, cosmetology, and athletic training fields to register for annual licenses.

Rules for Hourly and Salaried Employees

As an employer, you have a lot of latitude when it comes to how much you pay employees, but you do have to conform to the Federal Labor Standards Act (FLSA), which is administered by the U.S. Department of Labor. In short, the FLSA sets standards for minimum wages and overtime, which we discuss in a moment.

Employers often try to classify as many employees as salaried as possible because this fixes annual payroll costs. Some employees relish knowing what their paycheck will be each pay period, while others might want the opportunity to earn overtime pay.

Hourly Workers

As of this writing, the federal government requires that every employee age 16 and over be paid at least $7.25 per hour. If an employee works 40 hours a week for 52 weeks, this translates to an annual pay of $15,080. Some cities and states mandate higher minimum wages, so be sure to check your local statutes. You're required to use the state minimum if it's higher than its federal counterpart.

Federal law also requires hourly employees be paid time and a half ($10.88 per hour for minimum wage employees) for any hours beyond 40 in a 7-day period.

There's no state or federal requirement to extend paid vacation to hourly workers, as you learn in Chapter 11. However, some states, cities, and counties have enacted legislation that requires paid sick time for certain workers.

Although there's no federal requirement to do so, some employers offer time-and-a-half or even double-time pay to employees who work on holidays. Doing so can make it easier to staff a business that operates on holidays and can yield goodwill with employees.

Some businesses try to skirt certain employment regulations by limiting certain workers to less than 30 hours per week. Such part-time workers usually aren't entitled to most of the employee benefits we discuss in Chapter 11. Although the cost savings might appear enticing, you'll likely experience higher employee turnover—and incur the costs related to hiring and training new employees often. Also, customer service could suffer if your employees don't feel invested in your company.

Salaried Workers

The FLSA governs both hourly and salaried employees. Salaried employees—often referred to as exempt employees, meaning the employee is not eligible for overtime pay—are expected to complete their job responsibilities each week even if those tasks require more than 40 hours of time. Salaried employees are typically part of a company's management or professional staff.

Exempt employees must earn at least $455 per week ($23,660 a year), although some states require an even higher minimum. At the time of this writing, new federal guidelines are being proposed to raise the $455 limit so be sure to check the current guidelines.

Salaries provide a fixed cost for employers, but unfair expectations with regard to job responsibilities can send salaried employees running for the door. As we discuss in Chapter 11, your business might offer paid vacation time or sick leave. Depending on the arrangement you strike with your employees, even salaried employees can have their pay docked when they take sick or vacation time that exceeds company policies.

RED FLAG

Employee wages are serious business, and you might be surprised at the levels of government that have enforcement power over employee wages. Federal minimum wage changes require an act of Congress, which means the rate doesn't change very often. The current rate of $7.25 an hour took effect on July 24, 2009. However, state and local governments are authorized to set minimum wage levels that are higher than the federal level, and these can and do change more frequently. Disgruntled employees often have multiple governmental agencies that are interested in correcting unfair or illegal wage practices so keep your pay practices on the right side of the requirements.

Paying Owners

Technically, an owner of a corporation is within his or her right to decide to work for free and just take a share of the profits in the form of a dividend when the corporation is successful. However, the IRS frowns on this behavior and believes that if a corporation is functioning, someone must be doing some work on its behalf and, therefore, employment occurs. Yet beware of the nuances: sole proprietors (and partners in a partnership) normally aren't considered employees and do not receive a W-2. Owners of entities treated as corporations can be employees.

Some studies seem to indicate that a reasonable rule to apply is a 60/40 rule, wherein 60 percent of the distribution to a working owner is treated as salary, subject to payroll taxes, and the remaining 40 percent is treated as dividend. This percentage can, and should, change when an owner goes into semiretirement, the business has a reason to accumulate capital, or a number of other business-based circumstances occur.

The 60/40 rule is a starting point for determining the portion of employment of a business owner and by no means is written in stone. Your own calculation of what constitutes a reasonable salary should be well documented so you can support the logic of it should the IRS contest your determination.

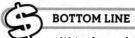

BOTTOM LINE

We've focused this discussion on taxable corporations and have not addressed salary rules for owners of other types of entities. There's more flexibility in determining a salary/dividend/draw split in S corporations, LLCs, partnerships, and other types of business entities. No matter what type of entity you choose, discuss your plans for ownership withdrawals with your tax adviser.

Payroll Processing Options

At this point, you might be realizing that the simple act of paying someone can mean a great deal of complexity. Fortunately, you do have options.

You could outsource payroll processing to a third party, or your accounting software might allow you to electronically calculate payroll and related taxes. But both of these options require some level of financial outlay.

If you're on a tight budget or have very minimal payroll processing needs, you can manually calculate the payroll tax amounts due. Let's look at the ins and outs of each of these processing methods.

Third-Party Providers

Many businesses enlist the services of a national fee-based payroll provider, such as ADP (adp. com), Ceridian (ceridian.com), or Paychex (paychex.com). These companies specialize in making payroll simple by providing the following options:

- Employees can be paid by direct deposit.

- Payroll taxes can be automatically remitted to the designated tax authorities.

- Periodic tax reporting, such the items discussed in Chapter 18, can be filed automatically.

When using these services, you report the hours worked by hourly employees, and the payroll provider automatically calculates the amounts due.

Of course, you also pay a fee for the payroll provider's services. These vary depending on the frequency of your payroll (weekly, biweekly, semimonthly, or monthly) and the number of employees you have. All national providers offer websites where you can set up new employees and administer pay rates and withholding requests. Some even offer apps you can use on mobile devices. They also can directly provide or connect you with resources for time clock options if needed.

You have many other options for payroll processing beyond national providers. Your bank may offer payroll processing, as do cloud-based payroll services such as Kronos (kronos.com), SurePayroll (surepayroll.com), and ZenPayroll (zenpayroll.com). Pricing varies, but typically, assuming some level of responsibility through a cloud-based provider gives you the best of both worlds, meaning reduced costs and reduced paperwork.

Payroll service providers such as these provide summary reports you can use to post your payroll expense to your books. Many businesses use journal entries to post payroll expenses, as we covered in Chapter 7, but you also can record a check, as we discussed in Chapter 6. In this case, the check would be made payable to the payroll provider and include all the salaries, wages, and related payroll taxes.

Accounting Software Options

Most desktop and cloud-based accounting software programs offer built-in payroll features.

However, the software vendors generally consider this a bonus feature that requires an additional fee. For desktop-based accounting programs, such as QuickBooks and Sage 50, you must purchase a separate payroll subscription each year—in addition to your software license—that unlocks the payroll features of your accounting software. Some programs only streamline payroll calculations (that is, the subscription enables you to calculate payroll taxes for any jurisdiction in the United States). Others enable you to electronically file your payroll tax returns. Some provide reports that allow you to determine your tax liability for a given time period, but usually you'll need to remit the taxes yourself, as we discuss in Chapter 18.

If you choose to process payroll within your accounting software, the first step is to enable the payroll feature, typically via the Help or Payroll menu. If you're using a desktop-based accounting program, you'll be prompted to periodically download tax updates that implement the latest payroll tax calculations. These updates are transparent within cloud-based accounting programs.

Within the accounting software, you'll set up each employee individually. For instance, in the desktop version of QuickBooks, you'll find an Employees menu at the top of the screen, along with Employee Center and Payroll Center commands.

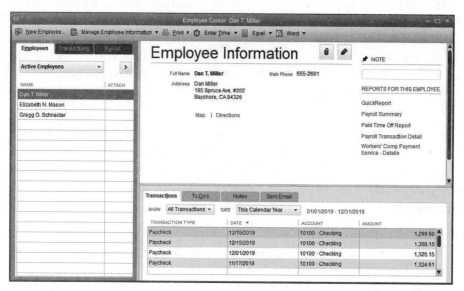

QuickBooks desktop centralizes all employee and payroll activities in the Employee Center.

Conversely, Sage 50 Accounting takes a more distributed approach. You need to choose Maintain and then Employees/Sales Reps to set up a new employee. A Payroll command on that same menu provides access to payroll configuration options. You initiate paychecks from the Tasks menu by choosing one of two Payroll Entry options.

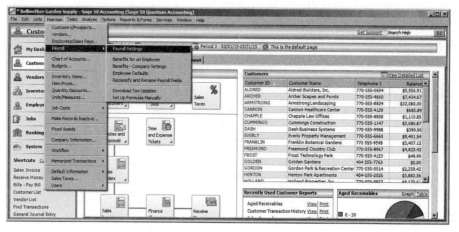

Sage 50 offers a decentralized approach to maintaining employees and processing payroll.

Your accounting software provides fields for you to specify both demographic and financial information about your employees. You'll utilize the employee's I-9 and W-4 forms for much of the data for these screens.

Employee Information

Title   First name   Middle name   Last name   Suffix

Email

Separate multiple emails with commas

*Display name as

Phone   Mobile

Print on check as ✓ Use display name

Billing rate (/hr)

☐ Employee's time is billable by default

Address
map

SSN

Street

Employee ID   Gender

City/Town   *State*

ZIP   *Country*

Hire date   Released

Notes

Date of birth

Cancel   Privacy   Save

Different accounting software asks for new employee information in slightly different formats.

After you complete the employee setup, your accounting software automates most of the calculations related to payroll.

Manual Calculations

Although many aspects of payroll processing can be automated, you still can perform all the calculations by hand if you prefer. The IRS offers Publication 15, commonly referred to as Circular E, that contains guidance on calculating payroll tax withholding, including tax tables you can use.

 **RED FLAG**

> Due to the complexities and vagaries of payroll processing, you might quickly abandon manual calculations unless you have a situation in which most calculations related to employee paychecks are relatively constant. Another downside of manually preparing the withholding is that rates different from the standard tables in Circular E may be required for supplemental pay or bonuses.

Many businesses outsource as much of the payroll process as possible, which is certainly understandable given the complexities. Outsourcing also reduces the potential exposure of missing a payroll tax remittance or reporting deadline. Fortunately, if try handling payroll on your own and decide it's too much, you can send it out. What's important is that you ensure you have mechanisms in place so you accurately and timely comply with the federal, state, and local payroll regulations that apply to your business.

The Least You Need to Know

- If your business is a corporation, you might need to treat yourself as an employee and pay yourself a reasonable salary in addition to any draws you take.

- The IRS provides rules that can help you determine if a worker is an employee or an independent contractor.

- Every new employee is required to fill out employment forms, and employers are required to report new employee information to the government.

- You must comply with pay laws and regulations for both hourly and salaried employees.

- As an owner, you might need to use a method such as the 60/40 rule as a starting point to determine how much to pay yourself in salary (60 percent) versus draws (40 percent). The actual amounts of reasonable compensation vary among regions of the country and other economic factors.

- You can use a payroll service or employ the payroll features in your accounting software to complete this task.

Understanding Insurance

Life is fraught with risk, and owning or managing a business often brings exposure to even more risks. Although you can't guard against every risk in life, you can share the burden of risks you can anticipate by purchasing insurance.

As with many aspects of running a business, there's an art to using insurance effectively. As you'll see in this chapter, if you have employees, you need to purchase workers' compensation insurance, at a minimum. You also could purchase other types of insurance to protect your business and your personal assets. You can offer insurance to your employees as a benefit as well.

In this chapter, we break down the various types of insurance you might consider purchasing to protect your business and employees, including those types of insurance you're legally required to buy.

In This Chapter

- Managing risk with liability insurance
- Protecting your things with property insurance
- Health and life insurance for your employees
- Accounting for insurance expenses

Liability Insurance

The purpose of liability insurance is to protect an insured party against unintentional acts or situations that cause some form of harm to others. Liability insurance takes many forms, and most are optional, but as you'll see, at least two forms are government mandated.

Even the tiniest of home-based businesses can encounter situations in which an expensive legal defense is required, even if the business isn't in any way at fault. If your business is sued, your liability insurance covers your legal defense fees. Further, if your company is found to be at fault, liability insurance covers any court-ordered monetary amounts up to your policy limits. This can protect your business from catastrophic financial payouts that could cripple or even bankrupt it.

Keep in mind that liability insurance does not offer any protection against criminal acts. Also, liability insurance policies are very tightly written, so you might need to purchase more than one type of coverage to protect your business from various risks.

Insurance companies continue to segment coverage into specialty protections that aren't listed in the following sections, but we can offer a general overview of the types of coverage you should consider for your business.

 BOTTOM LINE

> Insurance is a means of sharing risk, and for most policies, you're expected to provide some level of first dollar coverage. This means your policies likely have a deductible you need to pay in full before the insurance company pays any part of a claim. Deductibles also can be used as a financial tool. In some cases, your insurance premium amounts could drop if you're willing to shoulder a larger deductible, which lessens the insurance company's initial exposure should a claim against the policy arise.

Workers' Compensation

The underpinnings of workers' compensation date back as far as 2500 B.C.E., although in the United States, *workers' compensation* coverage is a fairly recent development that originated in the early to mid-1900s. In a previous era, this type of insurance was known as workman's compensation insurance.

The purpose of workers' compensation insurance is to provide a safety net for workers who are injured on the job. This insurance provides automatic benefits to injured employees and also protects employers from legal action for negligence stemming from such injuries.

Workers' compensation is not optional, although certain states allow employee-owners or *officers* of a business to opt out of workers' compensation. That is, only owners and officers can choose to opt-out; all other employees must be covered.

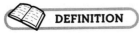 **DEFINITION**

Workers' compensation insurance provides a safety net for workers who are injured on the job. Employees in higher-level positions such as chief executive officer, president, vice president, secretary, treasurer, and so on are referred to as **officers** and are authorized to transact business and make decisions on behalf of the company.

Workers' compensation provides injured employees the following:

- Coverage for medical expenses

- Income replacement during periods of temporary or permanent disability

- Funeral and dependent benefits resulting from a loss of life

- Vocational benefits to retrain workers unable to carry out their previous line of work.

Although the U.S. Department of Labor (DOL) provides oversight, workers' compensation insurance is regulated by each of the 50 states, which means there are 50 different systems. We can at least provide a general overview of how workers' compensation works in many states.

Employers purchase workers' compensation insurance from a private company, or in the case of certain industries, a quasiprivate or public company designed to manage risks within certain industries. Certain large companies are permitted to self-insure, meaning they pay all worker benefits directly instead of paying premiums to an insurance company that would pay out the benefits.

The insurance premium is typically based on two primary criteria: the total payroll for each employee, and a risk factor assigned to each employee based on his or her job. For example, a clerical worker has a much lower risk factor than a deep-water oil rig worker.

At the beginning of a coverage period, employers pay an estimated premium based on the projected payroll and the associated risk factors for the period. The insurance company then performs an audit after the coverage period to calculate the exact premium due. Employers might have to pay for additional coverage if the initial estimate was too low, or they might receive a refund or premium credit if the coverage was too high. The audit typically provides copies of federal payroll tax returns to document the actual wages paid to each employee.

 **ACCOUNTING HACK**

Workers' compensation insurance is not optional. Although it might feel like a costly burden, the coverage protects your business from legal action and protects your employees. You or your business can be subject to severe penalties for not maintaining workers' compensation insurance for your employees. However, you do not have to accept the first quote you get. Compare prices among multiple insurance carriers to stay compliant while also controlling costs.

An internet search with your state's name and the words "workers compensation" should help you locate the government agency that has oversight over your state. You also can use the interactive map offered by the DOL at dol.gov/owcp/dfec/regs/compliance/wc.htm.

General Liability Insurance

This type of insurance provides a level of protection for business owners against civil litigation. For example, a customer could slip and fall in the lobby of your office and file a lawsuit. Business owners can purchase liability coverage in dollar amounts commensurate with the amount of perceived risk. As noted in Chapter 2, your choice of business structure might protect you personally from litigation, but litigation that consumes all the assets of your business could still be catastrophic to you personally.

Product Liability Insurance

This type of insurance protects businesses from financial losses when a product covered by the policy causes an injury or damage. For example, food recalls due to listeria, salmonella, and other bacterial agents can cause significant harm to customers. Just about any other product can spark unintended consequences, such as appliances with faulty wiring, baby cribs that cause injuries, or outdoor clothing with heating elements that cause burns.

Directors' and Officers' Liability Insurance

This type of coverage, often referred to as D&O coverage, protects directors and officers of corporations from legal defense costs for acts related to their role of running the company. Just as workers' compensation only protects employees while working on the job, D&O coverage is limited to acts carried out on the job.

Professional Liability Insurance

Lawyers, accountants, architects, consultants, and many other professionals purchase insurance protection for improperly rendering services, or failing to live up to their professional responsibility. This type of coverage is sometimes referred to as errors and omissions (E&O) insurance. This insurance doesn't protect against fraudulent acts, such as a tax adviser knowingly filing an improper income tax return, but the insurance can protect against negligent acts in the line of delivering professional services.

Medical professionals often have a special version of this type of insurance known as malpractice insurance.

Automobile Insurance

Any automobile you or your business owns must have a liability policy. The minimum amount of coverage varies by state, but often the minimum coverages are insufficient to fully protect your business. If you drive a vehicle without liability insurance, you run the risk of losing your driver's license; incurring civil penalties; and being personally liable for any property, medical, and legal costs of any car accidents in which you are found at fault.

BOTTOM LINE

Automobile liability coverage does not protect the vehicle itself. It reimburses injured parties for harm and property damage caused by the insured vehicle.

Cyber Risk Insurance

It seems like every day the news reports yet another breach of computer systems at retailers, insurance companies, and even government databases. If you have even one device connected to the internet, you face the potential risk of your computer being hacked. Although you can purchase internet security software and firewall devices that lessen the risk, no system is completely infallible.

Your risk of exposure isn't limited to someone electronically breaking into your computers. Confidential information can be inadvertently exposed through lost or stolen computers and devices, or disgruntled employees can misuse company data or computer privileges. It often can be difficult to quantify what's involved in repairing the damage from data breaches of any sort.

A cyber risk policy might be available under a variety of names, including computer hacking, computer fraud, and data breach coverage.

Personal Umbrella Insurance

All the coverages we've discussed thus far are considered primary coverage, meaning the insurance company pays for covered events when warranted. However, in certain cases, litigation could result in judgments that exceed the policy limits of your primary coverage. For instance, if a customer successfully sues your business for $1,000,000 for a car accident caused by an employee but your liability insurance has a policy limit of $500,000, you or your business could be responsible for the remaining $500,000 beyond what your insurance pays.

It's a good idea for every business owner, as well as high-net-worth individuals, to purchase personal umbrella insurance. This type of coverage is known as secondary coverage because it doesn't take effect until the limits of one of your primary policies have been exceeded. Umbrella insurance is typically purchased in $1 million increments and is usually rather inexpensive, particularly when compared to primary coverage.

Umbrella insurance raises the limits of your primary liability coverage and helps protect your business or personal assets by providing a higher level of coverage than you might be able to afford. With that said, your umbrella policy might include a clause that requires you to increase your current liability coverage amounts to a higher level than you presently have. In the end though, you'll have a much greater level of protection.

Property Insurance

We've discussed the various types of liability insurance that protect others. Now let's look at insurance that protects your business directly.

You're probably familiar with homeowner's or renter's insurance that protects you personally should something happen to your home or your possessions within your home. Chances are, such policies exclude home-based businesses, so check your policies carefully.

Businesses located outside the home need similar property insurance that covers damage to the premises and its contents. Commercial property insurance policies can cover your premises, any outdoor signage, furniture and equipment, inventory, and even property belonging to others that's stored in your building. However, a general-purpose property insurance policy might not be specific enough to cover some of the risks that your business might face.

Boiler and Machinery Insurance

This type of coverage, now often referred to as equipment breakdown coverage, protects against exposure from key pieces of equipment breaking down or causing damage. Any sort of machinery or equipment can be subject to malfunction. This type of policy doesn't just cover the cost of repairs or replacement of almost any type of equipment you want to cover in your business. The policy also can replace lost business income as well as the value of damaged or spoiled products caused by the mechanical failure.

Despite the name, you can purchase coverage for small equipment, including computers, larger items such as kitchen equipment, and even production machinery.

Business Interruption Insurance

Earthquakes, tornadoes, flooding, hurricanes, and other natural disasters often strike without warning and wreak large swaths of havoc. Property insurance can reimburse you for losses of physical property, such as buildings, automobiles, and certain equipment. However, such coverage doesn't provide any protection from situations in which you have a loss of income caused by property damage. Business interruption insurance can reimburse you for lost revenues attributed to a property loss. You typically must purchase this coverage as an addition to property insurance.

Inland Marine Insurance

Property insurance typically covers items within the premises of your business. This means it might not cover items you frequently use *outside* your premises, such as laptop computers, cameras, and other equipment that's easily mobile.

Even though your business might not have anything to do with shipping goods on water, you might still need specialty coverage for portable equipment, known as an inland marine policy. The scope of this sort of policy has expanded over the years to cover modern technology equipment.

ACCOUNTING HACK

Insurance policies are available to cover just about every imaginable risk and exposure your business faces. However, insurance can be expensive. A knowledgeable insurance agent or broker can help you determine which risks you should insure against and can often help you identify multipolicy discounts.

Health Insurance

Most of the types of insurance we've covered so far are rather staid, and the rules and coverages don't change very often. Health insurance is the exception to the rule, and lately, it seems like the requirements shift on an annual basis. (We'll keep our discussion of health insurance here brief because the ground continues to shift on a regular basis.)

Depending on the size of your business, you might be subject to state or federal requirements that require you to provide health insurance for your employees.

Historically, health insurance has been optional and was primarily provided by employers to full-time employees. This left a large swath of part-time, unemployed, or individuals not in the workplace without coverage. The Affordable Care Act, signed into law in 2010, requires that every U.S. citizen have health-care coverage. As of January 1, 2015, employers with 50 or more full-time employees must provide affordable health care or incur a financial penalty.

The terms of this law are broad and complex, and some of the rules are coming into effect over a period of years. For instance, under the law, the definition of full-time employees includes part-time workers who work 30 or more hours per week, which differs from the traditional definition of full-time being those who put in a 40-hour workweek.

Businesses with fewer than 50 full-time employees are not required to provide health-care coverage at this time, but keep an eye on the regulations that are still being fine-tuned as the implementation of the law rolls out.

Even if you don't provide health insurance for your employees, you do have to provide insurance coverage for yourself. In the past, individuals were often priced out of the health insurance market, particularly people with a preexisting health condition. The Affordable Care Act makes it much easier to purchase individual coverage from a health insurer at an affordable price, or you can use the health-care marketplace website at healthcare.gov. There's even a section specifically for small businesses.

Usually you can get free advice and guidance from a health insurance broker, who is typically compensated by the health insurance companies directly. Businesses usually can secure group coverage for employees at a lower cost than what it would cost individuals to get health insurance coverage on their own.

The Internal Revenue Service (IRS) has been tasked with ensuring compliance with the Affordable Care Act, so you'll want to get advice from a tax adviser as well to ensure you operate within the confines of the law.

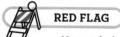 **RED FLAG**

You might have difficulty securing individual health insurance if you miss the annual open enrollment period that runs from November 1 through January 31. The Affordable Care Act requires that all taxpayers provide proof of health coverage on their tax return or pay a penalty that can be as much as 2 percent or more of your taxable income.

Life Insurance

Life insurance pays out a designated amount of money if an insured person dies. Some businesses arrange for group-based life insurance as an employee benefit.

Recently, a major retailer was found to have secretly taken out life insurance policies on employees from which the *company* received the payout if the employee died while in their employment. Most states prohibit this type of secret coverage and also require what's known as an insurable interest of the buyer.

Businesses that offer life insurance as a paid benefit typically provide no more than $50,000 coverage per employee. As you'll see in the next section, the IRS considers employer-paid coverage in excess of this amount to be a taxable benefit.

It might be worthwhile for your business to consider a special type of coverage commonly referred to as key man or key person insurance. This type of policy protects a business against financial loss in the event of the death or disability of an important employee. Such coverage may be applicable for corporate officers, partners in a partnership, key salespeople, and other employees who significantly contribute to a business's revenue. Key person insurance also can be used as a mechanism of *succession planning.*

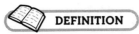 **DEFINITION**

All businesses must plan for the eventual planned or unplanned departure of key employees or stakeholders. **Succession planning** involves grooming existing employees for future promotions to leadership and other key positions, as well as using insurance and other tools to minimize the financial ramifications of a change in succession.

Special tax rules apply to the deductibility of key man life insurance, so be sure to check with your tax preparer before purchasing.

Tax Advantages

You can deduct the benefits you offer your employees, and they're possibly tax free for your employees, too.

All the types of insurance we've discussed in this chapter are tax-deductible expenses for your business. We cover personal and business tax returns in Chapter 19, but in short, a business can deduct what it pays for business-related insurance against its taxable income.

What's more, certain types of insurance, such as health and life insurance for your employees, often can be provided as a tax-free benefit for them.

The IRS provides an exclusion for the premiums on group term-life insurance policies of up to $50,000 per employee. Policies that provide coverage in excess of $50,000 can trigger a taxable fringe benefit.

Health Insurance for the Self-Employed

Self-employed individuals who report their income on Schedule C or whose income is reported by a pass-through entity such as a partnership or an S corporation are subject to different rules when it comes to the deductibility of health insurance. The rules relate directly to the profitability of the business and your percent of ownership of that business.

If you're self-employed and purchasing health insurance for yourself and your family, be sure to seek the advice of a tax professional to help you determine if, how, when, and where to deduct health insurance costs.

Health Insurance Paid by Individuals

If, as an individual, you're paying for your own health-care insurance, specific tax rules govern the deductibility of your premiums. If you're buying insurance on your own as opposed to getting it through your job, you can list the full cost of your premiums for you and your family on Schedule A, Itemized Deductions, which accompanies your Form 1040, Individual Income Tax Return. Additional rules govern who actually gets to itemize deductions and how much of those deductions you ultimately get to claim, so talk to your tax adviser if you're in this situation.

If you're paying part or all of the cost of your and your family's share of health insurance through your employer's group plan, more than likely your employer is handling your payments through payroll withholding, and those payments are treated as "pretax payments." This means the amount of your income withheld to pay for health insurance isn't subject to income tax and isn't allowed as an itemized deduction.

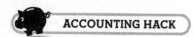

ACCOUNTING HACK

If your business is taxed as a S corporation, there's an advantageous rule that permits you to deduct, dollar for dollar, every penny of health insurance premiums paid by you. It requires a proscribed treatment of the health insurance costs on your W-2. If this is applicable to you, be sure to check on it before your last check of the year.

Recording Insurance Costs and Reimbursements

Insurance policies typically cover 6 or 12 months at a time, which means you might pay for several months of insurance all at once. If you arrange with your insurer to pay by the month, you can simply record your insurance payments within your accounting software directly to an Insurance Expense account. However, if you pay your insurer for multiple months of insurance at once, you'll need to record this a bit differently.

As we discussed in Chapter 4, you need to establish a special type of account known as a prepaid expense account. This is an asset account that temporarily reflects the amounts of an expense, such as insurance, you've paid in advance for future months. So when you pay an insurance premium, your accounting transaction debits prepaid insurance, for instance, and credits cash. Each month, you'll move a portion of the insurance premium to the Insurance Expense account, until the prepaid expense is exhausted. (You can automate this type of entry within your accounting software. See Chapter 17.)

Many small business owners tend to record the entire insurance premium payment as an expense in a single month, but doing so distorts your monthly operating expenses and can result in you taking an unwarranted income tax deduction. IRS Publication 535, Business Expenses, states "You generally cannot deduct expenses in advance, even if you pay them in advance. This rule applies to both the cash and accrual methods. It applies to prepaid interest, prepaid insurance premiums, and any other expense paid far enough in advance to, in effect, create an asset with a useful life extending substantially beyond the end of the current tax year." Thus, booking insurance premiums to a prepaid account is not only a best practice with regard to your accounting, it's also the law.

Insurance reimbursements represent cash received by your company, but this type of cash isn't taxable revenue, per se. Presumably, you incurred some expense for which you're being reimbursed in the form of repair of storm damage, repair to an automobile that was in an accident, etc. The insurance reimbursement you receive should offset the expense you incurred, so you record this amount as a credit to the expense account, reducing the amount of expense.

 **ACCOUNTING HACK**

Sometimes you experience a delay between the time you pay for insurance repairs and the time you receive your insurance reimbursement. If this delay results in the expenses being paid in one year and the reimbursement being received in the next year, the IRS does not want you to take a tax deduction for the expenses the insurance will cover. Set up a current asset account called Anticipated Reimbursements or something similar. Reduce your expense by the amount you expect to receive in reimbursement, and debit the amount to the new asset account. Then, in the next year when you receive the reimbursement, you'll clear—or zero out—the asset account.

The Least You Need to Know

- Liability insurance typically results in payments to others and protects your business from potentially devastating claims.
- If your company has employees, workers' compensation insurance is a liability requirement.
- Property insurance protects you from incurring great costs if items you own are damaged.
- Health and life insurance represent key benefits you might offer your employees.
- The insurance benefits you offer your employees can be tax deductible for your company.
- There may be some nuances in how you record business insurance policy costs and any reimbursements your business receives.

Other Benefits and Reimbursements

Small businesses typically have many options when it comes to the benefits you offer employees. Although you have flexibility in what benefits you offer, you're often required to provide the same benefits to all full-time employees. Exceptions are sometimes possible for part-time employees.

In this chapter, you learn about the various types of retirement plans small business owners can establish, including SIMPLE, SEP, 401(k), and Keogh plans. We also explain how to remit retirement plan contributions and what points of government oversight to anticipate. Finally, we discuss auto and other business expense reimbursements, as well as paid vacation and sick leave issues.

In This Chapter

- Retirement plans for you and your employees
- Reimbursements for business use of a vehicle and other expenses
- Section 125 cafeteria plans
- Vacation, sick, and other leave

Retirement Plans

Many people have already accumulated some amount of retirement savings through current or previous employers, so your employees likely have started saving a nest egg for their retirement.

As an employer, you can choose from several different offerings to help your employees continue their retirement savings. Small businesses have access to many of the tools larger companies do, with some special options specially geared toward small businesses. Let's take a look at the various retirement plan options.

SIMPLE IRAs

Savings Incentive Match Plan for Employees (SIMPLE) Individual Retirement Account (IRA) plans are designed for employers that don't presently offer any type of retirement savings vehicles to employees. These plans can be set up through many mutual fund companies such as Vanguard (vanguard.com), Fidelity (fidelity.com), and T. Rowe Price (troweprice.com). There's usually a low fee structure for both employers and employees.

With SIMPLE IRAs, employees can direct a portion of each paycheck into a tax-deferred retirement savings account, and employers are required to match up to 3 percent of an employee's compensation.

Businesses with up to 100 employees are eligible to establish SIMPLE IRA plans. The amounts employees can contribute each year are indexed for inflation, but as of the 2016 tax year, the contribution limit is up to $12,500 per employee. Employees 50 or over can contribute an additional $3,000 as of the 2016 tax year.

One caveat of SIMPLE plans is that employers must match employee contributions on a dollar-for-dollar basis up to as much as 3 percent of the employee's compensation. Let's say an employee earns $50,000 per year and contributes $5,000 toward his SIMPLE IRA. The employer is required to contribute the lesser of 3 percent of $50,000 or the employee's contribution. In this case, 3 percent of $50,000 is $1,500, so the employer is required to contribute at least $1,500. Any employer contributions to a SIMPLE IRA plan are immediately *vested*.

DEFINITION

In terms of retirement plans, **vested** means the contributions made on an employee's behalf by an employer are permanent and cannot be taken away. If the employee leaves the company, he or she has access to all the money in the vested plan. Public companies often grant stock options to employees that only vest if the employee stays with the company for a specified period of time.

Simple Employee Pensions (SEPs)

This type of retirement plan gives small business owners more latitude on contributions. The maximum annual contribution is the lesser of 25 percent of compensation or $53,000 per year as of the 2016 tax year.

Employers can decide on a yearly basis how much to contribute. The catch is that each employee gets the same percentage match. Owners can't elect to contribute 25 percent of their own compensation, for instance, without also contributing 25 percent of each employee's compensation as well. This type of plan might be best suited to self-employed individuals with no employees.

401(k) Plans

You likely have some amount of savings already in a 401(k) plan. 401(k) plans share some similarities with SIMPLE IRA plans in that employees can make tax-deferred investments. However, 401(k) plans cost employers more to administer and require that Form 5500 be filed with the U.S. Department of Labor annually.

Employee participants can contribute up to $18,000 for the 2016 tax year, and employees age 50 or older can contribute an additional $6,000 per year.

Employers have discretion with regard to determining matching contributions for 401(k) plans, but they must follow the rules written into the plan. For 2015, a limit of $53,000 can be contributed to 401(k) plans, combining both the employee and the employer contribution. As with SIMPLE IRA plans, employer matching contributions vest upon deposit into an employee's account.

There's a special 401(k) provision called solo 401(k) or the one-participant 401(k) for businesses with no employees or businesses in which the only employee is the owner. (The owner's spouse can be an employee as well.) The contribution limits are the same as for regular 401(k)s, but because the business owner is both the employer and the employee, the company can create a matching program and take advantage of both employer and employee contribution limits.

Keogh Plans

Historically, one of the main types of retirement plans for self-employed was the Keogh plan. Over time, these plans have fallen into disuse in favor of the easier-to-administer SIMPLE IRA and SEP plans discussed earlier.

Remitting Retirement Contributions

Employee retirement contributions are withdrawn from employee paychecks in the same fashion as an employee's payroll taxes. However, instead of remitting funds to a government agency, you send the funds to the financial institution that administers your retirement plan.

Your business has a *fiduciary* responsibility to ensure the contributions are remitted timely. Delayed contributions can have serious ramifications, including the following:

- Employees miss out on potential investment income and gains during the delay.

- Civil or criminal penalties can apply to businesses that misuse employee retirement contributions.

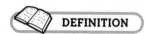

> **DEFINITION**
>
> **Fiduciaries** are individuals or entities entrusted with a legal or financial responsibility on another's behalf.

Government Oversight

Every retirement plan falls under the jurisdiction of the Employee Retirement Income Security Act (ERISA). This law, enacted in 1974, is administered by the U.S. Department of Labor (DOL). You might have noticed earlier that Form 5500 is filed with the DOL instead of the Internal Revenue Service (IRS). ERISA sets forth specific requirements for the fiduciary responsibilities of employers as well as the reporting requirements for employers and financial institutions.

This law is designed to protect the interests of employees who work for private employers. It does not apply to governmental entities or churches.

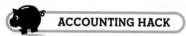

> **ACCOUNTING HACK**
>
> It's not uncommon for an employee to overcontribute to a retirement plan. It's not the employer's responsibility to oversee how much an employee contributes; however, it's helpful if the employer ensures employees are aware of the plan contribution limits. If an employee contributes more than the statutory limit in a given year, he or she needs to contact the custodian of the plan—typically the financial institution or brokerage house that maintains it—and make a request to withdraw the excess. There are tax penalties associated with contributing too much, so contributions should be made and carefully tracked throughout the year. You have until April 15 of the following year (the individual tax return filing date) to arrange for the refund without penalty.

Vehicle Reimbursements

Any employee or business owner who uses a personal vehicle in the course of business is engaging in a tax-deductible activity. Many businesses provide reimbursements for the vehicle expenses, but this is completely optional.

Employers can choose to reimburse for actual vehicle expenses, such as gasoline and maintenance costs, but an easier method is to utilize the standard mileage rate set by the IRS. The business miles driven are tracked and recorded in either a written log, your accounting software, or an app, and the employer reimburses based on the miles driven.

The standard mileage rate amount is published by the IRS and typically changes once a year, although the IRS has been known to change the rate mid-year during periods of severe gasoline price changes. The standard mileage rate is intended to compensate a vehicle owner for all costs of operating the vehicle or business on a per-mile basis. If you or an employee opts for the standard mileage rate, you cannot also deduct any direct costs related to operating the vehicle.

If you opt to utilize a mileage-based reimbursement plan within your business, be sure to maintain detailed records, such as a spreadsheet that tracks your mileage (see Chapter 22).

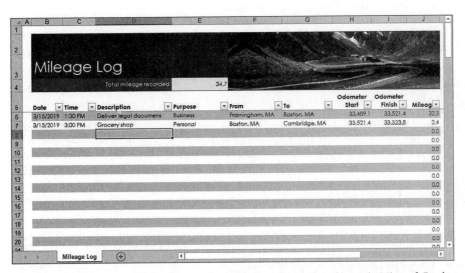

Your spreadsheet program might offer a ready-made mileage log, such as this one in Microsoft Excel.

Your accounting software might offer built-in mileage tracking capabilities as well. In the desktop versions of QuickBooks, you can maintain a list of vehicles and then use the Enter Vehicle Mileage window to log individual trips. You can then run reports for any time period you choose that show the mileage for all or specific vehicles.

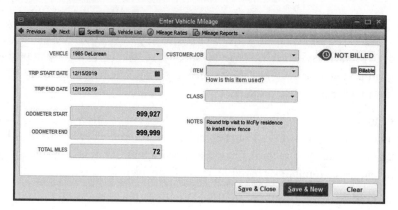

Your accounting program might offer built-in tools for tracking mileage, such as this example from QuickBooks desktop.

The downside to spreadsheet and accounting software-based mileage tracking is that employees are often relegated to writing down mileage on a piece of paper so the information can be entered into the spreadsheet or accounting program later. The IRS doesn't mandate a specific logging method, but your records must be consistent and accurate to pass muster with an auditor.

The mileage rate fluctuates with the economy. It was as low as 31¢ a mile in 1999 and as high as 58.5¢ per mile during the second half of 2008. As of this writing, it's 57.5¢ per mile. An internet search for "standard mileage rate" and the year can show you the current mileage rates.

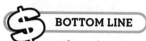

BOTTOM LINE

If your business is taxed as a partnership or sole proprietorship, be sure to write yourself a reimbursement check for any mileage or other expenses applicable to your business. It's possible to deduct unreimbursed expenses, such as mileage, on your personal income tax return (more on this coming up). However, sole proprietorships and businesses taxed as partnerships must pay self-employment tax (currently 15.6 percent) on net income of the business. Such owners pay more taxes than necessary opting not to run this expense through their business.

Other Reimbursements

Employers have a wide degree of latitude when it comes to reimbursing employee expenses. The expenses being reimbursed must have a valid business purpose, such as costs incurred while traveling for business, continuing-education classes, professional licenses, or other expenses that relate specifically to an employee's work or compliance with professional standards. And they should be documented with paper or electronic receipts.

Some employers require specific documentation for travel expenses, and others opt to use perdiem rates set by the General Services Administration (GSA). The GSA sets these rates for each fiscal year to define the maximum amounts appropriate for lodging and meals in each geographic area within the United States.

Employees are not required to provide receipts for per-diem-based reimbursements, and these amounts are not taxable to the employees. If you choose to reimburse any employee expenses, be sure to document the policy in writing. You also might want to provide a standard expense report document to provide a formal reimbursement structure. Or you could use a productivity app to automate expense reimbursement tracking.

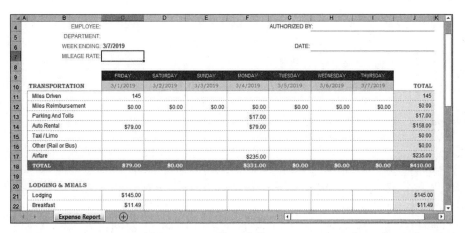

Most spreadsheet programs offer prebuilt expense report templates.

ACCOUNTING HACK

Many employers provide reimbursements for business vehicle usage. However, this is optional, and not all employers comply or reimburse at the full IRS standard mileage rates. If there's no reimbursement, or only a partial reimbursement, the employee has the option of filing Form 2106, Employee Business Expenses, with his or her individual income tax return and claiming the unreimbursed vehicle expenses as an itemized deduction on Schedule A.

There are no set rules governing how you remit reimbursements to employees. Some employers add reimbursement amounts as line items on employee paychecks. Others write separate checks to the employee for the expense. With the latter, you might need to set up your employee as a vendor to issue them a nonpayroll check. (Contrary to popular belief, some reimbursements are actually taxable to your employees. Consult IRS Publication 463 to determine the specifics for your situation and any corresponding reporting requirements.)

In the case of nonemployee owners, you'll simply issue a check directly to the owner.

Whether owner or employee, when we say "issue a check," we mean handwrite or print a check, transfer funds through online banking, or remit the money through another agreed-upon reimbursement avenue. Even if you make the transfer electronically, you'll still record this as a check in your books unless you include it as part of payroll.

Cafeteria Plans

A cafeteria plan allows employees to set aside a portion of each paycheck, income tax free, to put toward certain accident and health benefits, adoption fees, dependent care assistance, group-term life insurance coverage, or health savings accounts.

Cafeteria plans, sometimes called Section 125 plans for the Internal Revenue Code section that authorizes them, enable employees to pay for certain personal expenses with pre-tax income, while employers have a reduction in payroll taxes.

Cafeteria plans must be approved by the IRS and are administered by approved third-party companies. They can be limited to enabling employees to pay health and life insurance premiums with pretax dollars or to establish flexible spending accounts (FSAs), which allows employees to purchase certain medical expenses with pretax dollars.

You'll be happy to know that the IRS does not typically require any type of annual filing for a cafeteria plan. Employers that offer a special type of plan known as a welfare benefit plan to retirees are required to submit Form 5500 to the DOL, but otherwise, your cafeteria plan shouldn't require any ongoing governmental filings.

Paid Vacation and Sick Leave

The Fair Labor Standards Act (FLSA) does not require employers to offer paid vacation or sick leave for employees. However, this doesn't mean you can necessarily disregard this benefit.

As of this writing, California, Connecticut, Massachusetts, and Oregon require employers to offer some amount of paid sick leave. Several cities and at least one county have enacted similar legislation. As an employer, you not only have to stay compliant with the federal law, but also any local laws.

Paid Vacation

Presently, paid vacation is not mandated by any level of government. This means as an employer, you can decide whether or not to offer paid time off to your employees. Businesses that do offer paid time off often require employees to accrue time off throughout the year. For instance, an employee who is entitled to 5 days of paid vacation per year accumulates just under a ½ day of vacation per month.

Employers have wide discretion when it comes to allowing employees to take time off that they haven't formally accrued yet or not. Some employers grant an automatic block of paid time at the start of a new calendar year.

If you choose to offer paid vacation, your accounting software will likely have a built-in feature that enables you to track it, or your third-party payroll provider can handle the tracking for you.

The number of paid days earned and taken during a given calendar year should be reported on each employee's paystub.

Business owners can decide whether paid vacation not taken at the end of the year expires or can be carried forward to a future year. Certain employers allow employees to sell back vacation time they haven't taken. It's always best to encourage your employees to take paid time off, and in fact, doing so can be an effective measure of internal control. (We cover the concept of internal control in detail in Chapter 15.)

Sick Leave

As noted, there's no federal requirement for a business to offer paid sick leave, but a movement is afoot in some cities, counties, and states to require paid sick leave. Employers that don't fall under a mandate can offer both paid vacation and paid sick leave, or just one or the other. Some employers try to simplify things by offering a general bank of paid time off that can be used for sick or vacation days.

As with vacation time, your accounting software enables you to track and report sick leave, or you can outsource the task to a payroll provider.

Family and Medical Leave Act

Private businesses that have 50 or more employees, any public agency, and any public or private school is required to offer certain employees up to 12 weeks of unpaid time off per year.

Employers cannot fire employees for taking time off under the Family and Medical Leave Act (FMLA) and must protect the employee's job while the employee is away for any of these reasons:

- Birth or adoption of a child

- Care for an immediate family member with a serious health condition

- Temporary disability that prevents the employee from performing his or her job

- Situations arising from an immediate family member being called for active military duty

Employers have discretion whether or not to maintain an employee's pay during a FMLA absence, but they cannot penalize an employee for taking said time off.

The Least You Need to Know

- Small business owners have many attractive choices when it comes to offering retirement savings plans to employees.

- Reimbursing for the business use of automobiles is a common practice, and published rates are available for computing this. Employees can be reimbursed for other types of expenses as well, such as business-related travel.

- Employers can choose to offer cafeteria plans to their employees, giving the employees a menu of benefits choices.

- In general, employers are not required to offer paid vacation and sick leave, but the FMLA outlines certain situations in which employers must protect an employee's job during unpaid leave.

CHAPTER 12

Payroll Taxes

Benjamin Franklin is widely attributed as saying the only two certainties in life are death and taxes. As you'll see in this chapter, taxes are an absolute certainty of running any sort of business. Even if you don't have any employees, it's very likely that you'll be subject to payroll taxes in some fashion.

In this chapter, you might be astounded to learn about the number of different payroll taxes you have to pay and keep up with as a business owner. Some will be rather familiar to you if you've ever worked as an employee and lamented about the assortment of withholdings taken from your paycheck. However, some taxes are borne solely by employers.

You'll also see in this chapter that you'll be paying taxes at the state, federal, and sometimes even local level. We don't mean sales tax here, that's a separate discussion in Chapter 18. In this chapter, we explain the whats and whys about the most common taxes assessed on payroll.

In This Chapter

- Withholding federal, state, and local income taxes
- Calculating Social Security and Medicare withholdings
- Understanding federal and state unemployment taxes
- Determining if your company is subject to a disability tax

Withholding Taxes

Income tax withholding in the United States has been around in some manner since the Civil War, but most of its present structure was formed in the 1950s, including the setting of April 15 as the annual date all personal tax returns must be filed.

Withholding is a mechanism by which employers may have to set aside a prescribed amount of each employee's check for federal income tax withholding. (We say *may* because various factors can determine whether an employee has federal income taxes withheld from their paycheck.) Most states also assess a state income tax, and some jurisdictions, such as cities and counties, assess local income taxes as well.

In a perfect world, the amount withheld from each employee's check would exactly match their tax liability by the end of the year. However, that's rarely the case, and employees often end up withholding more than necessary, resulting in large income tax refunds the following year.

Federal Withholding

Federal withholding amounts are determined annually by the Internal Revenue Service (IRS) and vary based on income level and marital/household status. The IRS typically issues new withholding tables for the upcoming calendar year each December in a document known as Publication 15, or Circular E. This document provides instructions for knowing whether someone who works for you should be considered an employee, the definition of wages and other compensation, directions for determining how much to withhold from employee paychecks, and information on how to deposit taxes you've withheld. In essence, Circular E contains everything you need to know to determine payroll tax withholding by hand, if you choose to do so.

Unlike the other payroll taxes we'll cover, federal income taxes tend to be highly personalized. To start, there are two different sets of withholding tables. One covers unmarried individuals (referred to as single), as well as unmarried people who have one or more dependents (referred to as head of household). A second table covers married couples.

Another personal aspect to federal tax withholding is the number of *allowances* you and your employees opt for. The value of an allowance changes each year due to inflation, but for the 2016 tax year, each allowance an employee claims reduces their taxable income for withholding pur-poses by $4,050. This enables employees to match their withholding to their expected income tax liability. (However, allowances simply control withholding from one's paycheck. If you claim too many allowances, you might end up with a large income tax bill when April 15 rolls around.) The IRS requires all employees to submit a Form W-4 indicating the number of allowances claimed.

 **DEFINITION**

A withholding **allowance** gives an employee a measure of control over the amount of income taxes withheld from each paycheck.

State Withholding

If you and your employees are isolated to Alaska, Florida, Nevada, South Dakota, Texas, Washington, or Wyoming, you can skip this section. None of these states levies a state income tax. In addition, Tennessee and New Hampshire do have a state income tax, but both exempt wages.

So anyone living in the other 41 states must calculate, remit, and report state income tax withholdings in addition to federal income taxes. Most states have a similar tax structure to the federal tables, but be sure to investigate the requirements with your state's Department of Revenue.

Local Withholding

The U.S. Census Bureau reports that as of 2013, the United States contained 19,508 incorporated areas (cities, towns, townships) and 3,194 counties for a collective total of 22,702 jurisdictions. Specific information about local taxes is difficult to find, but a 2011 article published by the Tax Foundation indicated that nearly 5,000 cities and counties across the United States assess a local income tax. These numbers change regularly, and the totals are updated infrequently.

Suffice it to say, there's a roughly 1 in 5 chance you live in a local jurisdiction that assesses a local income tax.

Social Security and Medicare

The U.S. Social Security and Medicare programs are administered by the federal government, and taxes for these programs are collected by the IRS.

The Social Security Administration (SSA) was founded in 1935 and pays retirement, disability, and survivors benefits to U.S. citizens. Taxes have been collected under this program since January 1937, and regular monthly benefits have been distributed since January 1940. The SSA reports that the first payout under the program was a single lump sum of 17¢ in January 1937. Further, as of calendar 2009, the most recent year available, 55 million Americans received monthly Social Security benefits.

The collective Social Security and Medicare tax withheld from employee paychecks is often referred to as the FICA tax. The acronym stands for Federal Insurance Contributions Act, the legislation that authorized the tax. The FICA tax itself is actually a combination of two tax rates, with two distinct thresholds.

Ostensibly, this tax is shared on a 50/50 basis between the employee and the employer. However, self-employed taxpayers must pay both halves of the tax.

Social Security Withholding

The tax rate for Social Security withholding has remained mostly constant at 6.2 percent of the wage base since the early 1990s. However, both the employee and employer must pay this tax, so the collective rate is 12.4 percent of the wage base.

For calendar year 2015, the wage base is $118,500, which means employees must pay Social Security tax of 6.2 percent on the first $118,500 they earn during the year. Employers must match this, so for 2015, the collective tax can be as much as $14,694 for employees who are at or above the wage threshold.

A self-employed taxpayer earning above the wage threshold owes the entire $14,694, although offsets are sometimes available.

The wage base increases by a small percentage each year to reflect inflation.

 BOTTOM LINE

During the 2011 and 2012 tax years, Congress temporarily lowered the Social Security tax rate to 4.2 percent for employees (the employer rate remained at 6.2 percent), so the collective employer/employee total was 10.4 percent. That legislative provision, the 2010 Tax Relief Act, expired without renewal and the tax rates returned to 6.2 percent for both employee and employers in 2013 and beyond.

Medicare Withholding

A Medicare tax is withheld from employee checks in the same fashion as Social Security, however there's no wage base, so all wages are taxed for Medicare.

For the 2015 calendar year, the Medicare tax is 1.45 percent of all wages an employee earns. The employer matches this, so all wages are subject to a total of 2.9 percent for Medicare tax.

Certain high-income earners are now subject to an additional Medicare tax of 0.9 percent above designated thresholds, but these amounts are calculated and paid on one's personal income tax return and not subject to payroll withholding.

an the FICA withholding base should pay particular atten-
a given year. It's possible to have excess FICA withheld
oyer won't take into account the amount your previous
ind yourself subject to excess FICA withholding, you can
n you file your annual personal income tax return by claim-
ss.

es

for two different types of unemployment taxes, federal and

l to be a safety net for employees who have had their
loyer. If an employee willingly leaves a job, he or she is not
urance (also called unemployment compensation). However,
ss layoff, typically all those employees are eligible for
ever, that an employee terminated for misconduct or some
ualify to receive unemployment insurance.

ually provide full-wage replacement. It's intended to be a
mployees seek new employment.

is administered by each state, but you also pay a federal unemployment tax.

Federal Unemployment Taxes

Federal unemployment taxes need to be paid in addition to state unemployment taxes. You might
wonder why Uncle Sam wants to charge you for an insurance program administered by each of
the 50 states. There are several reasons for this:

- The federal government helps subsidize the cost of running each state's unemployment
  insurance program.

- Congress sometimes mandates that states extend the period of time they offer benefits
  to long-term unemployed citizens. The federal tax helps fund these congressional
  mandates.

- The need for benefits in a given state sometimes outstrips the unemployment taxes
  collected. In such cases, a state can borrow money from the federal unemployment tax
  program to fund benefits. Any such borrowings must be paid back by the state.

The Federal Unemployment Tax is often referred to as FUTA. In this case, the A in the acronym refers to the legislation that enabled the tax, the Federal Unemployment Tax Act.

This tax applies to the first $7,000 earned by each employee in a given calendar or fiscal year. Ostensibly, the tax is 6.2 percent of the first $7,000 of each employee's wages, or $434 per employee, per year. However, employers are allowed to claim a credit of up to 5.4 percent of the $7,000 based on the unemployment tax they pay to their state. This reduces the federal unemployment burden for most employers to 0.8 percent of the first $7,000 of wages, or usually $56 per employee, per year. This assumes an employee is on your payroll long enough to earn $7,000.

FUTA is based on the first $7,000 an employee earns in a year, so for most employees, the $7,000 meter starts at January 1. For any new hires during the year, the $7,000 starts accumulating as of the hire date.

Any other wages employees earn are exempt from the FUTA tax.

State Unemployment Taxes

State unemployment taxes are commonly referred to as SUTA (State Unemployment Tax Act). Each state is responsible for paying unemployment benefits to citizens who have had their job terminated by an employer. The criteria for qualifying for unemployment varies by state, and employees terminated for cause, such as fraud, not performing job duties, etc. might not be eligible for unemployment.

For the most part, states have a wide degree of latitude in how they fund and administer unemployment programs. Accordingly, the rules and regulations for state unemployment vary widely. Unlike FUTA, which is assessed on the first $7,000 of an employee's wages, some states, such as Washington, assess a state unemployment on as much as the first $41,300 for calendar year 2014. Conversely, Arizona and California had the lowest wage base in 2014 of $7,000. Other states fall somewhere in between.

Another difference between FUTA and SUTA is that each employer might have to pay a different percentage of the wage base. This is often based on several criteria.

For example, brand-new businesses are often subjected to a new employer tax rate that's higher than the average paid by most businesses. Over time, if the business doesn't have any former employees who file for unemployment, the tax rate is lowered. For calendar year 2014, Vermont had the lowest new-employer rate of 1 percent of its wage base, while Hawaii had the highest rate of 4.6 percent.

Also, businesses that have had many employees file for unemployment insurance are often subjected to a maximum unemployment tax rate. In 2014, Massachusetts had the highest maximum rate of 12.27 percent of the wage base; the lowest rate in 2014, 5.4 percent, was assessed by Alaska, Florida, Georgia, Mississippi, Nebraska, Nevada, New Mexico, and Oregon.

In addition, businesses that, over time, do not have any employees file for state unemployment benefits may see their wage rate drop to as low as 0 percent. This is true in states such as Iowa, Missouri, Nebraska, North Carolina, and South Dakota. In calendar year 2014, Pennsylvania had the highest minimum tax rate of 2.8 percent of the wage base.

ACCOUNTING HACK

At this point, your head might be spinning from the vagaries of each taxing authority's requirements. Most accounting software offers fee-based payroll processing services that range from streamlining payroll by providing prebuilt tax calculations so you don't have to perform any manual calculations, to full-service payroll options that calculate all the withholdings and prepare all the tax forms (see Chapter 18). You also can outsource your payroll processing to your software provider or a third-party payroll processing company.

As you can see, the states are all over the place when it comes to determining how much to charge for state unemployment taxes. Accordingly, we can't provide specific guidance for each state, but in general, we can say this about SUTA:

Every employer in a state pays an unemployment tax based on a certain threshold of each employee's wages, referred to as a wage base.

The percentage of the wage base each employer pays for its employees is based on a state's experience with that employer. States typically only change the wage base and/or tax rate for an employer once a year, but sometimes mid-year changes are implemented during periods of high unemployment. Each state is expected to keep its unemployment insurance fund solvent, so changes in demand for unemployment benefits may result in sudden and dramatic changes in the tax.

Unemployment taxes are typically remitted to the states by way of a quarterly unemployment tax return. This return usually includes a list of every employee the company has in a given state, along with their total wages. The unemployment return has a space to show the amount of exempt wages (those employees earned above the wage base) along with a net taxable amount. The tax rate is applied to this next taxable amount.

The unemployment insurance programs are typically administered by a Department of Labor in each state, but some states might have different names for their programs or departments.

Temporary Disability Insurance

If you live in California, Hawaii, New Jersey, New York, or Rhode Island, you might be subject to an additional tax levy to fund temporary disability insurance (TDI).

Much like unemployment insurance provides partial income replacement for employees who are terminated by employers, TDI is intended to provide similar protection for health-related issues. Employees who miss work for more than a few days due to illness, injury, or pregnancy-related issues may be able to recover a portion of their lost wages under this program.

The Least You Need to Know

- Employers are required to withhold income, Social Security, and Medicare taxes from employee wages and remit those amounts to the federal and state governments.
- In jurisdictions where income tax is incurred at the local level, employers are required to withhold and submit city, county, or township taxes.
- Employees who had too much (or not enough) tax withheld can settle up on their annual income tax returns.
- Unemployment insurance is required to be paid at both the federal and state level.
- Additional payroll taxes such as disability insurance are required in some states.

Financial Reporting

We've mentioned that accounting serves as a means to score how your business is doing. All the transactions you've learned about so far are just that—individual transactions. The reports you generate via your accounting software bring together those individual transactions to provide the higher-level scorecards you need to run your business and communicate with others about its health.

In Part 4, we go through the most essential accounting reports, including how and when to generate them, how to interpret them, and cues to act on. First, you learn how and why it's important to generate routine reports about accounts such as Accounts Receivable and Accounts Payable. Next, we explore the "big three" financial statements: income statement, balance sheet, and statement of cash flows. These overview reports provide information about the financial health and value of your company. Next, we cover security issues, including keeping your accounting information safely backed up and managing risk such as customer information theft, identity theft, and even business check theft. Part 4 concludes by giving you insights into how external stakeholders can use and interpret your business reports, including what the IRS may be looking for, what lenders and investors want to see, and what key ratios help you keep your financials on track.

Tracking Receivables and Payables

Unless you're the type of business that's able to get paid immediately when products are delivered or services are rendered, and you can pay all your vendors and service providers in the same fashion, you'll likely have accounts receivable. You'll have accounts payable to track as well, either within your accounting software or by keeping an eye on a stack of unpaid bills in both your physical and virtual inboxes.

Your accounts receivable is comprised of unpaid invoices you've sent to customers, while within your accounting software, your accounts payable includes bills for amounts you owe to vendors you've entered into your books but haven't paid yet.

If you opt to enter bills into your books at the time you write the payment checks, you may not carry any accounts payable on your books. However, whenever you have bills you plan to pay at some point in the future instead of immediately, it's always best to enter a bill in your accounting software, as we discuss in Chapter 6.

In This Chapter

- Setting payment terms for customers
- Using the Aged Accounts Receivable report
- Making refunds for overpayments
- Writing off bad debts
- Tracking payables with an Aged Accounts Payable report

If the nature of your business is such that you handwrite invoices to customers for work performed in the field, always be sure to record the invoices in your accounting software as soon as possible so you don't lose track of the money due to you.

This chapter introduces you to all the best practices for tracking receivables and payables.

Payment Terms

Each business has the flexibility to set its own policies on how quickly payment is expected from its customers. You've likely received bills that say "payable upon receipt," but a more standard convention is referred to as "net 30 terms." This is how accountants signify that payment for the entire bill is expected within 30 days.

You also might encounter situations when a bill shows payment terms of "2%/10 net 30." In this case, the vendor is saying you can pay 98 percent of the bill within 10 days (a 2 percent discount) or 100 percent of the bill within 30 days.

In your books, you'll record the entire expense in the usual fashion and add a line item for the discount that has a negative amount posted to an Other Revenue account called Discounts Taken.

If you choose to offer such terms to your customers with the hope of speeding up your cash flow, you'll record the early payment discount in much the same fashion as the credit card transaction fees we discuss in Chapter 6.

Your accounting software enables you to set payment terms for customers on a global basis, but you can always override this global setting for specific customers.

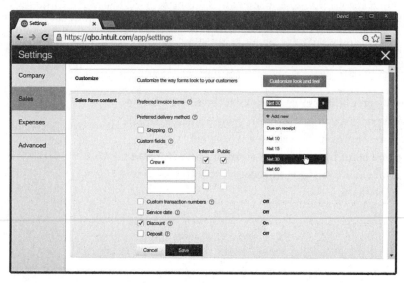

Customer payment terms are typically set at a company level within your accounting software.

Aged Accounts Receivable Report

Your Aged Accounts Receivable report provides a detailed accounting of all the money owed to you by customers, as well as any credits you've issued to customers that have not yet been applied against an invoice or refunded. If you maintain your books on the accrual basis, the amount of this report should match the balance of the Accounts Receivable account on your balance sheet and General Ledger. If you use cash basis accounting for your books, you won't have an Accounts Receivable account because invoices you issue don't truly affect your books until your customer pays you.

The following figure shows a typical aging report. The standard configuration, which you might be able to change to suit your needs, is as follows:

- Customer name and/or customer ID

- Invoice date

- Invoice number

- Aging bracket columns typically in 30-day segments, such as 1 to 30 days, 31 to 60 days, 61 to 90 days, and 91 days and older

- Total due by invoice

The report then reflects a subtotal of the amounts due by customer along with grand totals for each column at the very bottom.

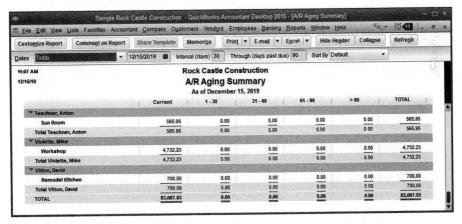

The Aged Accounts Receivable report gives you an overview of how much money each customer owes you as of the report date.

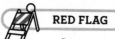

RED FLAG

Some accounting programs, notably the desktop versions of QuickBooks, use the number of days past the due date to age invoices and bills. In effect, the report shows you the number of days past due a transaction is, as opposed to the number of days old. So a transaction that's due within 30 days of the invoice date but is 15 days past due would appear in the 1-30 Past Due column based on this convention. If you set your accounting software to age based on the transaction date, this amount will appear in the 31-60 Past Due column. Be cognizant as to which approach your software uses so you don't misjudge the age of unpaid bills and invoices.

As noted in Chapter 17, many accounting reports have a drill-down feature that allows you to easily dig deeper into the source of amounts shown in your accounting records. In the case of an Aged Receivables Report, you can click on an invoice amount to see the supporting detail of the amount. Depending on your software, you'll see either the unpaid invoice or a new version of the aging report that shows all unpaid invoices for that customer. You might have to click one more time to display the actual unpaid invoice.

Once the invoice is on your screen, you can print another copy if you want to send a reminder by mail, or you can email a copy of the invoice from within the software. Some accounting programs add the word DUPLICATE prominently to invoices you print or email more than once so customers don't inadvertently pay the same invoice twice.

Customer Statements

An alternative to sending additional copies of invoices to your customers is to use the Customer Statement feature if its offered by your software.

You can typically run statements two different ways:

Open transactions: This type of statement allows you to generate a list of open invoices and credit memos for your customers. This format is helpful for reminding customers they might have missed one or more invoices, or to give them a quick overview of their account.

Customer activity: This type of statement reports all activity on a customer's account for a given period of time, including their payments. In effect, it's a mini general ledger just for that customer for a specific period of time. This is helpful in eliminating discrepancies that arise when you post a payment from a customer in a different fashion than they expected. For example, you might have applied a customer payment to a different invoice than the one the customer intended the payment for.

			Amount Due	Amount Enc.
			$9,397.33	
U/M	Date	Transaction	Amount	Balance
	11/25/2019	2nd story addition- INV #1081. Due 12/25/2020. Orig. Amount $5,418.00.	5,418.00	5,418.00
	10/15/2019 11/25/2019 12/11/2019	Kitchen- INV #1066. Due 11/14/2020. Orig. Amount $3,100.00. INV #1080. Due 12/25/2020. Orig. Amount $1,636.69. INV #FC 6. Due 01/10/2021. Orig. Amount $5.95. Finance Charge	700.00 1,636.69 5.95	6,118.00 7,754.69 7,760.64
	12/15/2019	INV #1098. Due 01/14/2021. Orig. Amount $1,636.69.	1,636.69	9,397.33

CURRENT	1-30 DAYS PAST DUE	31-60 DAYS PAST DUE	61-90 DAYS PAST DUE	OVER 90 DAYS PAST DUE	Amount Due
9,397.33	0.00	0.00	0.00	0.00	$9,397.33

This excerpt from a customer statement shows only unpaid invoices and unapplied credit memos, if any.

			Amount Due	Amount Enc.
			$9,397.33	
U/M	Date	Transaction	Amount	Balance
	11/15/2019	Balance forward		11,590.71
	11/25/2019 11/25/2019	2nd story addition- INV #1081. Due 12/25/2020. PMT	5,418.00 -4,085.30	17,008.71 12,923.41
	11/25/2019 11/25/2019 11/25/2019 12/11/2019 12/15/2019	Kitchen- INV #1080. Due 12/25/2020. PMT PMT INV #FC 6. Due 01/10/2021. Finance Charge INV #1098. Due 01/14/2021.	1,636.69 -2,580.00 -4,225.41 5.95 1,636.69	14,560.10 11,980.10 7,754.69 7,760.64 9,397.33

CURRENT	1-30 DAYS PAST DUE	31-60 DAYS PAST DUE	61-90 DAYS PAST DUE	OVER 90 DAYS PAST DUE	Amount Due
9,397.33	0.00	0.00	0.00	0.00	$9,397.33

This excerpt from a customer statement displays all activity that occurred on your books for a given period.

Although your accounting software might enable you to send a statement to every customer, every month, it's usually best to reserve customer statements to an as-needed basis. Some customers might want you to submit a statement periodically, and don't be surprised if some customers only pay from a statement rather than individual invoices.

Keep in mind that only customer invoices, credit memos, sales receipts, and invoice payments appear on a statement. Estimates, quotes, and sales orders don't affect your general ledger and, therefore, won't appear on an aging report.

 BOTTOM LINE

Statements provide documentation of what your records show for a given customer as of a certain point in time. Statements serve as a useful collections tool for you, as well as a research aid for your customers when their records differ from yours. Keep this type of document in mind should you encounter discrepancies on what you think you owe to a vendor. Most likely their accounting software enables them to prepare a statement on your behalf so you can quickly see how your payments to them have been applied.

Collectability Risk

Always keep an eye on your Aged Accounts Receivable report. There's a distinctly inverse relationship between the age of an invoice and its collectability. In other words, the farther to the right the amount moves on your aging report, the odds of the customer paying it drop precipitously.

Some companies take excessively long periods to pay their bills. This is often referred to as vendor financing, as by exceeding the agreed-upon payment terms, your customer is using your business as a de facto lender. It could be that the invoice got lost by the U.S. Postal Service if sent by mail. Keep in mind that, occasionally, emailed invoices don't make it to their intended inbox. Or your customer could be continually promising, "the check is in the mail" when it's actually not. The person making the promise likely has the best intentions but either can't pay the invoice due to financial constraints or they simply don't have authorization to do so.

As invoices age beyond the 30-day past due column, it might be time to consider your options.

Unfortunately, the saying "nice guys finish last" is often true when you allow customers too much leeway. Be proactive but polite when pursuing what's due to you. Do give the benefit of the doubt when first following up on invoices. If you email invoices electronically, you've likely noticed that most, but not all, of your electronic correspondence gets to its intended destination. As for paper mail, you've likely seen news stories trumpeting a letter finally delivered after lingering in the postal system for sometimes decades.

The reasons why invoices are paid late are legion, but sometimes the late payment occurs because the person who needs to approve the invoice is on vacation, traveling, or simply swamped with work. A gentle "just making sure you saw this" follow-up by email within a couple days of an invoice exceeding your payment terms could prevent many collection issues. Being proactive also helps you temper your frustrations, because most customers can and want to pay their invoices timely.

Be prepared to gently ratchet up the pressure as needed if an invoice payment continues to slip into the future.

Finance Charges

Your accounting software might allow you to assess finance charges on unpaid balances. It's doubtful that a customer who consistently pays invoices late will honor a request for finance charges, but some will, and by assessing extra charges, you'll then have that fee on record should you need to send the customer to collection.

Your software won't automatically charge interest on unpaid invoices, and not every program offers this capability. If this feature is available, you'll be able to choose which customers you want to charge in this fashion.

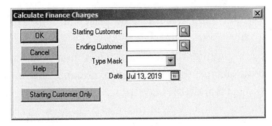

Your accounting software might allow you to specify which customers you want to assess finance charges.

Keep in mind that states set *usury* limits on the amount of interest you can charge. These caps on past due invoices vary by state, and businesses may be subject to different rules than consumers. States periodically change their maximum permitted interest rates, and some make a distinction between *simple interest* and *compound interest*. Check your state's regulations to determine whether late fees in lieu of or in addition to interest are permitted.

DEFINITION

Usury interest rates are generally exorbitant or excessive. **Simple interest** means you can only charge interest on the original amount due, while **compound interest** means you can charge interest on unpaid interest amounts as well.

The penalty for violating usury statutes typically entails some amount of monetary forfeiture and could include criminal penalties as well. Tread carefully when applying finance charges so you don't inadvertently run afoul of the law.

Refunding Credit Balances

From time to time, a customer might inadvertently pay an invoice more than once, and you might cash the check before realizing it's a duplicate payment. For instance, many banks offer lockbox services where customers mail payments directly to a post office box controlled by the bank. The bank opens the envelopes, creates an electronic copy of the checks and any supporting documents, and provides you with electronic documentation of the deposit made. If a bill is paid twice accidently using this system, your customer must issue a stop payment notice when they realize their error.

If it's too late, you can post a credit memo to your books on behalf of the customer to be applied against future services. Or you could issue the customer a refund. Your accounting software might offer two different ways to issue refunds.

The screen you use to pay bills might allow you to choose a customer instead of a vendor. In such cases, you should have the option to select the invoices and/or credit memos you're applying the refund against. Keep in mind that accounting programs sometimes make a distinction between paying bills and writing checks. A "write checks" window likely won't allow you to choose a customer, so check the bill payments window if necessary. In some cases, you might be refunding a remaining balance; in others, you might need to first apply the credit against one or more unpaid invoices and then refund the difference. If you issue a check without applying it against open invoices and/or credit memos, the open balance remains on your books even though you'll have given the customer their money back.

In some software, the screen you use to issue credit memos may offer a "Use Credit to Issue Refund" button. If available, this approach helps you avoid leaving an open accounts receivable balance on your books.

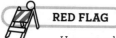 **RED FLAG**

Use care when recording payment transactions that involve your customers. If you write a check to a customer for an amount other than a credit balance due, your accounting software might try to be helpful and set up a receivable balance for the amount you paid. For instance, you might need to purchase products or services from your customer. To avoid such situations, set up your customer in your accounting software as a vendor as well so you don't inadvertently record receivable balances for purchases you make to the vendor.

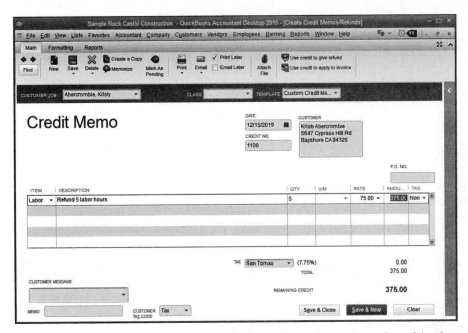

Some accounting programs make it easy to issue refunds to credits; you have to do some legwork in others.

Writing Off Bad Debts

Unfortunately, you might reach the inevitable point that you determine one or more invoices are simply uncollectible. The one saving grace about a bad debt is that if you're an accrual basis taxpayer and already recorded the revenue on your books, you'll receive an income tax deduction in the amount of the foregone revenue. In that regard, it's important to keep your books up-to-date so at least you're not unnecessarily paying income taxes on money you'll never see (even though you will recoup the tax amount paid at the point you write off the debt).

Accrual basis companies that maintain an Accounts Receivable account are allowed to create a contra-asset called Allowance for Bad Debts. In particular, if you have a history of a certain percentage of your receivables being uncollectible, the IRS encourages you to set up this offsetting asset so your Accounts Receivable, net of the Allowance for Bad Debts, reflects a realistic total of what you actually expect to collect.

You'll use your past history as a guide for how much to aggregate in the Allowance for Bad Debts account. When you record the initial amount and update the allowance account periodically with a journal entry, the offsetting entry goes to a bad debt expense. This expense reduces your revenue for tax purposes so you're not paying taxes on amounts you don't plan to collect.

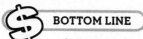

BOTTOM LINE

If you maintain your books on the cash basis, you aren't entitled to an income tax deduction for bad debt because you were never taxed on the revenue. As we discuss in Chapter 2, cash basis accounting recognizes revenue upon receipt from the customer, while accrual basis books recognize revenue when earned.

Managing Credit Risk

You often can minimize the risk of lost revenue by doing some homework in advance. As shown in the following figure, Microsoft Word offers a free business credit application template. An internet search using the term "business credit application" can unearth other alternatives.

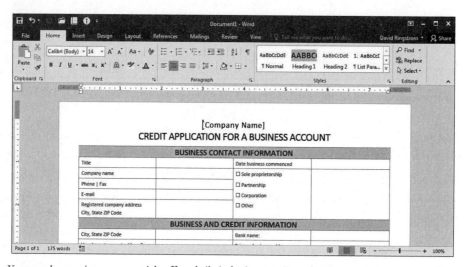

Your word processing program might offer a built-in business credit application template you can modify to suit your needs.

You also might be able to purchase the equivalent of a consumer credit report for many, but not all, businesses from Dun & Bradstreet (dnb.com). Indeed, you may have seen customers make reference to their D-U-N-S number, a program offered by Dun & Brandstreet to make it easy for businesses to share their credit profile with prospective vendors.

Your accounting software likely enables you to establish credit limits for your customers. These can often be set globally, such as a $5,000 maximum for every customer, although you can also permit larger or smaller thresholds as needed. When utilizing this feature, you might have the following options:

- View a notification prompt that the invoice you're entering will cause a customer to exceed their credit limit, with the option to override the credit limit.

- Prevent a user from posting the invoice they entered because the credit limit would be exceeded.

Some accounting programs show the current balance for a customer when you add a new invoice. In other cases, you might not realize the credit limit conflict until you go to save the invoice, which can cause a frustrating loss of your work.

Aged Accounts Payable Report

Just as the Aged Accounts Receivable report shows what's owed to you, your Aged Accounts Payable report displays what you owe to others.

Every accounting program offers such a report, but if you don't record your vendor bills until you're ready to pay them, there won't be any items listed on this report and you won't have a need for it. As discussed in Chapter 6, you have the option to enter vendor bills into your accounting software in advance of paying them, or you can streamline the process by writing checks when payment is due and skip the bill-entry step.

You might be able to get away with bills initially being added to your books when you write the payment check, but as your business grows, you'll likely gravitate toward entering bills as they're received. The vendor bills you enter will appear on the Aged Accounts Payable report.

Among other things, the Aged Accounts Payable report can help you keep track of bills you're purposely not paying, such as a bill you're holding due to a delayed completion date or goods damaged in shipment.

Eliminating Zero Balances on Aging Reports

From time to time, you might encounter situations in which a customer or vendor shows an amount due of, for example, $100 alongside a credit balance of $100. You'll need to purposefully match these transactions to clean up your aging reports.

Within your accounting software, go to the screen where you apply customer payments or pay vendors, respectively. Depending on the software you use, you might be able to simply select both the amount due and the corresponding credit to create a 0 balance transaction you'll post. Or you might have to click a Credits button to instruct the software that you want to apply a pending credit against the invoice. This, too, generates a 0 balance transaction that will clean up your aging report.

The Least You Need to Know

- Payment terms vary from one business to the next. Check any bills you receive to determine if any early payment discounts are available.

- Your Aged Accounts Receivable report shows how much is owed to you at a particular point in time and how long those accounts have been lingering on your books.

- Use the Aged Accounts Payable report if you enter vendor bills when you receive them, and you'll always know how much you owe and to whom.

The Big Three Financial Statements

As noted in Chapter 1, accounting can be thought of as a means of keeping score within your business. Therefore, financial reports can be thought of as the scorecards for different periods of time.

The financial reports discussed in this chapter—the P&L (or income statement), balance sheet, and statement of cash flows—consolidate transaction information from a variety of accounts in your accounting software. Most programs are already set up to generate these reports automatically, but you generally can customize them to suit your specific needs.

Because these reports gather key metrics that indicate the relative strength of your business, you might be asked to share them with lenders or investors when seeking a loan or capital investment, for example.

This chapter helps you learn about the key aspects of each report and how you can use the reports to interpret the health and status of your business.

In This Chapter

- A look at your P&L, balance sheet, and statement of cash flows
- Reviewing the big three to check your business health
- Correcting errors

The Profit and Loss, or Income, Statement

Although most financial reports are referred to by a single name, an income statement has several monikers. You might have heard the terms *P&L, profit and loss, profit and loss statement,* or just *income statement.* These are all names for the same report.

In essence, an income statement is a summary of revenues and expenses for a specific time period. Businesses usually run the P&L for both the current month and the calendar year to date.

A special characteristic of the income statement is that it's reset to 0 at the start of each new fiscal year. However, this doesn't mean your business' income and expenses simply vanish. Your accounting software automatically moves the prior year's income and expense activity into the *Retained Earnings* account on your balance sheet.

DEFINITION

> The **Retained Earnings** account on your balance sheet reflects the accumulated net income your business has generated from inception to date, less any dividends or distributions that have been paid out to owners or shareholders. The Retained Earnings account is a required element in every set of books.

Included on the P&L are various types of accounts that reflect the money from all sources your business is earning from and offsetting expenses to—the places where your business is spending money. Sample income accounts might include Sales and Service Revenue. Sample expense accounts might include Salaries and Wages, Supplies, Rent, Utilities, Advertising, Depreciation, and Employee Benefits.

It's important to note that when you start using a software program to track your business's financial activity, there will likely be a list of accounts (called a chart of accounts, which we discussed in Chapter 4) available. You can add any account names appropriate for your business to that list. So for a pet boarding business, you'd add an account for Pet Food. You also can remove account names that don't apply to your business.

The P&L is also a place where you reflect income that belongs to your business but actually isn't part of your business purpose. Typically, income or expense in this category is placed at the very bottom of the P&L statement to highlight that it's not part of income from the normal business operations. For example, if you have your extra money in an interest-bearing bank account or mutual fund, the interest or dividend earnings on that money appear on your P&L. Also, if you sell assets that belong to the business, like a company car, the profit or loss on that sale appears on the P&L.

Ideally, your income statement always reflects net income (more income than expenses) at the bottom, but you might sometimes reflect a loss when you have more expenses than income in a given period. The term *P&L* or *profit and loss* actually is a misnomer, because this report won't typically reflect both a profit and a loss. A better name would be the profit *or* loss report, reflecting that your business either made a profit or incurred a loss.

The income statement typically reflects the activity for your business through the end of a fiscal year—which for most businesses, is a calendar year. At the start of each new fiscal year, say January 1, the income statement starts over at 0 and begins accumulating new information again.

The fiscal year is the year you use for tracking your business financial activity. As noted, for most companies, this is a calendar year. Some companies, however, can choose a year that's more appropriate to the ebb and flow of their business activity. The federal government, for example, uses September 30 as the last day of its fiscal year, so the financial statements for the government cover the period from October 1 through September 30 instead of a calendar year.

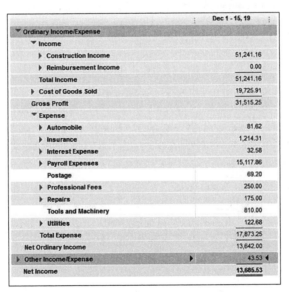

	Dec 1 - 15, 19
▼ **Ordinary Income/Expense**	
▼ **Income**	
▶ **Construction Income**	51,241.16
▶ **Reimbursement Income**	0.00
Total Income	51,241.16
▶ **Cost of Goods Sold**	19,725.91
Gross Profit	31,515.25
▼ **Expense**	
▶ **Automobile**	81.62
▶ **Insurance**	1,214.31
▶ **Interest Expense**	32.58
▶ **Payroll Expenses**	15,117.86
Postage	69.20
▶ **Professional Fees**	250.00
▶ **Repairs**	175.00
Tools and Machinery	810.00
▶ **Utilities**	122.68
Total Expense	17,873.25
Net Ordinary Income	13,642.00
▶ **Other Income/Expense**	43.53 ◀
Net Income	**13,685.53**

*Your income statement is a scorecard for a period of time that shows
revenue you've generated and expenses you've incurred.*

ACCOUNTING HACK

Many accounting software programs enable you to expand and collapse various levels and categories of information in generated reports to just what you want to see. Expanding or collapsing information does not affect the calculated subtotals and totals in the reports.

The Balance Sheet

By nature, accountants tend to be pragmatic, so the balance sheet is aptly named. Simply put, it's a listing of account balances at the end of a given time period. Balance sheets are broken down into three major sections:

Assets: This section contains the book balances of accounts of what your business owns or is owed.

Liabilities: This section contains the balances of what your business owes to others.

Equity: This section reflects what would be distributed to stakeholders of your business should you close the business and liquidate your assets. The amount of equity is the difference between your assets and your liabilities.

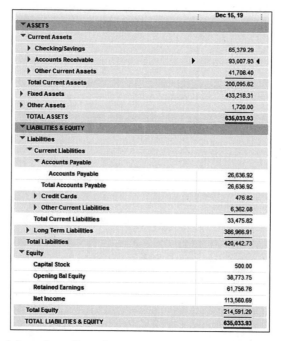

Your balance sheet reflects what you own and owe. The difference between those two amounts is the net worth of the business, or the equity.

The historical nature of accounting reports means that the amounts you see in the assets section do not necessarily reflect the current reality. A building listed at a $500,000 *book balance* on the books might be worth a multiple of that amount, or a fraction, today. If a balance sheet reflects equity of $1,000,000, that doesn't necessarily mean you can close up shop and pocket a million dollars.

In short, accounting records do not reflect current *fair market value* for assets. They only reflect fair market value at the point that an asset purchase is first recorded. After that, the value of the asset might rise or fall, but these fluctuations aren't recorded in the accounting records until the asset is sold. The true value of your business equity can be determined only by appraising all the assets you own and then subtracting any liabilities presently due.

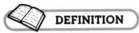

DEFINITION

The **book balance** of an asset on the balance sheet may differ from its fair market value. For instance, if your business owns a building, the book balance on your balance sheet is whatever you paid for the building less accumulated depreciation. The **fair market value** of an asset is the amount an unrelated third-party would willingly pay to purchase that asset.

The major headings within the balance sheet—Assets, Liabilities, and Equity—are further broken down into subcategories so you can get a better sense of what the business owns. Let's look at a handful of typical balance sheet subcategories next.

Current Assets

This section reflects assets your business owns that can be converted to cash either immediately or fairly readily. Examples include bank balances, accounts receivable, inventory, employee loans, security deposits, and prepaid expenses.

ASSETS	
Current Assets	
Checking/Savings	
Checking	46,969.10
Petty Cash	500.00
Savings	17,910.19
Total Checking/Savings	65,379.29
Accounts Receivable	
Accounts Receivable	93,007.93
Total Accounts Receivable	93,007.93
▶ Other Current Assets	41,708.40
Total Current Assets	200,095.62

Anything on your balance sheet that's either cash or can be readily converted to cash is considered a current asset.

Long-Term Assets

This section reflects assets your business owns or is owed but that might take some time to convert to cash, including investments, real estate holdings, equipment, notes receivable, and construction in progress.

Current Liabilities

This section reflects amounts you'll need to pay in the short term, typically within 1 year. You also might see these referred to as short-term liabilities. They include accounts payable and long-term debt that must be paid back within the current fiscal year.

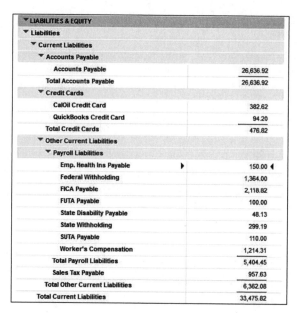

▼ **LIABILITIES & EQUITY**	
▼ **Liabilities**	
▼ **Current Liabilities**	
▼ **Accounts Payable**	
Accounts Payable	26,636.92
Total Accounts Payable	26,636.92
▼ **Credit Cards**	
CalOil Credit Card	382.62
QuickBooks Credit Card	94.20
Total Credit Cards	476.82
▼ **Other Current Liabilities**	
▼ **Payroll Liabilities**	
Emp. Health Ins Payable	150.00 ◄
Federal Withholding	1,364.00
FICA Payable	2,118.82
FUTA Payable	100.00
State Disability Payable	48.13
State Withholding	299.19
SUTA Payable	110.00
Worker's Compensation	1,214.31
Total Payroll Liabilities	5,404.45
Sales Tax Payable	957.63
Total Other Current Liabilities	6,362.08
Total Current Liabilities	33,475.82

Current or short-term liabilities represent money your business will be required to pay to others in the near future.

> **RED FLAG**
>
> When reviewing a balance sheet, ideally the Total Current Assets value should exceed the Total Current Liabilities line. Current assets represent the short-term liquidity of a business, meaning the ability to handily cover any bills that will come due in the near future. If current liabilities are close to or exceed current assets, it's very likely that a cash crunch is imminent for your business.

Long-Term Liabilities

This section reflects amounts your business owes but won't have to pay back until some point in the future. Subcategories here include things like mortgages and car loans.

Equity

This section reflects the net earnings or loss from inception to date, along with investments made into the company, less distributions made to owners. In other words, these types of equity items represent the *book value* owned by the owners of the business, which would be a starting point for valuing the business in the event the business was sold. Examples include capital contributions, common stock, and retained earnings.

▼ Equity	
Capital Stock	500.00
Opening Bal Equity	38,773.75
Retained Earnings	61,756.76
Net Income	113,560.69
Total Equity	**214,591.20**

Equity represents the book value of the business, a starting point for valuing the business as a whole.

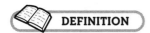

DEFINITION

> Within financial statements, **book value** is a theoretical figure that shows what the owners would get if the company was liquidated as of the financial statement date. We say theoretical, because items on the balance sheet could be sold for more or less than their book value. This differs from fair market value.

The Statement of Cash Flows

Accounting reports are all interrelated, in that no one report stands on its own. As we've seen, the net income or loss from an income statement rolls into the Retained Earnings section of your balance sheet. Although your income statement reflects the revenue and expenses for given periods, it doesn't necessarily reflect the actual cash in and cash out for your business.

For example, when you make a loan payment, only a portion of that amount may affect your income statement. For a loan payment of $1,000, $200 might be interest and $800 would be principal. The $200 in interest appears on your income statement as an expense but the $800 principal amount does not appear there. Instead, this amount reduces a short-term liability on your balance sheet.

Rock Castle Construction
Statement of Cash Flows
January 1 through December 15, 2019

	Jan 1 - Dec 15, 19
▼ **OPERATING ACTIVITIES**	
Net Income	113,560.69
▼ Adjustments to reconcile Net Income	
▶ to net cash provided by operations:	
Net cash provided by Operating Activities	42,584.17
▼ **INVESTING ACTIVITIES**	
Furniture and Equipment ▶	-11,500.00 ◀
Net cash provided by Investing Activities	-11,500.00
▼ **FINANCING ACTIVITIES**	
Loan - Construction Equipment	-431.79
Loan - Vehicles (Van)	-5,789.05
Note Payable - Bank of Anycity	-28,487.31
Net cash provided by Financing Activities	-34,708.15
Net cash increase for period	-3,623.98
Cash at beginning of period	71,443.27
Cash at end of period	67,819.29

The statement of cash flows reflects cash in and cash out for a business.

Thus, the statement of cash flows helps you follow the money. The report starts out with your ending cash balance as of the previous accounting period, typically the prior month. It then has three sections: cash flow from operations, cash flow from investing activities, and cash flow from financing activities.

Cash Flow from Operations

The cash flow from operations (Operating Activities in the preceding figure) is the actual net cash in or out of your business. This isn't necessarily equivalent to the Net Income line amount at the bottom of your income statement. Indeed, net income in your income statement may reflect invoices customers haven't paid yet, bills from vendors you haven't paid yet, noncash accounting adjustments such as depreciation and amortization (see Chapter 7 and the later "Depreciation on Fixed Assets" section for more about depreciation), and the current month's portion of a prepaid expense.

From an accounting perspective, income and cash flow are two very different measurements.

Cash Flow from Investing Activities

Cash flow from investing activities (the Investing Activities section in preceding figure) includes money related to ownership stakes in your business, such as contributions you make to get the business started or to fund ongoing operations or distributions you make to yourself and other owners to share profits from the business.

Cash Flow from Financing Activities

Cash flow from financing (called Financing Activities in the preceding figure) reflects cash in or out of your business related to money you've borrowed to help fund the business. This section includes both new money you've borrowed as well as monies you've paid back, such as money borrowed on or repaid for a credit card, activity related to a working capital line of credit, funds borrowed on or repaid to car loans and mortgages, and money you or a related party loan to the business temporarily.

Reviewing Your Financial Statements

Each report derived from your accounting software gives you insight into your business from a different perspective.

For example, the balance sheet shows what you own, what you owe, and what the book net value (as opposed to the fair market value) of your business is. Reviewing the balance sheet is helpful to understand where things stand, but another purpose for reviewing financial statements is to catch accounting errors. In this section, we review some common issues you might find when reviewing your financial statements.

We assume you're going to be using accounting software. Further, we assume you'll be viewing your financial reports on-screen. Your accounting software certainly allows you to print reports on paper, but the primary benefit to viewing reports on-screen is that corrections are just a click or two away. Most accounting programs allow you to drill down into an underlying transaction so you can view the source of that information. If you find that you've put all or part of a transaction in the wrong spot in your books, you can fix it easily.

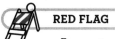 **RED FLAG**

Be sure to review your financial reports regularly and in a timely fashion. Corrections you make within a month or so of the end of the accounting period have little to no ramifications. Finding errors down the road means you could end up paying more or less income tax than you should, so the impact can be magnified. Indeed, depending on the magnitude of the correction, it's possible you could have to file an amended income tax return, which could lead to unintended and unwanted regulatory scrutiny. Corrections are always easiest if you haven't yet filed your income tax return.

Reviewing Your Income Statement

Your income statement starts over again at 0 at the start of each fiscal year, so the effect of any errors you make on the income statement are limited to affecting a single accounting year. However, it's still important to perform a review to ensure that your records are in order.

First, you'll want to be able to compare your financial results from one month to the next, as well as one year to the next. Over time, this can help you identify trends and determine which of the products and services you offer are doing well and which are starting to lag.

Second, the amount of federal and state income tax you pay each year is predicated by your income statement. Errors on this report can result in over- or underpaying your income taxes. Overpaying is simply a monetary penalty, but underpaying due to poor accounting can result in criminal prosecution.

With that background in mind, let's look at some typical income statement issues.

If you have multiple income accounts, you'll want to ensure that items are categorized properly in each account. For example, if your business offers both consulting and training services, you'll likely have a Consulting Income account as well as one or more Training Income accounts. Ensuring that amounts are classified correctly gives you the ability to monitor trends based on each of these lines of service.

Also, when reviewing expenses, be on the lookout for accounts that don't show any expense when they should. For instance, let's say your company's monthly health insurance premium is paid by credit card. If you forget to reconcile your credit card statement in a given month, you might not have a health insurance premium amount. This can give you the false impression that your net income is higher than it truly is. Plus, you potentially miss out on a valuable income tax deduction if you don't record every expense for your business in a timely fashion.

 **RED FLAG**

Some accounting programs let you enter transactions without specifying an account on each line. The intent is to simplify data entry, but this convenience comes with potential problems. Transactions entered this way get lumped into either Uncategorized Income or Uncategorized Expense on your income statement, and as a result, you can't meaningfully compare revenue and expenses by type from one period to the next. Also, say you write a check for a security deposit. This is an asset to you—money you'll get back at some point in the future. However, if it's lumped into Uncategorized Expenses, you won't carry the asset on your books and will claim an invalid income tax deduction on it.

Reviewing Your Balance Sheet

Now, let's move on to the balance sheet and look at some typical corrections you might need to make. Unlike the income statement, your balance sheet never gets zeroed out until you liquidate your business, so any errors here could potentially linger for years.

Cash account: The cash balance on your balance sheet should always be reconciled with your bank statement. (Chapter 8 covers reconciliation.) No matter how closely you think you're watching your cash, it's easy to miss transactions. Here are some common occurrences:

- You record a payment or deposit twice.

- You forget to record an automatic withdrawal from your account, such as bank fees or an automatic payment.

- You neglected to record an ATM transaction.

- If you're fortunate enough to have customers who pay invoices by Automated Clearing House (ACH), you might not notice when a payment posts to your bank account so you didn't record it in your books.

- You handwrite a check, and when posting it into your accounting software, you enter it into the wrong bank account.

Fortunately, you'll catch all these issues when you reconcile your bank account, so cash account errors on your balance sheet usually take care of themselves.

Accounts Receivable: Accounts Receivable represents the amount your customers owe you. The amount in your Accounts Receivable account on your balance sheet should always match the bottom line total on your Aged Accounts Receivable report. Typically, your accounting software takes care of this for you. However, your Accounts Receivable account can get out of balance.

For example, when recording customer invoices in your accounting software, you might post a line item detail transaction to the Accounts Receivable account. In other words, the invoice amount automatically increases your Accounts Receivable account in your software, but when you enter the description of what this income is for, it's easy to forget and post the offsetting amount to Accounts Receivable as well. This results in a debit and a credit to the same account, which in effect fails to record the revenue and results in a 0 amount transaction on your books, even though the invoice itself reflects an amount due.

Also, be especially careful when recording journal entries that affect your Accounts Receivable account. Only in rare instances should you need to force activity into your Accounts Receivable account with a journal entry. This account should only be affected by posting invoices, credit memos, and customer payments. If your Aged Receivables Report doesn't match your Accounts Receivable account on your balance sheet, something's gone awry in your books.

One way to track down an error is to review the detail of the Accounts Receivable account in your general ledger and look at the Type (or Transaction Type) column. The exact transaction type codes might vary based on your accounting software, but valid transactions in the Accounts Receivable account typically appear as one of these items:

- Invoice (sometimes abbreviated IN)

- Credit memo (sometimes abbreviated CM)

- Customer payment (sometimes abbreviated PMT)

- Check (sometimes abbreviated CK; any checks that post to this account should solely be to issue a refund to a customer)

RED FLAG

Transactions that have a type of general journal or that look anything like general journal entry should be scrutinized closely, as journal entries cannot affect the Aged Accounts Receivable report. Your general ledger report typically includes a Transaction Type column, and general journal entries typically are indicated by the abbreviation *GJ* or the word *Journal*. This differs from accounts receivable related indicators like INV (Invoice), CHK (Check), PMT (Payment), or RCPT (Receipt).

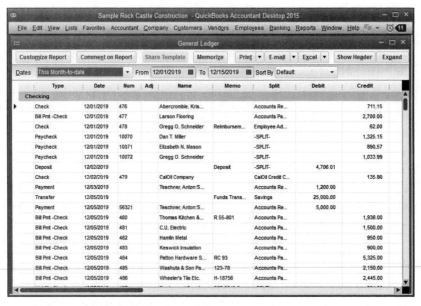

The Type column for your Accounts Receivable account within your general ledger helps you identify misposted transactions.

Inventory: Another account you should never affect by way of a general journal entry is your Inventory account. Your ending inventory balance on your balance sheet should always match the inventory valuation report your accounting software provides. Always use transaction forms in your accounting software to record the purchase, sale, and write off of inventory.

Discrepancies in inventory balances can be tracked down in the same fashion as misposted accounts receivable transactions. If you use a journal entry to try to make a correction to your inventory account balance, the other inventory management reports your software provides will no longer tie back to the ending inventory balance on your balance sheet.

Now, let's go back to our pet boarding business example. It's the end of the year, and you find that you still have some pet food on the shelves that's expired, or perhaps a bag tore and the food spoiled. Your accounting software has a means you can use to record an inventory adjustment, which removes the unsalable food from your books and record an expense. In this case, what was an asset—the bag of pet food—has become an expense.

Always ensure that you use inventory adjustments and not journal entries to make corrections to inventory balances.

Prepaid Expenses: Most accounting programs don't offer a means of reconciling prepaid expenses, so you might want to use a spreadsheet to maintain *supporting schedules*. Examples of prepaid expenses include insurance premiums you pay in advance, such as for a vehicle.

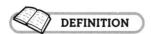 **DEFINITION**

Your Aged Accounts Receivables report is an example of a **supporting schedule,** which provides additional detail a standard accounting report isn't suited to display.

Let's say you get a discount for paying $1,200 for a full year of insurance in advance. You wouldn't post the entire $1,200 in a single month, as this is really 12 monthly expenses of $100 each. Instead, when you pay the initial bill for your vehicle insurance, you'll post the transaction to a Prepaid Expenses account. Then, each month by way of a journal entry, you'll debit Insurance for $100 and credit Prepaid Expenses for $100. At the end of 12 months, the Prepaid Expenses account should have a balance of 0.

Typically, you can use a single Prepaid Expenses account to temporarily store all your prepaid expenses in one spot. However, because the prepaid expenses will likely be amortizing over different time periods, you might want to maintain a spreadsheet where you can log and reconcile the ins and outs of the prepaid expenses account. We provide an example of such a schedule in Chapter 22.

Fixed Assets: Economists like to use the term *durable goods* to describe appliances and equipment consumers purchase. Fixed assets are much like durable goods for your business.

It's important to properly account for these items, which usually have a longer life within your business and a greater expense than day-to-day purchases like office supplies. The federal or state tax codes that apply to your business might require that you not record the expense for these items all at once, but rather over a period of years. Further, your local government might assess a personal property tax, sometimes referred to as an *ad valorem* tax, on such items.

When reviewing your fixed assets, be sure equipment such as office furniture, laptops, cash registers, machinery, and so on have been categorized properly on your balance sheet. Otherwise, your operating expenses may be improperly distorted.

Depreciation on Fixed Assets: The theory behind depreciation is that the cost of major expenditures relates to a period of time longer than the current year. If you purchase a piece of equipment, say for $3,000, there's an assumption that you're going to use the equipment to generate income for several years. So you should expense the cost of the equipment over those same years to present a fair picture of your income, offset by appropriate expenses.

We use depreciation expense to represent the wearing down or the usage of fixed assets over a period of time. Ideally, that period of time relates exactly to how long the asset is expected to last, but in reality, some assets last seemingly forever, like a building or a file cabinet.

The IRS has taken the guesswork out of determining the life of an asset by preparing tables that tell you how much to depreciate and over how many years the depreciation should occur. You can view online or request a printed copy of IRS Publication 946: How to Depreciate Property. It gives you the life expectancies and depreciation options for all your fixed assets.

BOTTOM LINE

Depreciation is a complicated area and one most small business owners turn over to their accountant because there are many different ways items can be depreciated and choices to make. Typically your accountant calculates the depreciation for you and gives you a journal entry to make monthly or once a year.

Other Assets: This catch-all category reflects assets that don't fit into the other categories on your balance sheet, such as security deposits that have been refunded.

When a landlord or utility company refunds a security deposit, be sure to zero out the amount that appears on your balance sheet. If you record the deposit on your income statement as revenue, you'll inadvertently pay income tax a second time on money you've already paid income tax on once.

Current Liabilities: When reviewing your balance sheet, be sure to reconcile the Accounts Payable account in the same way we described for Accounts Receivable. In some cases, you might enter a bill to be paid later but then in haste write a check you post as an expense without applying it to the unpaid bill. If you've paid the bill separately but the liability remains, this can result in double-counting one or more expenses. Such transactions distort your net income and could result in an improper income tax deduction.

As with Accounts Receivable, you should never try to make an adjustment to your Accounts Payable account with a general journal entry. Doing so puts your balance sheet out of step with the supporting schedule.

Other issues that can arise in the current liabilities section of the balance sheet report are mismatched payroll tax liabilities. Your accounting software is designed to handle most of the payroll tax tracking for you, but if you work outside the built-in forms, you can end up with discrepancies.

Similarly, if you remit a payroll tax amount but use the Payroll Tax Expense account for your check instead of a liability account like Federal Withholding, you'll end up with a double-counted expense as well as a fictitious liability on your books.

Long-Term Liabilities: Many small businesses won't have long-term liabilities if they've used short-term financing options such as credit cards or contributed capital. However, if you do have some sort of long-term financing, when reviewing your balance sheet, be sure to compare the balance of any long-term debt with the associated *amortization schedule* for the loan.

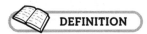 **DEFINITION**

> An **amortization schedule** shows how each loan payment you make is allocated between principal and interest. Principal reduces the remaining balance of the loan; interest is an expense for holding someone else's money. We show how you can create an amortization schedule on your own in Chapter 22.

Equity: You shouldn't have to make entries in this section very often. However, one thing to be on the lookout for is your retained earnings amount dropping below 0. This can signify that your business is consistently losing money, or that the ownership of a profitable business is making excessive distributions.

Typically, a business should only distribute any net income that remains after all expenses are recorded, although in certain circumstances, you might temporarily overdistribute to meet external cash requirements or fulfill previous commitments.

When You Find an Error

If you review your financial reports on a monthly basis, you'll typically catch issues immediately and can fix them in the same accounting period. In other cases, it could be months or years before you realize a mistake was made in a prior accounting period. The actions you take will be driven by the amount of the error as well as the type of account:

Income statement accounts: If the incorrectly reported activity is in your current fiscal year, simply fix the transaction. If the activity is in a previous fiscal year, you'll need to decide whether it's *material* enough to fix. If you determine that the activity is material, a journal entry is necessary to make the correction.

 **DEFINITION**

Materiality means is the amount significant enough to have a meaningful impact on the financial statements. The concept of materiality varies from one business to another.

Balance sheet accounts: These accounts never get zeroed out until you close down and liquidate your company, so mistakes you leave in place on your balance sheet can haunt you into the foreseeable future. The balance sheet is intended to be a clear picture of what your business owns, is owed, and has earned over the years. Always make corrections to the balance sheet so you have a clear picture of your financial standing.

The Least You Need to Know

- Financial reports interrelate to each other, and your accounting software consolidates information from various accounts to create them.
- The profit and loss, or income, statement is a summary of revenues and expenses for a specific time period.
- The balance sheet is a listing of account balances at the end of a time period and is intended to be a picture of what your business owns, is owed, and has earned.
- The statement of cash flows reflects cash in and cash out for a business.
- Review your financial statements to find and correct any underlying errors, both for accuracy and to avoid any resulting concerns such as tax liabilities.

CHAPTER 15

Internal Control and Minimizing Fraud Risk

Internal control means that, as a business owner, you take precautions to secure both your accounting records and the assets of your business. With reports of identity theft, customer account information theft, and more in the media seemingly daily, it's smart to take basic precautions to keep your company information safe.

In this chapter, we touch on core security measures such as password protection, data backup, identify theft prevention, and disaster recovery options, among other commonsense measures.

In This Chapter

- The importance of securing your records
- Maintaining your software
- Backup, backup, backup
- Preventing identity theft
- Securing customer information and checks

Securing Your Accounting Records

If you're using desktop accounting software, it might be optional for you to assign a password to your accounting records. Cloud-based programs don't give you an option. They require a password for you to access your records.

We know. You don't want yet another password in your life, but the nature of securing financial information requires that you do so. Even if you're the only person who accesses your accounting records, it's still important to password protect your books. You never know when or if your home or office might be burglarized. Plus, accounting software can be full of information identity thieves seek, such as employee names, addresses, and Social Security numbers.

As with all aspects of your online life, you should change your accounting software password from time to time, and be sure not to use that same password anywhere else.

 **ACCOUNTING HACK**

Keep a list of all your passwords in a secure location such as a locked desk or safety deposit box, and update the list as needed. Or use an app such as LastPass (lastpass. com) or Dashlane (dashlane.com).

Also be sure to protect your computer with antivirus software such as Norton Internet Security (norton.com/Internet_Security), Trend Micro Internet Security (trendmicro.com), or McAfee (mcafee.com). It's entirely possible for unprotected computers to be compromised by hackers who might surreptitiously spirit away copies of your accounting records or hijack your computer in exchange for a ransom.

Here are some basic rules for selecting a strong, secure password:

- Make the password at least eight characters long. You don't need to use complete words, but a memorable phrase works.

- Don't use only letters. Use a combination of uppercase and lowercase letters, along with numbers and special characters such as $, &,), or !. Use spaces if you can; if they're not allowed, substitute an underscore.

- Use abbreviations or alternate spellings, or substitute numerals for words (*4* instead of *for*, for example).

- Avoid personal information others could easily guess or find, such as your name, birth date, or pet's name.

So using these guidelines, a password like *L0v34eveR* is stronger than *loveforever*, for example.

Updating Your Accounting Software

Computer software in general is fraught with complexity, and despite software companies' best efforts, many times software bugs emerge. These errors in the underlying programming code can cause calculation errors, data integrity issues, or worse.

One of the benefits of cloud-based accounting software is that you don't have to perform any maintenance. Any bug fixes are applied to the platform automatically.

With desktop software, vendors often push out software updates to fix bugs or add new features, but it's your responsibility to download and install these updates. If you opt not to update your software, it's possible that software errors could affect your accounting records.

Sometimes bug fixes or updates cause *new* problems in your software, but software vendors generally correct such issues very quickly. Still, to protect yourself, always back up your accounting software and company data before you install any new software updates, and particularly before you install a new version of your desktop-based accounting software.

Backing Up Your Accounting Records

Backing up means making a copy of your records as of a given point in time for safekeeping. In effect, backing up makes a snapshot of your accounting records you can restore, or copy from, later if necessary. Ideally, your backup copies shouldn't reside on your accounting computer itself because bad things can happen to your accounting computer.

It's best to make backup copies of your accounting data and store them in various other, separate locations, such as these:

USB flash drive or an external hard disk: Either can be connected to your accounting computer so you can save the backup files to the drive and then disconnect when you finish. Be sure to store the drive or disk in another, secure location.

Writeable DVD-R disc: Many newer computers include a drive that can burn backup files to discs. Store these in a secure location away from the computer.

Cloud-based storage service: Even the free basic plans for services such as Microsoft's OneDrive, Google Drive, or Dropbox provide enough room to upload and store multiple backup files for a typical company.

The penalty for not maintaining proper backups of your accounting software can be harsh. You might have to reconstruct months of activity from paper records you may or may not still have available.

No matter what type of accounting software you use, whether desktop or cloud-based, it's essential that you create backups of your data.

Backing Up and Restoring Desktop-Based Data

Although the exact procedures vary depending on your software, when backing up your data in desktop-based accounting software, you'll typically go to the File menu and then look for a command named something along the lines of Backup. Or it might be under a Utilities submenu. Backing up is important enough that most software programs usually make the process easy to find.

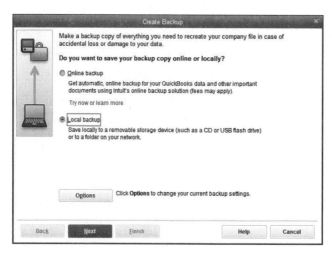

Desktop-based accounting software programs often walk you through the steps involved with backing up your data.

You can and should back up your company data manually from time to time. However, you also should set up scheduled backups for your accounting software, so in case you forget to back up your data manually, a backup copy is still made.

Depending on your accounting software, in addition to backing up your data, you also might be able to create an archive copy of your accounting records. An archive lets you open a snapshot of your books so you can run reports and view transactions, but you won't be able to make any changes to the archive copy. Archive copies are particularly helpful for providing supporting documentation to auditors.

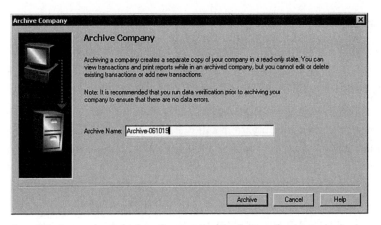

An archive is a read-only backup of your accounting data as of a given point in time.

If your accounting software does not include backup capabilities or if you have trouble with the backup procedure, look for the company file or folder on your computer's hard disk, make a copy of it, and paste the copy in another location, such as those mentioned earlier.

The process for restoring accounting records from a backup is similar to creating the backup file, but in reverse. You choose a command in your software and then choose which backup file to restore from.

Some programs enable you to keep incremental copies of the accounting data over time. You might choose to restore an older file rather than the latest one, for example, if you know last week's entries introduced some errors and you want to return to two weeks ago, before those errors were introduced.

 **RED FLAG**

Bear in mind that if you get into your backup files and restore your books on your existing computer, you might be overwriting any previous work you did in the software subsequent to the date you created the backup file.

When it comes to backing up your accounting data and documents, your mantra should be trust but verify. Most of these systems generally perform flawlessly, but anything a human creates or maintains has fallibilities. Randomly perform a backup or check online storage sites to confirm that your backup data and copies of documents are appearing where you expect so that you'll have the information when you need it.

Backing Up Cloud-Based Data

With cloud-based accounting software, you don't have to back up your data. In theory, that is. However, no human-based system is completely infallible. In recent years, we've seen gigantic companies collapse overnight. It's unlikely that your cloud-based accounting software provider will suddenly fail, but it is a risk to consider.

A much more likely risk is that a hacker will guess or use a technique like *social engineering* to get your password, get into your account, potentially steal your data, and change your password so you're cut off from your financial records. Many times a single combination of an email address and password is the only thing standing between a perpetrator absconding with money from your bank account or holding your accounting records ransom.

One way to guard against such intrusions is to implement two-factor security. More and more online service providers allow you to turn on a feature that requires you to enter a confirmation number they text to you when you sign into an online account. This means if someone steals or guesses your online credentials, they'd also need to have your cell phone in their possession. Two-factor security isn't a perfect solution, but it does make it harder to illegally access your online accounts or services.

DEFINITION

Social engineering takes many forms, but commonly hackers or others intent on ill will pose as someone reputable in order to gather passwords or information they can use to determine passwords or access to protected spaces or data.

Your cloud-based accounting software may not offer a means for you to back up your entire set of books, but sometimes clever workarounds exist. For instance, with QuickBooks Online, you can export all your data to a backup you can then restore to the desktop versions of QuickBooks. Performing this export doesn't mean you have to cancel your account, but doing so gives you a comprehensive backup copy of all your online accounting records.

In other cases, you might have to piecemeal your backups by exporting reports from the online software. As we discuss in Chapter 7, the General Ledger report provides a comprehensive listing of all your accounting transactions for any period of time you choose. Periodically exporting this report to an Excel spreadsheet gives you an electronic copy you can use if you need to reconstitute your accounting records. You'll want to do the same thing with customer, vendor, and employee lists so you always have backup copies of the information.

When you use cloud-based accounting software, you give up an element of control you normally have over data that resides in a desktop accounting program. The upside is that the data is automatically backed up for you, and your service provider may be able to restore your books to a certain point upon request. Most cloud-based accounting programs offer little to no functionality with regard to importing transactions, so if something goes awry with your books, you might have to resort to manually rekeying your data. However, by their very nature, cloud-based programs aren't susceptible to many of the risks desktop accounting programs pose.

Managing Identity Theft Risk

Identity theft is a widespread and insidious risk individuals as well as companies face every day. Data, money, merchandise, and more is potentially exposed or stolen if someone spoofs your identity or gains access to a bank, retailer, or other entity with whom you have an account.

The key to reducing your chances of identify theft is to keep personal information such as Social Security numbers and dates of birth for you and your employees as secure as possible.

Within your accounting software, keep access to employee records on a need-to-know basis. Both cloud-based and desktop accounting software programs allow you to establish roles for users within the software. Thus, if you have salespeople, you might grant them access to inventory, customers, and sales screens, but not access to vendors, writing checks, or the payroll sections of your software. This concept is often referred to as separation of duties.

Securing Customer Information

If your business accepts credit cards, you need to take special precautions to protect the credit card numbers you collect.

Fortunately, modern accounting programs no longer allow you to store credit card numbers within the software itself. Instead, customer credit card numbers are stored in a secure fashion online that integrates with your accounting software. This ensures that if a malicious party does get a copy of your accounting records, they won't get all your customers' card numbers.

Therefore, it's doubly important to secure your accounting records, not only for your own protection, but to protect your customers as well.

Using Magnetic Swipe Card Readers

Many businesses have started using magnetic swipe card readers that attach to smartphones or tablets. You plug the reader into your device, activate the related app that records the transaction, and swipe credit cards on the spot.

Square Reader (squareup.com) is a popular example, and it synchronizes with QuickBooks, Xero, and other popular programs. Intuit QuickBooks offers its own GoPayment Reader, which works in a similar fashion, accepting credit card payments and recording the payments automatically in your books.

These devices offer even solo businesspeople a secure method for accepting credit cards while protecting customer credit card data. The transaction is encrypted, and the numbers aren't stored in your device nor your accounting software.

Securing Checks

Credit card fraud runs rampant, but check fraud does as well. All the information anyone needs to empty your bank account is printed along the bottom of your checks: your bank's routing number and your account number.

Always keep blank checks secured in a locked drawer, safe, or other secure location. Even if you closely monitor the sequence of your check numbers, it might take you months or possibly years to notice checks stolen from the bottom of the box.

Most office supply stores sell blank check stock, magnetic ink, and computer software anyone can use to create fake checks. However, check fraud takes many forms, and thieves sometimes steal checks from the mail. The payee and/or the amount of the checks are altered before the checks are cashed. Fortunately, many banks offer a service called Positive Pay that can head off this issue. If you participate in Positive Pay, whenever you issue checks to anyone, you provide a list of the payees and amounts to your bank. Any checks presented for payment on your account that don't appear on the Positive Pay list are returned.

RED FLAG

When possible, spell out the full name of a vendor or governmental agency when you print or handwrite checks. In particular, if you're writing a check to pay taxes to the federal government, take the time to write out "Internal Revenue Service" on the check. If your check was somehow stolen, the abbreviation "IRS" could easily be converted to "MRS." along with any name a thief wishes to use.

If your business is of such a size that you're not reconciling your bank statement on your own (see Chapter 8), a good safeguard is to have your business' bank statements mailed to your house or available online so you can view them at any time. Unfortunately, much employee theft is perpetrated by trusted employees who have access to both check writing and bank reconciliations.

As a business owner, you should make a point of always reviewing your bank and credit card statements at least monthly to ensure your accounts haven't fallen prey to theft or fraud.

Destroying Records

Even the smallest of businesses can generate a mountain of paperwork, some of which can be discarded quickly and some that must be kept for several years or more.

You completely relinquish control over paperwork you put in a trash can, so anything that can be remotely tied back to your business, customers, or employees should go through a shredder, unless it falls under the record retention policies we discuss in Chapter 18.

One of the best investments you can make in your business is a heavy-duty paper shredder that can accommodate 20 pages or more at once. Further, choose a cross-cut shredder that minces paper into tiny pieces, not just long shreds that can be easily taped back together by a thief with time on his or her hands.

Also, be sure to properly destroy electronic records. When it's time to replace any computers you've used in your business, it's essential that you ensure no data is left on the hard drives. Simply deleting data from your hard drive is insufficient because data you delete still remains on your drive until something else is saved over it. Data is saved on your hard drive randomly, so deleted data could still have a long life.

Reformatting a hard drive resets the drive to its original, blank state. This action can be carried out within the operating system of your computer, but isn't a foolproof method. Modern data recovery tools can still find data on even reformatted drives. The best software-based solution is to use a tool that wipes your computer's hard disk, which means the entire disk is overwritten with 0s and 1s that obliterate any previous data.

 **RED FLAG**

Formatting or wiping your hard disk leaves your computer without an operating system, so if you plan on repurposing the computer, you'll need to reload the operating system and any software you want to use. Many computers either ship with a recovery drive built-in or offer the option to create your own recovery CDs or DVDs for reloading the operating system.

Another method of destroying everything on a hard drive involves using a piece of equipment called a degausser, which magnetically erases all data on a hard drive. You can purchase these for as little as a few dollars to tens of thousands of dollars.

Or to keep it simple, you can just remove the hard drive from your computer and physically destroy it with a sledgehammer or other means.

Disaster Recovery

There's no limit to the number of ways your business can be affected by a natural or human disaster, so it's important to have a disaster recovery plan, no matter what size business you have.

Let's consider a real-world example. An Atlanta-based chocolatier was forced to close down one of its stores due to smoke damage from a fire in an adjacent space. This could have been devastating if the business only had a single location. As you can see, it's not only your accounting records that can be at risk, but the actual operation of your business as well.

Storing records in the cloud provides an easy way for businesses to protect themselves from disasters, as at least copies of key business documents and records will be available from a new location.

To help prepare your business for a potential disaster, establish on-demand financing such as a working capital line of credit or available room on a credit card should you encounter an unanticipated cash crunch. (This can happen even during normal business operations, much less during a disaster.)

Also, if your business has employees, establish a phone tree for communicating news about the business so no one person is responsible for reaching out to everyone.

If your business needs a physical space, identify potential temporary working quarters you can use should your primary place of business become inaccessible for a period of time.

And as we discuss in Chapter 10, business interruption insurance policies can provide financial protection against events that prevent normal business operations.

Finally, cloud-based accounting are great when disaster strikes because your books won't be tied to any particular computer. As long as you can get online, you'll be able to access your books.

The Least You Need to Know

- Use strong passwords to secure access to your accounting records, and create backups you can pull from in the event of a data loss.
- Take commonsense measures to secure your identity, information such as credit cards, and blank checks for your business bank account.
- Magnetic swipe card readers offer a secure way to accept credit cards.
- Shred old paper records, and remove the hard disk before disposing of any computer that held company accounting or other confidential data.
- Even small businesses need a disaster recovery plan.

Financial Reports and Stakeholders

Even if you're the sole owner of your business, you're by no means the only stakeholder with an interest in your company's activities. As you'll learn in later chapters, various governmental agencies levy a dizzying array of taxes, including payroll taxes, income taxes, business license taxes, property taxes, and more. The Internal Revenue Service (IRS) in particular carefully watches the financial results you report on your tax returns.

In some situations, you might seek financing to help get your business off the ground, expand, or function on an ongoing basis. Lenders rely on your financial statements for much of the basis for their lending decisions. We explain some of the tools that quickly give them insights into the current state of your business.

We also cover what primary stakeholders look for in your business financials, as well as introduce you to financial ratios, which are quick ways to measure the health of your business.

In This Chapter

- What the IRS looks for in your tax returns
- Information lenders and investors want to see
- Understanding financial ratios

How the IRS Reviews Your Financials

The IRS projects it will receive around 11 million corporation and partnership tax returns for the 2015 tax year. This doesn't include Schedule C returns for sole proprietorships.

One of the ways the IRS tests the reasonableness of your income tax returns is to compare your results to other businesses like yours. To do this, it looks at your *NAICS* code, one piece of information every business must provide, no matter the tax form. When filing your tax return, choose the NAICS code that corresponds to the largest percentage of your revenue. In addition to the NAICS code, you need to provide brief written descriptions of your primary line(s) of business.

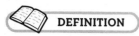 **DEFINITION**

> The North American Industry Classification System, or **NAICS,** is a numbered list of business activities comprised of around 1,000 six-digit codes that group businesses by sector, subsector, and group. The list provides a means for governmental departments to track and compare economic activity. NAICS supersedes the previous four-digit Standard Industrial Classification (SIC) codes used for several decades.

The IRS also maintains the National Research Program through which it develops statistical norms for each type of business. Although your revenue can vary drastically from other businesses in your industry, certain patterns emerge when large cross-sections of data are compared. It's through this research that the IRS can identify outliers, such as extraordinarily large amounts of meal and entertainment expenses or unusually high travel expenses.

The IRS makes these determinations in part based on ratios, such as those we'll discuss later in this chapter. Some ratios are based on percentages of revenue; others may center on percentages of net income. Not only does the IRS compare your tax returns to your industry peers, but it also looks at your historical returns. Large fluctuations in revenue or expenses can be cause for additional scrutiny.

 **RED FLAG**

> Although your odds of being audited are rather low, keep in mind that the IRS has up to 3 years to request an examination of your books. This time period can be extended if the IRS determines there are material mistakes in your books. Keep in mind that mistakes aren't necessarily fraud. Many IRS audits are conducted by mail, when the IRS requests information and you mail it in. Serious inquiries often result in an on-site visit by an IRS auditor who expects immediate access to your books and records—hence the on-site visit instead of you going to an IRS office.

What Lenders Are Looking For

Periodically during the life of your business, you might need to borrow money from a bank, investor, or even a family member. Many businesses can't get off the ground without borrowing money, while some business owners can *bootstrap* their way off the ground.

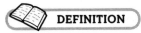 **DEFINITION**

In a business context, **bootstrap** means to use one's own resources instead of relying on others. Instead of borrowing money, bootstrappers rely on their own savings or personal credit cards, and plow profits back into the business.

In this section, we give you an idea of what lenders look for in your financial reports should you seek to borrow money.

Consistency

Lenders like consistency in revenue and expenses. This doesn't mean your revenues and expenses have to be the same year after year, but rather that the overall trend is consistent. Lenders first and foremost want assurance you'll be able to pay back a loan.

Your financials can only tell a portion of your story, so when meeting with a lender, be sure to disclose any extraordinary circumstances within your financial statements that have caused significant changes in your revenues and/or expenses. Sometimes, the inconsistency can be caused by something positive, like acquiring a large customer. You can use this type of variation to explain the need for a new equipment loan or other costs of growing your business.

Collateral

The paradox of borrowing money is that it often seems banks only want to loan money to people who don't need it. In some cases, your money may be tied up in illiquid assets, such as equipment or real estate—items that can be converted to cash but usually not quickly. The ability to guarantee some portion of the loan with *collateral* increases the odds of you being approved for a loan.

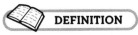 **DEFINITION**

Collateral is business or personal assets that you pledge as security as repayment for a loan. You must have full title to any item you want to use as collateral. In the event that you fail to repay the loan, the bank either claims ownership of the collateral or forces you to sell the asset to repay the loan.

In addition to any collateral your business may have, lenders also look to the owners of the business to personally guarantee any loans made. As discussed in Chapter 2, many businesses choose some form of incorporation to protect against litigation and isolate business activities from personal activities.

When it comes to financing, no matter what business structure you have, lenders want you to have some personal interest in the game. The term you'll see is *guaranteeing* the loan, so each owner is likely to be considered a guarantor. This means if the business fails to pay back the loan, the lender can look to each guarantor personally for repayment.

Cash Flow

Lenders want to ensure that your business has an ongoing cash flow. In most cases, you'll need to make monthly loan payments, so lenders will want assurance your business has the *liquidity* each month to easily make the loan payments.

If your business has seasonal peaks, having sufficient cash reserves to cover *debt service* during slow periods can make a difference in your ability to get the loan.

Some lenders entice borrowers by agreeing to waive interest and principal for a period of time. Others might offer to collect monthly interest payments only and let the principal ride. Most loans require payment of both interest and principal on a recurring monthly basis.

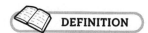 **DEFINITION**

In business terms, **liquidity** is a measurement of the amount of cash on hand, as well as assets that are easily converted to cash. Liquid assets include your business bank account(s), accounts receivable you expect to collect in the near term, stock and bond investments, certificates of deposit, and in certain cases, inventory. **Debt service** relates to repayment of a loan over time.

Minimal Revenue Concentrations

Lenders have to weigh lending money to your business versus other uses of their funds. Many of the tests we discuss in this section fall under the umbrella of *risk management*.

The interest you pay on the loan compensates the lender for the risk they're taking. Therefore, lenders are going to be looking for potential exposures, such as how diversified your revenues are. If an overwhelming amount of your revenues are derived from a small number of customers, the lender might not be comfortable with that exposure.

 **DEFINITION**

> **Risk management** is a discipline that focuses on identifying risks and their potential impact on an organization. Lenders weigh the risk of lending money. In turn, businesses weigh the odds of customers paying their invoices in a timely fashion. Businesses of all sorts face exposures that must be managed.

Financial Ratios

Lenders might review multiple sets of financial statements in a single day. You may have experienced the blur that can set in from just reviewing your own numbers. Accordingly, lenders employ financial ratios such as those we discuss later in this chapter to get a quick read on whether or not they should employ more time and money to make a formal investigation into the creditworthiness of your business, or if the application should be disapproved without more time or thought.

In the first section of this chapter, we explained how the IRS compares your tax returns with those of like businesses to try to identify irregularities. Banks use financial ratios in much the same fashion.

Depreciated Assets

Earlier in this section, we discussed how lenders look at the type of collateral you have that serves as security for a loan. Your balance sheet might not always offer the best representation of the collateral you have, particularly if some of your major assets are highly depreciated. For example, a piece of equipment you've owned for 5 years might reflect a near zero net value on your books, but it could have significant market value.

When applying for a loan, be sure to inform your lender of any assets that might have a low book value but a higher market value. Depending on the asset, the lender might order an appraisal of the asset to determine the amount a third party would be willing to be pay for the item.

Discretionary and Owner Expenses

Businesses have wide discretion on how to spend their money. As a business owner, you can't treat truly personal items, such as clothes for your children, groceries for your house, and your home cable television bill, as business expenses. However, many expenses do fall in a gray area known as discretionary expenses. These might include subscriptions to business newspapers and industry websites, and in some cases, advertising expenses. *Discretionary* means you have a large amount of control over whether or not to spend money on these items, which means you could eliminate the expenses to free up money for debt service if necessary.

Owner expenses are items you, as an owner, may choose to incur but that another owner might eschew. Examples of this might be golf club memberships, cost of the owner's automobile, and entertainment expenses not directly related to the business.

Using Financial Ratios

We touched on financial ratios a bit earlier in this chapter. Now let's take a closer look.

Every business has different combinations of revenue and expense, which can make comparing financial statements difficult. Financial ratios serve as an equalizer to condense even the most complex financial statements into easy-to-grasp measurements. In this section, we discuss some of the ratios lenders use to determine the creditworthiness of your business. You also might find these ratios useful in determining the health of your business, as well as in comparing yourself to industry standards in your field.

Public libraries and certain websites provide free or paid access to industry benchmarks that make it easy to see how your business measures up against its peers. And of course, you can be assured that the ever-present IRS is using some of these measurements to test the reasonableness of the figures presented on your income tax return.

Current Ratio

The current ratio is a liquidity measurement that identifies how easily your business can repay *short-term* debt obligations. As shown in the following figure, the current ratio is your current assets divided by your current liabilities. (We defined these terms in Chapter 4.)

A current ratio of 1 means your current assets exactly equal your current liabilities. This is a fragile liquidity state because not all current assets are likely to be cash. If a significant portion of your current assets are accounts receivable, there's a chance customers will be unable to pay some of their invoices, which can make your business unable to pay its short-term bills in full.

A current ratio of .9 means your business only has current assets on hand to cover 90 percent of your short-term liabilities, which can mean your business is technically insolvent.

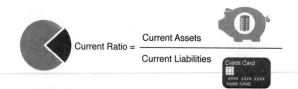

$$\text{Current Ratio} = \frac{\text{Current Assets}}{\text{Current Liabilities}}$$

A current ratio of 1.5 means the business has one and a half times
as many current assets as current liabilities.

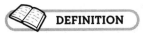

DEFINITION

From an accounting perspective, **short-term** means 12 months or fewer. You might have a 30-year mortgage on a building you use in your business, but only the amount that's presently due within the next 12 months is considered short-term. The balance of the loan is considered long-term debt.

Quick Ratio

Whereas the current ratio includes inventory, which depending on the industry, can be a somewhat illiquid asset, the quick ratio strips inventory out of total current assets to determine the ability of a business to fund short-term liabilities without involving inventory. This is done because a business might not receive full value for inventory that must be sold off quickly to cover the debts of the business.

$$\text{Quick Ratio} = \frac{\text{Current Assets} - \text{Inventory}}{\text{Current Liabilities}}$$

A quick ratio of 1 means the business has the liquidity to pay short-term bills without having to sell inventory.

The quick ratio is sometimes referred to as the acid test for a business.

Debt-to-Equity Ratio

As we noted earlier, lenders very much want to see that owners have a personal interest in their business. A ratio that immediately shows how much money owners have either invested directly or indirectly by leaving profits in the business is the debt-to-equity ratio. You also might see this referred to as debt to worth.

The closer this ratio is to 1, the more the owners have put into the business. Conversely, the closer the number is to 0, the more *leverage* the business is using, which raises the likelihood that the debts may not be able to be repaid. These amounts can be derived from your balance sheet.

Bankers or other lenders usually exclude shareholder loans (money the owners invest in the business) from this equation because the bank subordinates debt from the owner(s) to the debt from the bank. Subordination is a lender's term that means the lender's debt legally comes ahead of the shareholder's debt.

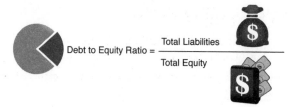

Debt to Equity Ratio = $\dfrac{\text{Total Liabilities}}{\text{Total Equity}}$

The debt-to-equity ratio identifies how much owners and investors have put into a business versus how much lenders have contributed.

DEFINITION

Leverage represents the ratio of a company's debt to the value of its equity. The higher the leverage, the more it appears the business is using debt to finance its operations rather than increasing its earnings or managing its expenses. When used properly, leverage can help you multiply the impact of money you've invested in the business. When used improperly, the business can be put at risk, which can detrimentally impact the livelihood of owners, employees, and stakeholders.

Cash Flow Coverage Ratio

You're probably starting to see a pattern in the ratios here, where the goal is to determine a business's ability to pay back borrowed money. Even if you don't formally take out a bank loan, every business, in effect, borrows money in some form by utilizing services that are used today but paid for later.

Lenders considering extending credit always seek assurance that their money will be repaid. In that regard, they often use the cash flow coverage ratio to determine how much cash flow a business has with respect to its total liabilities. In this method, the annual cash flow from operations amount comes from the year-end version of the statement of cash flows report (Chapter 14).

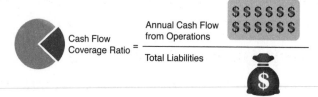

Cash Flow Coverage Ratio = $\dfrac{\text{Annual Cash Flow from Operations}}{\text{Total Liabilities}}$

The cash flow coverage ratio compares the annual cash flow of a business to its total liabilities, or total debt.

Performance and Probability Ratios

Depending on your industry, lenders might use one or more performance measurements to compare your business to other similar businesses, and to your company's prior financial history. Each of these measurements focuses on different operational aspects of your business, which isn't necessarily related to servicing debt.

Gross profit margin determines the profit a business is making from selling products. This can be an indication of pricing strength and effectiveness, and it also reflects a company's ability to pay its overhead and administrative expenses. In this case, the calculation is multiplied by 100 percent to return a percentage amount instead of a decimal value like some of the other ratios.

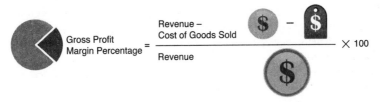

The gross profit margin is a measure of pricing effectiveness and ability to cover other expenses of the business.

Profit margin is also often referred to as *net profit margin*. This bottom line–oriented ratio makes it easy to compare the effectiveness of different businesses by dividing the net income by total revenue. As with gross profit, this can be multiplied by 100 percent to return a percentage amount.

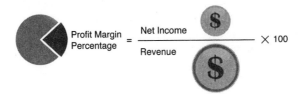

Profit margin, or net profit margin, measures the bottom line effectiveness of a business.

Accounts Receivable Turnover Ratio

Some businesses, such as fast-food restaurants, coin laundries, and retail stores, have the luxury of getting paid at the time of sale for their products and services. Most businesses, however, extend credit in some form by providing goods and services that customers pay for later. This ratio is predicated on the payment terms you offer your customers. Some businesses expect payment within 10 days of an invoice being presented, while many businesses allow 30 days for payment.

A turnover ratio of 12 or higher for a business with 30-day payment terms means most customers are paying their invoices in a timely fashion. A lower turnover ratio tends to wave a caution flag that the business may be headed into cash flow challenges.

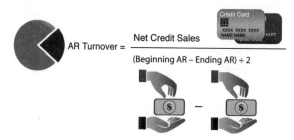

The accounts receivable (AR) turnover ratio shows how effective a business is at extending credit to customers and collecting on its invoices.

 **RED FLAG**

The older a customer's invoice gets, the less likely you'll collect the money. Always pay close attention to your Aged Accounts Receivable report. Unfortunately, many people are more than willing to take advantage of generous payment terms. Payment terms are a powerful constraint you can use to ensure the health of your business and your cash flow.

Accounts Payable Turnover Ratio

This ratio is the inverse of the accounts receivable turnover in that it measures how effectively a business pays its vendors. Lenders can identify trends by looking at this ratio for different accounting periods.

When the ratio trends lower, the business may be having difficulty paying its bills. A higher ratio may not necessarily be better because although it's good to pay bills on time, it can be better to take advantage of payment terms, such as paying bills within 30 days instead of immediately to help smooth out cash flow and enable the business to hang on to its cash for a bit longer.

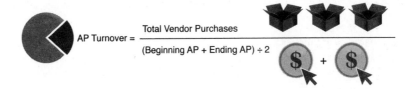

The accounts payable (AP) turnover ratio shows how effective a business is at paying what it owes to its vendors and suppliers.

Inventory Turnover Ratio

By now, we hope you've realized that a constant theme in business is that it's all about flow and movement. This is particularly important with regard to inventory. Inventory that lingers can cost your business in many subtle and indirect ways:

- Increased rent for storage

- Less space to store products that are selling well

- More time spent inventorying the same items over and over

- The possibility of money down the drain for items that become unsellable

The inventory turnover ratio determines how effective your business is at moving inventory as a whole. Keep in mind that this ratio can enable some problematic items to lay around unnoticed on your shelves, but overall, it gives an indication of how effectively you're managing your inventory. In this context, we use the words *annual sales* to distinguish sales of inventory items. Your business may derive revenue from services and nonrelated inventory activities, which should not be factored into this ratio.

The inventory turnover ratio indicates the number of days inventory items remain in your possession before you sell them.

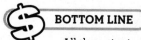 **BOTTOM LINE**

All the ratios in this section help lenders quickly compare your business to its peers. Be sure to clearly describe the operations of your business, and provide the same NAICS code you use on your income tax returns. This ensures that lenders perform a fair comparison. Ratios also can help you manage your business more effectively, as exposures that concern lenders should also be of concern to owners.

Take the time to calculate these ratios yourself before meeting with lenders and investors. By doing so, you'll notice where your weaknesses lie before your discussions and can better prepare yourself by anticipating questions lenders might have.

The Least You Need to Know

- The IRS can analyze your business by comparing the amounts on your tax returns with other similar businesses.
- Banks, lenders, and investors use a series of ratios to take the financial temperature of your business and determine how healthy it is.
- The accounts receivable turnover ratio can help you determine if you've been lackadaisical with regard to ensuring customers pay you timely.
- The inventory turnover ratio enables you to objectively see if inventory is lingering on your shelves.

Monthly, Quarterly, and Annual Activities

Scorecards are finite in that they always cover a particular time period. Similarly, some accounting activities and filings must total the transactions from a particular time period. These activities might consist of sensible checkpoints for monitoring your company's finances. In other cases, they serve as the trigger for filing and paying tax returns or submitting other regulatory reporting. In Part 5, we help you stay on top of these ongoing requirements for your business.

First, we go over the end-of-month procedures you should perform and what to look for in the balance sheet and trial balance each month end. From there, we move on to quarterly activities, which typically involve employee and vendor tax reporting. Next, we look at the annual activities: business and personal tax returns. The part concludes with a rulebook for how long you need to keep particular types of business and accounting information.

Closing Your Books and Other Accounts

Larger businesses have dedicated employees who review and close the books each month, but even the smallest of businesses need to review the books at least monthly. As you'll see in this chapter, users sometimes try to fix one problem in their books and inadvertently cause another problem. Even the most mindful of users can distractedly enter the same transaction twice, for example. The sooner you catch mistakes in your accounting records, the easier it is to fix the problem and avoid potential financial ramifications such as unrecoverable payments or inflated income tax bills.

Some accounting software requires you to carry out certain actions at the end of a month before you can start entering transactions in a new month. Even if your software doesn't mandate it, always schedule time to review your books at least monthly. The activities we recommend in this chapter help you keep your business on track and make filing the requisite tax forms much easier. In the following pages, we show you how to make corrections if you find errors while completing your monthly analysis. In addition, we discuss the steps for closing your books at the end of the year.

In This Chapter

- Tasks to perform at the end of each month
- Working with the trial balance
- Finding errors in your account balances
- Tasks to perform at the end of each year

Monthly Accounting Procedures

Depending on the type of accounting software you use, you might be obligated to perform some monthly procedures, or you may be able to roll along from month to month. Similarly, you might be required to take specific actions to move into a new year, or the year-end might be a nonevent.

There's a benefit to the formalized closing procedures in an accounting program. If the software puts a fence around a specific accounting period, you're less likely to post a transaction to an incorrect period. However, even the more informal accounting programs generally allow you to set a closing date for your books so you can prevent inadvertent changes to previous accounting periods.

In this section, we look at the accounting tasks you might need to perform at month end.

Program-Specific Tasks

Depending on whether you use a desktop-based accounting program or a cloud-based version, you might have some specific month-end tasks to complete.

Some desktop-based accounting programs take a regimented approach to accounting periods. For instance, Sage 50 allows you to modify transactions during a 2-fiscal-year period. You typically work in a single accounting period at any given point, although the software allows you to edit or add transactions in other periods without physically changing the accounting period. The desktop versions of QuickBooks, on the other hand, don't require formal accounting periods.

In Sage 50, each month you need to choose Tasks, System, and Change Accounting Period to advance your accounting program to a new month. You're limited to a 2-year span of accounting periods in this program, but not every program enforces such limitations.

You still can enter transactions in prior or future months, but the catch in this case is that all transactions default to the first day of the accounting period when the accounting period doesn't match the calendar month. This increases your odds of posting transactions into the wrong month, or requires you to continually change the date on each transaction you enter. The transaction date automatically defaults to today's date when the accounting period and calendar month match.

This isn't a limitation of every desktop program, but rather a peculiarity to be on the lookout for with any other desktop-based accounting program.

Most cloud-based accounting programs tend to be agnostic with regard to accounting periods. You simply post transactions to your accounting software without worrying about which accounting period the transactions post in. This can be liberating for users who have little or no accounting background, as it gives you the freedom to work with few limitations. However, the downside is that your accounting software might not warn you if you inadvertently date a transaction, say, 3 years in the past or 5 years in the future.

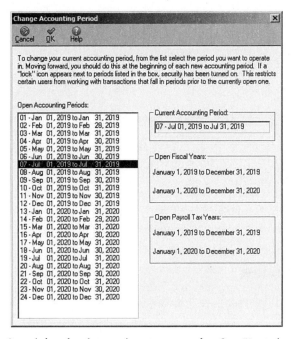

Some desktop-based accounting programs, such as Sage 50, require
you to switch periods at the end of a month.

Many desktop programs provide a prompt that alerts you if you enter a transaction unreasonably far into the future or the past. The desktop version of QuickBooks provides the warning, for example, but the online version of QuickBooks doesn't.

Some accounting programs warn you if you attempt to post a transaction too far in the past or the future.

ACCOUNTING HACK

Even if your accounting software doesn't require a formal closing process for a month or year, you can often set a closing date for your books that locks them so changes cannot be made prior to the closing date without a password. This is an important level of protection for your books, particularly for protecting your documentation for tax returns. Governmental auditors might want to look at your books several years after the fact, and if your books don't match the amounts you filed on your tax returns, you could be exposed to additional scrutiny.

Bank and Credit Card Reconciliation

One of the most important actions you can carry out each month is reconciling your bank and credit card accounts. (We discuss the specifics of the reconciliation process in Chapter 8.)

Reconciling your bank account ensures that the cash amount on your balance sheet is accurate. Reconciling credit card accounts ensures that you properly report the outstanding liabilities on your balance sheet, and guarantees all expenses for the month appear on your income statement.

Balance Sheet Review

It's important to run a Balance Sheet report at least once a month so you can keep track of what your business owns, owes to others, and the book value of your ownership stake (see Chapter 14).

Here are some common items you should look for on your balance sheet:

Accounts Receivable should match the total on your Aged Accounts Receivable report (Chapter 13). If you find a discrepancy, use the techniques in Chapter 7 to review your general ledger for your Accounts Receivable account to find the misposted entries. Common errors include crediting revenue to the Accounts Receivable account instead of a revenue account, or using a journal entry to write off bad debt instead of using credit memos within your accounting software as discussed in Chapters 6 and 13.

Accounts Payable should match the total on your Aged Accounts Payable report (Chapter 13). Your Accounts Payable account can be subject to errors similar to those for your Accounts Receivable account.

Payroll tax liability accounts should reflect the unpaid amounts due. Users sometimes inadvertently post tax deposit payments to a Payroll Taxes expense account instead of the corresponding liability account. This can distort your actual expenses, lower your income, and create a liability on your balance sheet that doesn't actually exist.

Inventory should match the Inventory Valuation report (Chapter 5). Users sometimes incorrectly attempt to write off damaged or spoiled inventory by using journal entries.

Remember, when reviewing your Balance Sheet report on-screen in your accounting software, you often can click on an account balance to view the underlying detail. This displays a report similar to the general ledger (see Chapter 7). You can then click on a line item within that report to drill down to the actual transaction.

RED FLAG

The sum of your Retained Earnings, Capital Distributions, and Net Income on your balance sheet should always be a positive number. If the amount falls below 0, you might have more misposted accounting transactions, or you might be withdrawing too much from your business in the form of distributions. Excess distributions can result in an additional capital gains tax of 10 to 15 percent of the excess amount. Limit distributions to the amount of net income for a given year, or distribute up to the amount of your retained earnings account. You can withdraw shareholder loans without adverse tax affects if they've not been used to claim prior losses.

Income Statement Review

The end of each month is a good time to review your income statement for missing and misposted transactions. When reviewing, compare the current income statement to the one from the same period last year so you have something to use as a guide.

Here are some common items you should look for:

Accounts that have a lower balance than usual. Check particularly for expense accounts that should reflect a monthly expense, such as a health insurance premium payment.

Revenue accounts that have negative balances. (Except discount accounts.) Expenses may have been inadvertently posted to a revenue account.

Expense accounts that have negative balances. Revenue activity may have been inadvertently posted to an expense account. Expense accounts can legitimately have a negative account balance if you've received a refund for an expense paid in a prior year.

Expense accounts that have unusually high balances. A user might have entered a bill twice or posted a transaction to the wrong account.

Inventory Analysis

As we discuss in Chapter 5, inventory can present an exposure to your business. At least once a month, it's important to review how much inventory you have on hand. Doing so may help you identify excessive quantities of slow-moving products, or perilously low quantities of fast-moving products.

Your accounting software offers a report along the lines of the Inventory Valuation Report shown in the following figure. If available, the Percent of Inventory Value column can help you identify concentrations in your inventory where you might have excessive amounts of money tied up.

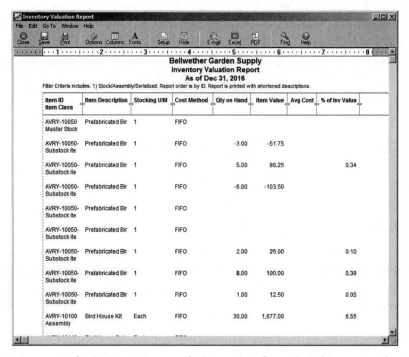

An Inventory Valuation Report gives you a bird's-eye view of your physical inventory on hand.

Aging Reports Review

In Chapter 13, we show how to run the Aged Accounts Receivable and Aged Accounts Payable reports in your accounting software. In addition to confirming that the overall amounts are reasonable, you should have procedures in place for handling receivables and payables that have aged beyond a reasonable time.

This could include working with a collection service to collect old receivables and working with a debt consolidation service if you're having trouble keeping your Accounts Payable up to date.

Payroll Liabilities

You should establish separate liability accounts for each payroll tax your business is responsible for (see Chapter 4). As noted in Chapter 12, you might find yourself remitting taxes to multiple levels of government, including federal, state, and local.

At the end of each month, quarter, and year, the amounts in your payroll liability accounts should exactly match the amounts you're required to remit. For instance, if you submit state withholding taxes monthly, then at the end of the month, your state income tax withholding account should match the amount you'll remit on the fifteenth of the following month (or whichever date your state requires).

Understanding the Trial Balance

A concise listing of every account balance on your books, your Trial Balance report gives you an at-a-glance look at your business. Even though you may review your balance sheet and income statement carefully, you also should review your trial balance because situations you might not see in other reports can pop out immediately in this report format.

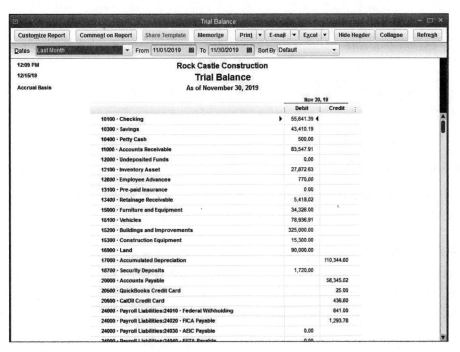

A Trial Balance report summarizes your balance sheet and income statement in a single report.

Despite your best efforts, accounting errors can and will occur within your books.

Adjusted Trial Balance

Your accounting software might offer an Adjusted Trial Balance report (sometimes called the Working Trial Balance). Historically, accountants used this report to mark up transfers that needed to occur between accounts. Increases or decreases to accounts are written in the middle columns, and the balances on the right are updated manually.

This old-school practice might feel out of date, but it does allow you to see the impact of the changes you're contemplating before you actually make them.

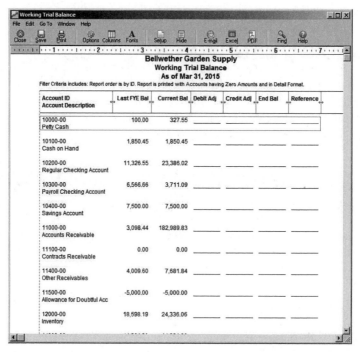

An Adjusted or Working Trial Balance report enables you preview account adjustments before you make them in your books.

This report is designed to be a paper-based tool as opposed to the on-screen modifications you can make in most other reports we mention in this chapter.

Accounts with Opposite Signs

Typically, asset accounts have a debit balance, which means they appear on the left of the two amount columns on your trial balance. As you learned in Chapter 4, certain accounts, known as contra-asset accounts, naturally have a credit (right column) balance.

The following list shows whether certain types of accounts typically have a debit balance or a credit balance. You can refer to this list when reviewing your trial balance to help identify any account that may be out of line:

- **Assets:** Debit, except for contra-assets

- **Liabilities:** Credit

- **Equity:** Debit or credit, depending on the context of the account

- **Revenue:** Credit, except for accounts that record discounts

- **Expenses:** Debit

Asset or liability accounts with the wrong type of balance are often indications of an accounting error or missing transaction. A revenue account with a debit balance could be an indication of a mistaken entry or of credits given for prior year sales. An expense account with a credit balance could mean you received a refund or rebate for something you expensed in a prior year.

 **RED FLAG**

Misposted entries in your accounting software are sometimes, but not always, the result of a user making an error when entering a transaction. More often, the errors arise when inventory items are set up incorrectly. As covered in Chapter 5, you're required to specify revenue, Cost of Goods Sold, and inventory accounts for stock items. If the wrong account numbers are used for any of these settings, when you sell inventory items, the automatic entries your accounting software makes will be incorrect.

Amortizing Prepaid Expenses

Chapter 11 explained that the Internal Revenue Service requires your financial statements to reflect only actual expenses incurred in your business. So if you prepay a 6-month insurance policy on December 1, you're only entitled to record [1/6] of that amount as an expense in December. The other [5/6] must initially be recorded to a Prepaid Expenses account. Then, for each of the next 5 months, you'll transfer 1 month of the insurance premium to Insurance Expense from Prepaid Insurance.

You'll do this by creating a journal entry to move the money between accounts. Your accounting software may offer a Transfer feature, but that's intended for transferring money between bank accounts, such as between checking and savings, as opposed to transferring amounts between other nonbanking accounts.

ACCOUNTING HACK

You might be able to use your accounting software to automate certain month-end journal entries; look for "memorized" or "recurring transactions" in your program. For instance, you can set up a journal entry that automatically moves $150 from your Prepaid Insurance account to your Insurance Expense account, request it stop after 6 months, and your books will update themselves. Automatically recording monthly depreciation, amortization expenses, and other recurring transactions ensure that ongoing revenue and expense items post to your books automatically, which can simplify your monthly review process.

Checking and Correcting Balances

Beyond accounts that have the wrong type of balance (debit versus credit and vice versa), other types of problems can cause nagging issues in your books. This section helps you identify and correct a couple other account error situations.

Lingering Balances

When reviewing your Balance Sheet, General Ledger, or Trial Balance reports, you might notice accounts that have remaining balances of a few dollars or pennies. This sometimes occurs in your payroll tax liability accounts. As we discuss in Chapter 12, Social Security and Medicare taxes on employees are 7.65 percent of wages. Your accounting software automatically computes this amount for each employee's paycheck. However, Form 941 (see Chapter 18) computes the tax as 7.65 percent of total wages for the quarter. This can result in rounding differences of a few cents.

When you encounter these amounts, you can use a journal entry to adjust the balances to 0 or to match the exact balance the account should have. If your Federal Withholding Taxes account has a credit balance of 3 cents, for example, you can correct this by creating a journal entry that debits Federal Withholding Taxes for 3 cents and credits Payroll Tax Expense for 3 cents.

Duplicate and Mistaken Transactions

Given the nature of numbers, and depending on the number of transactions you're juggling, you might inadvertently post the same transaction more than once in your books. Examples include recording an adjusting journal entry twice, invoicing a customer more than once, or recording a duplicate bill from a vendor.

Your accounting software will likely notify you if you enter the same vendor bill with an identical invoice number more than once, but only if you enter the bill before writing the check. There's no safety net with regard to accidentally recording other types of transactions more than once.

Duplicate transactions may distort an account balance enough to make the mistake noticeable, or you might need to carry out a detailed review of your general ledger, as we discuss in Chapter 7.

When given the option, you should generally void rather than delete duplicate transactions. Voided transactions don't affect your general ledger or financial statements, but they do provide an audit trail should questions arise about the transaction later. Deleted transactions don't necessarily vanish forever, however. As mentioned in Chapter 7, most modern accounting programs provide an audit trail report that records every transactional change in your books. So if you discover that a transaction has vanished, you can use the audit trail to determine which user eliminated the transaction.

You sometimes might need to make a correction to a paid invoice or bill. Your accounting software locks these transactions after a payment is applied against them, but you can still make changes by temporarily unapplying the customer or vendor payment. To do so, choose the payment transaction from your list of previous entries, clear the checkbox that relates to the bill or invoice, and save the payment transaction. You can then open the bill or invoice in a similar fashion, make the correction, and save the bill or invoice. Then return to the payment transaction, and reapply the payment.

Double-Checking Your Work

Even experienced accountants sometimes fumble debits and credits when entering journal entries. If you enter a journal entry backward by reversing the debit and credit amounts, you'll double the impact of the mistake or situation on your books you were trying to fix.

When entering journal entries, always double-check your balance sheet, income statement, or trial balance to ensure the affected account balances changed as you intended. If you find a goof, simply edit the journal entry to swap the amounts between the debit and credit columns.

Year-End Procedures

At year-end, you need to carry out all the month-end procedures discussed throughout this chapter, along with these few extra procedures:

Print your General Ledger and financial reports to PDF documents, and save the files, preferably somewhere other than your main computer hard drive. Also back up your accounting records using the techniques we discuss in Chapter 15.

If you're using a desktop program such as Sage 50, use the Year-End Wizard to close the fiscal year. Programs that don't require a formal year-end close should allow you to specify a closing date for your books. By doing this, you can typically choose between a warning or require a password before users can add or edit transactions dated prior to the closing date you set.

Although storage space usually isn't a consideration in a cloud-based accounting program, the physical size of your books can grow over time in desktop-based programs. This can result in performance issues that make reports take longer to appear on-screen as well as other delays. Your accounting software provides a feature that allows you to eliminate transactions from previous years. Such a command will typically appear on the File menu or sometimes tucked away under a Utilities submenu. Look for something along the lines of Purge.

Always create a backup of your data before performing a purge procedure so you can restore your records if needed.

BOTTOM LINE

Unlike many situations in life, most aspects of your books can be easily fixed, particularly if you catch mistakes in time. Take time each month to carry out the month-end procedures we recommend in this chapter. Doing so can save you money by ensuring that you don't inadvertently pay more or less taxes than you should. Accurate books result in accurate financial statements, which can help you secure financing, should you need to borrow money to grow your business.

The Least You Need to Know

- Monitoring your account balances monthly helps you ensure your books are correct and current.
- Tools provided in your accounting software make the monthly and annual review go smoothly.
- Reviewing your trial balance can help you find errors subject to correction.
- Save a backup copy of your accounting records at the end of each year so you'll always have the detailed support for your financial statements.

CHAPTER 18

Remitting and Reporting Taxes

The Congressional Budget Office estimates that for fiscal 2015, $1.5 trillion in individual income taxes are due, along with $1.1 trillion of payroll taxes. That collective $2.6 trillion dwarfs the estimated $628 billion due from corporate income taxes and other sources. There's no doubt, payroll taxes have an impact on your business.

Payroll taxes fund much of our federal government, but sales taxes are a significant source of funding for most cities, counties, and states. The U.S. Census estimates that sales tax collections for the 12 months ended March 2015 will exceed $355 billion. As you've seen elsewhere in this book, your business will likely collect payroll and/or sales taxes on behalf of governmental agencies. In this chapter, we provide an overview of how to account for these taxes and remit them to the appropriate parties.

We assume here that you plan to process and remit payroll and sales taxes directly to the respective governmental agencies, as opposed to using an outside accountant or third-party payroll provider. To that end, we'll demonstrate the typical abilities of accounting software to help you determine what you owe and then generate the corresponding reports.

In This Chapter

- Paying payroll-related taxes
- Quarterly estimated taxes
- Reporting on various business taxes
- Other types of business taxes

As you've seen in Chapter 9, you can outsource payroll processing to third-party companies. Sales tax reporting can be outsourced in the same manner, although the ease of which you do this may depend on your choice of accounting software.

Remitting Payroll Taxes

Each paycheck your business issues is subject to a number of withholdings (see Chapter 12). Some payroll taxes are the shared responsibility of both employee and employers; others are borne solely by employees or employers. For example, income tax withholding is an employee responsibility, Social Security and Medicare taxes are split between employee and employer, and employers bear the entire cost of unemployment and disability taxes.

As you'll see later in this chapter, all businesses follow the same approach for reporting payroll tax liabilities and reconciling the amounts due. However, there are marked differences when it comes to *remitting* (paying) payroll taxes. Generally, there's an inverse relationship between the amount you need to remit and the length of time you're given to make the remittance. This section gets you up to speed on paying various payroll taxes.

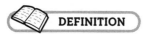

DEFINITION

In the context of payroll taxes, **remit** means to send the money to the appropriate governmental agency. In this chapter, the terms *remit, deposit,* and *send* all indicate the same thing. Depending on which agency you're paying, you may be required to pay electronically or you can pay by check.

Federal Payroll Taxes

The Internal Revenue Service (IRS) now requires that all regular tax payments be made electronically through the Electronic Federal Tax Payment System (EFTPS). Publication 966 provides an overview of this system, but in short, every business must register with EFTPS either online at eftps.gov or by telephone at 888-725-7879. Within 7 *business days* of registering, you'll receive a personal identification number (PIN) that's required so you can pay your business's taxes online or over the telephone.

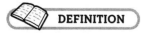

DEFINITION

In the context of payroll tax deposits and reports, **business days** are typically Monday through Friday, with the exception of state or federal holidays. If a tax deadline falls on Saturday, Sunday, or a holiday, the deadline is extended to the next business day. The term *business day* is used interchangeably with *banking day*.

Although the IRS still accepts paper checks for payments due on tax forms, the EFTPS system is generally faster and easier. You must arrange EFTPS payments no later than 8 P.M. Eastern Standard Time the day prior to the tax payment's due date. Late payments can be subject to interest and tax penalties. Although you shouldn't count on it, the IRS sometimes notifies you it's elected to waive the interest and penalties for certain late payments, but these are limited situations when the IRS perceives that taxpayers are striving to be compliant when a deadline has been missed.

The frequency with which you'll remit federal payroll taxes depends on the amount of taxes you've remitted in the previous year. All new businesses are considered monthly payers, meaning all federal payroll taxes for the previous month must be remitted by the fifteenth of the following month, as shown in the following table. Use the dates shown when due dates fall between Monday and Friday; otherwise, use the following business day when the fifteenth falls on a weekend or a federal holiday.

Remittance Schedule for Monthly Payers*

Month	Remit Taxes By
January	February 15
February	March 15
March	April 15
April	May 15
May	June 15
June	July 15
July	August 15
August	September 15
September	October 15
October	November 15
November	December 15
December	January 15

Between $2,500 and $50,000 annually

Businesses that remit more than $50,000 in payroll taxes per year will receive notification from the IRS that the business must start depositing payroll taxes on a semiweekly schedule. In effect, this means payroll taxes are typically remitted 3 business days after the payroll date. The following table provides a breakdown of this schedule.

Deposit Schedule for Semiweekly Payers*

Pay Day	Deposit Required By
Saturday	Following Friday
Sunday	Following Friday
Monday	Following Friday
Tuesday	Following Friday
Wednesday	Following Wednesday
Thursday	Following Wednesday
Friday	Following Wednesday

$50,000+ annually

If at any point you have payroll taxes of $100,000 or more on a given day, the taxes must be deposited in full the next business day. Regardless of prior status, your business is reclassified as a semiweekly depositor for the remainder of the current calendar year, as well as the following year.

At the opposite end of the spectrum, if your payroll taxes are consistently less than $2,500 per quarter, the IRS might inform you that you can deposit payroll taxes quarterly when you file Form 941 (which we discuss later in this chapter).

 **BOTTOM LINE**

With regard to payroll taxes, governments try to strike a balance between risk management and paperwork reduction. As you may have noticed, the more you owe in taxes, the sooner the government expects to have the money in hand. This reduces the government's risk that the funds will be misappropriated within your business before they're paid. On the other hand, if your business generates little taxable activity, you'll get some relief by having to make fewer tax deposits throughout the year.

Federal Unemployment Taxes

Federal unemployment taxes (FUTA) are usually deposited on a quarterly basis, but you might be able to make as few as one deposit per year. The magic number in this case is $500 in accumulated tax liability.

As long as your accumulated unemployment tax liability remains below $500, you can defer a quarterly payment to the next quarter. If at any point your liability exceeds $500, you must make a deposit for that quarter. At that point, the $500 threshold starts over again.

Quarterly FUTA tax deposits must be remitted electronically through the EFTPS system on the same schedule you use for filing your other federal payroll taxes on Form 941. If your total FUTA liability for the year is less than $500, you can remit the entire amount due when you file Form 940, Employer's Annual Federal Unemployment (FUTA) Tax Return (more on this later in the chapter).

State Withholding Taxes

As you learned in Chapter 12, most but not all states levy some form of state income tax. We can't provide specific guidance for all the states here, but we can tell you that most states follow the federal thresholds we discussed earlier.

Depending on your state, you might have the option of remitting taxes by mailing a paper deposit form and a check, although remitting payroll taxes electronically is often much easier. State withholding taxes are remitted to your state's version of a Department of Revenue. Check to see if your state offers an online portal where you can remit taxes.

Your federal taxes deposits likely will be much higher, so don't be surprised if you're required to submit federal taxes on a semiweekly basis but are allowed to remit state withholding on a monthly basis.

State Unemployment Taxes

State unemployment taxes (SUTA) typically are remitted to your state's version of a Department of Labor. As noted in Chapter 12, all 50 states levy unemployment taxes.

Many states require quarterly deposits and reporting of state unemployment taxes. As with federal unemployment taxes, you might pay SUTA on a different schedule than the remittance schedule for state income tax withholding. You'll likely be able to make electronic deposits, but you might have to use a different website for the deposit than you use for state withholding taxes.

Local Withholding Taxes

Deposit requirements for paying local income taxes can differ even beyond the state and federal levels discussed here. Rest assured that if your local county or city levies a local income tax, the information for complying with the regulations will be easy to find via an internet search.

 **RED FLAG**

State and federal governments will use every means necessary, including hefty monetary penalties and criminal prosecution, to ensure taxes collected on their behalf are paid in a timely fashion. In situations when you have to choose who to pay first, always pay the government first. The punitive actions creditors and vendors can apply against you pale in comparison to what governments can bring to bear. The Official Payments website (officialpayments.com) allows you to pay federal taxes with a credit card.

Reporting Payroll Taxes

Reporting the payroll taxes you owe or have paid typically occurs on a quarterly and/or annual basis. This means you need to submit reports for each type of payroll tax to the corresponding governmental agency.

As we noted earlier in the chapter, remitting and reporting occur on different timetables. Businesses with significant tax liabilities must send the taxes due to the respective government agency as frequently as the next banking day, while businesses that owe minimal taxes may only have to pay quarterly or sometimes annually.

No matter how often you pay, every business follows the same schedule with regard to filing payroll tax returns, even if no tax is due for a given period.

Federal Payroll Taxes

At the end of each calendar quarter, you must prepare and submit Form 941 to the IRS. This tax form is used to report the amount of federal income tax withheld from your business's employee paychecks during the quarter, as well as to calculate the amount of Social Security and Medicare taxes due. This form also serves to reconcile the tax deposits you made with the actual taxes due. You can request a refund of overpayments, or use this return as a vehicle for catching up underpaid payroll taxes.

Form 941 must be filed by the end of the month following each quarter, as shown in the next table.

Form 941 Filing Dates*

Quarter	Tax Period	File Form 941 By
First	January 1 to March 31	April 30
Second	April 1 to June 30	July 31
Third	July 1 to September 30	October 31
Fourth	October 1 to December 31	January 31

Within a month of the end of each calendar quarter

At the end of each year, you'll also prepare and file annual Forms W-2 and W-3. Each employee who received a paycheck at any point during the year must be issued a Form W-2 that reports the total wages paid and the employment taxes withheld during the year. Employees use this form as documentation for their personal income tax returns.

Employers use Form W-3 as a transmittal document that informs the IRS and the Social Security Administration of the total payroll taxes withheld during the year, as well as the number of W-2 forms being submitted. The total payroll on Form W-3 should always match the sum of the payroll you reported on the four 941 forms you submitted during the year.

At the end of each year, you'll also need to prepare and file Form 940, Employer's Annual Federal Unemployment (FUTA) Tax Return. You use this form to report and remit the federal unemployment taxes for a given year.

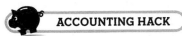

ACCOUNTING HACK

Don't panic if you discover you've made an error when filing Forms 940 or 941. The IRS has a somewhat confusing mechanism for filing amended returns. Certain forms, including Form 941, have an *X* series of forms used for filing amended returns, so you can submit Form 941X if you find an error in a previously filed Form 941. Form 940 doesn't have a 940X equivalent, so you'll simply file a replacement Form 940 to correct any errors.

State Withholding Taxes

Your state's equivalent of a Department of Revenue likely requires you to report the state income tax withheld on a quarterly and annual basis. These deadlines likely follow the quarterly federal file schedule given earlier, but be sure to check your state's specific requirements.

If you happen to live in a state that doesn't levy state income taxes, your periodic payroll tax reporting burden is a bit lighter than for most of us.

State Unemployment Taxes

You assuredly will be required to file a state unemployment tax return on a quarterly basis. As we note in Chapter 12, all 50 states levy unemployment taxes. Your state's equivalent of a Department of Labor can provide specific guidance on the filing requirements for your state.

ACCOUNTING HACK

Many states allow payroll tax returns to be filed online via state-run websites, although as of this writing the IRS does not. However, you can use many accounting programs to file payroll tax returns electronically. This might entail an additional fee from your software vendor, but it can greatly streamline the reporting process. You'll typically need to make payroll tax deposits outside your accounting software or through your third-party payroll provider. The latter also can file federal, state, and local payroll tax returns on your behalf.

Sales Tax

Most states and municipalities collect some level of sales tax on consumer purchases. Sales taxes are most often levied on goods, but your local jurisdiction might tax services instead of or in addition to physical goods. Within a given state, each county and city can have different tax rates.

The reporting and remittance schedule for sales taxes varies by state and municipality. As with payroll taxes, you'll find an inverse relationship between the amount of tax you collect and the frequency with which you must remit and report sales taxes collected. Unlike payroll taxes, many jurisdictions do provide a modicum of compensation for complying with sales tax reporting. For instance, Georgia companies are entitled to keep 3 percent of timely sales tax deposits as vendor compensation.

Typically, you'll need to register for a sales tax account with your state's equivalent of a Department of Revenue. The sales tax rate you collect may be based on the city or county where your business is located, or it could be based on your customer's location. Be sure to research your sales tax requirements, if any, because failure to collect sales tax from your customers means the government will look to your business to cover the shortfall.

The frequency with which you remit and report payroll taxes is based on the amount of taxes you collect. Businesses with minimal sales tax activity may only be required to remit and report once per year.

Sales tax collections can get very complex very quickly, but your accounting software can help. As shown in the following figure, your accounting software typically allows you to set up sales tax items or codes you'll assign to each customer. Further, you can indicate whether inventory items, which may be products or services, are taxable or nontaxable. By setting up sales tax in advance, your accounting software keeps track of your taxable and nontaxable transactions, as you're required to report the totals for both on your sales tax return. Some accounting programs offer more hand-holding than others. The following example shows a typical sales tax liability report that can be used to report and remit sales taxes due.

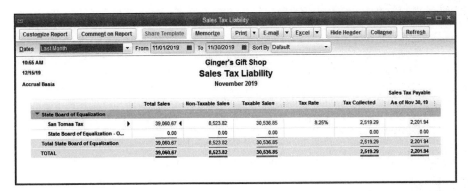

Your accounting software likely offers something along the lines of this Sales Tax Liability Report, from QuickBooks desktop.

If you have any complexity in your sales tax reporting, consider outsourcing sales tax compliance to a third party such as Avalara (avalara.com), Exactor (exactor.com), or Vertex (vertexsmb.com). If you collect sales tax in only a single county, you can easily configure your accounting software to perform the necessary calculations. However, sales tax returns often require you to detail your sales by county and further break those down into separate tax amounts per county. For instance, a 7 percent sales tax could be comprised of a 4 percent state tax, a 2 percent local tax, and a 1 percent local transportation tax. Multiply this by several counties, and you'll quickly be seeking a better way.

RED FLAG

Don't be surprised if you're required to collect, remit, and report sales taxes for more than one state. If you have an office or even single employee based in a state, or if you make sales to a customer in a state, your business may be required to collect sales tax or other taxes for that state. You also might have to file a use tax return to your own state for purchases you've made where no sales tax was collected. Although typically out-of-state and international customers are exempt from your local sales tax, sales tax enforcement is changing as state and local governments seek to recoup tax revenues. Enlist the help of a tax adviser or third-party service to help navigate the ever-changing rules.

Other Taxes

The taxing authority of government agencies knows few bounds. Your business could be subject to taxes beyond the scope of this book. Your county, city, or township might level an annual business license tax based on a percentage of your annual revenue. If your business owns property or equipment, likely you'll need to file and prepare some type of property tax return on an annual basis and then separately remit that tax payment.

The federal government assesses excise taxes on certain goods and services, while state and local governments have their own assortment of special purpose taxes.

Annual State Registration Fee

Your business might be required to file an annual registration return and fee with your state. This is a separate tax from what we've covered in this chapter, and the deadlines and requirements vary by state. These returns usually inform the state of the physical and/or mailing addresses of your business, as well as the names of general partners or corporate officers.

Penalties apply for late or missed filings, so be sure to mark your calendar each year.

Business License Tax

Depending on where your business is located, you might be required to pay a business license tax to your county, city, or township. Business license taxes are used to fund local government activities and are often some combination of a percentage of your annual revenue and number of employees.

You might be required to file a business license tax annually by a certain date and remit the tax due within a short period of time thereafter.

Ad Valorem Taxes

The Latin term *ad valorem* means "according to value" and is often used to refer to taxes that are based on the value of real estate and personal property. Such taxes are usually enacted at the county or township level, based on an annual assessed value.

In the case of real estate, local tax assessors make an annual determination of the market value of each property. Exemptions are sometimes available, and each taxing authority has a mechanism by which taxpayers can appeal what they feel are unfair assessments.

Separately, your business also might be required to file a personal property tax return. In this context, personal property is considered equipment, furniture, computers, and other assets owned by the business. Your return typically reports the initial purchase price of these items.

Excise Taxes

The federal government assesses an excise tax on certain goods, primarily gasoline, but also sport fishing gear, archery equipment, tires, and even vaccines. States and local jurisdictions often charge excise taxes on alcohol and tobacco products.

Excise taxes are typically borne directly by manufacturers and retailers, but ultimately, they make up part of the final price of products paid by consumers. Be prepared to either research the tax requirements of your industry thoroughly or enlist the assistance of a qualified tax professional.

Tourist Taxes

Your state or local government might collect special taxes that are primarily borne by out-of-town visitors. These taxes are often referred to as tourist taxes and may be special assessments on hotel rooms, vacation properties, rental cars, and other visitor-oriented services.

If these taxes apply to your business, you might have to file special returns above and beyond those listed in this chapter. It's always best to consult with a tax adviser to determine if your business is subject to this or any of these other unique tax situations.

The Least You Need to Know

- If your business has employees, you must calculate, withhold, and remit federal, state, and sometimes local payroll taxes in a timely fashion.
- Along with income tax, state and local governments get their revenue through a variety of taxes, including sales tax, property tax, franchise tax, and more. Check with your state authorities to find out which taxes you are liable for.
- Paying taxes isn't an option. Pay all your federal, state, and local taxes first and on time.
- In addition to paying taxes in a timely fashion, you typically have to report on taxes owed to federal, state, and local taxing authorities on a regular schedule.

Filing Business and Personal Tax Returns

As a business owner, your personal income tax return has some new complications. You might look back fondly on the days before you had a business of completing Form 1040EZ or the simplified Form 1040A, but the rewards of business ownership often outweigh the additional complexities at tax time.

In this chapter, we offer an overview of what to expect when April 15 rolls around each year. As we discussed in Chapter 2, your choice of business structure has a significant impact on your income tax return. Here, we cover federal returns for the various business types, including due dates and extensions. Then we review state business returns, and finish the chapter with information about completing your personal federal and state returns, including incorporating the relevant information from the business returns.

Business Income Tax Returns

Every business is required to file an annual tax return with the Internal Revenue Service (IRS). One of the most important reasons to utilize accounting software is to document the amounts you'll report on your business tax return.

Most businesses must file a separate income tax return to both their state government and the federal government, but there's one exception to the rule. This section covers the ins and outs of federal tax returns for various types of business structures.

 BOTTOM LINE

An ownership stake in a business means your annual tax return is at least a few pages longer, as you'll need to account for your share of the profit or loss of the business in some fashion on your personal tax return, as you'll see later in this chapter.

Sole Proprietorship

As described in Chapter 2, a sole proprietorship is the most basic form of a business. In short, you are the business, so you report the activities of your business on your personal income tax return instead of on a business tax return.

The primary form you'll use for reporting your business income and expense is the IRS form known as Schedule C, Profit or Loss from Business. As you'll see later in this chapter when we discuss personal returns in more detail, Schedule C is part of what's known as the long version of Form 1040.

In short, this 2-page document requests the following types of information:

- **Accounting method:** cash, accrual, or other

- **Income:** total sales from your profit and loss report less cost of goods sold

- **Expenses:** a summary of the expenses section of your profit and loss report

- **Inventory:** a summary of the net activity of your inventory activities during the calendar year

- **Vehicle information:** questions about whether you used a personal vehicle in your business

- **Other expenses:** documentation of other expenses that don't fit into one of the categories provided in the Expenses section

ACCOUNTING HACK

If you run your business out of your home, you might be able to deduct a portion of your household expenses on your tax return. Starting with the 2013 tax year, the IRS enacted a streamlined home office deduction of $5 per square foot up to a maximum of $1,500. So if that spare bedroom you use as your office measures 10 feet by 15 feet (150 square feet), you can take a deduction of $750 ($5 × 150 square feet). Or you can file Form 8829, Expenses for Business Use of Your Home, to allocate portions of your personal expenses to your business.

Partnerships

As noted in Chapter 2, a partnership is a business typically owned by two or more individuals. Partnerships are required to file Form 1065, U.S. Return of Partnership Income, to report their financial activity for the year.

This return documents the overall income and expenses for the partnership itself as well as the allocation of partnership profit or loss for each of the partners themselves on associated copies of Form K-1. As we'll discuss later in this chapter, Schedule K-1 holds the income or loss information you transfer to your personal income tax return. The partnership pays no income tax itself, but must file an income tax return nonetheless.

S Corporations

From an income tax standpoint, S corporations share some characteristics with partnerships. The corporation itself pays no income tax, and each owner's share of income or loss is reported on Schedule K-1. Each S corporation is required to file Form 1120S, U.S. Income Tax Return for an S Corporation.

C Corporations

As you've seen, the income or loss from partnerships and S corporations is taxed on each owner's personal tax return at their individual income tax rate.

C corporations, on the other hand, are taxed separately, meaning that the corporation itself pays its tax liability directly to the U.S. Treasury. C corporations file Form 1120, U.S. Corporation Income Tax Return.

The taxation of C corporations doesn't stop at the corporate level. Earnings of the corporation are shared with stakeholders through stock dividends, and the stakeholders (these can be individuals or other corporations) are taxed again on the same earnings, thus the confusion often referred to as "double taxation."

Limited Liability Companies

Like partnerships and S corporations, limited liability companies (LLCs) generally pay no income tax directly. However, this depends on the tax treatment the LLC elects with the IRS, from one of these choices:

Schedule C treatment: Single owner LLCs do not file separate tax returns for their business. Instead, the owner reports the income or loss of the LLC on his or her Form 1040, Schedule C, and pays tax at the individual income tax rates.

Partnership treatment: The LLC files Form 1065 annually and pays no income tax directly. Income (or loss) flows through to the partners to be reported on their individual income tax returns. This is the default status for LLCs with multiple owners.

S corporation treatment: The LLC files Form 1120S annually and pays no income tax directly. Income (or loss) flows through to the shareholders to be reported on their individual income tax returns.

C corporation treatment: Corporate income tax rates for income below \$75,000 are less than personal income tax rates. Corporations pay a tax of 15 percent of their first \$50,000 in income and 25 percent of any additional amounts up to \$75,000. Conversely, the 15 and 25 percent tax rates start at lower thresholds for personal taxpayers. Thus, in some cases, a LLC might opt to file Form 1120 as if it were a C corporation to take advantage of these lower tax rates. In this situation, the LLC pays its tax liability directly instead of passing the income or loss through to the owners.

As you can see, limited liability companies are a hybrid of other corporate structures in more ways than one. Unlike the other business entity structures, where there's only one tax form to choose from, in case of an LLC, you can have a variety of tax return options. Be sure to only file a single return that best suits your business needs.

Due Dates

Tax returns for S corporations and partnerships are due on March 15 each year unless your business requests an alternate tax year by filing Form 1128, Application to Adopt, Change, or Retain a Tax Year.

C corporations using a calendar year are due on April 15 or, if using a fiscal year, the fifteenth day of the fourth month after year-end. Recent law changes provide special due date rules for C corporations that use a June 30 year-end. Your tax preparer can provide the phase-in rules for a June 30 fiscal year company.

Sole proprietorships get an extra month. Schedule C must be filed as part of the business owner's personal Form 1040 on April 15 of each year.

Partnership returns are due on the fifteenth day of the fourth month following the last day of the partnership's year.

Tax Return Extensions

Business owners often need more time to file personal and business tax returns. Partnerships, corporations, and limited liability companies all use Form 7004 to request an automatic extension.

Partnerships and LLCs that opt to file as a partnership get an automatic 5-month extension, while corporations get 6 months. This means all these business entities have until September 15 to file tax returns if they've filed for an automatic extension.

Sole proprietorships and personal tax return filers can request an automatic 6-month extension by filing Form 4868. This form extends the due date of the various versions of Form 1040 to October 15 of a given year.

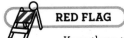 **RED FLAG**

Keep these two caveats in mind should you choose to extend a tax return. First, the IRS and your state expect you to have paid your full tax liability for the year by the statutory due date of your return. This means you may need to submit an estimated tax payment with your request for an extension. Second, procrastinating until the end of your 6-month extension means you're almost perpetually stuck in a mode where you're preparing a tax return. When you can, file tax returns as scheduled. Otherwise, there's no real downside to extending when circumstances warrant asking for more time.

Estimated Tax Payments

No matter what structure you choose for your business, you likely will be required to pay some manner of estimated tax payments throughout the year. This includes you personally if you have an ownership stake in a sole proprietorship, partnership, S corporation, or an LLC that files its taxes as either a partnership or S corporation.

The IRS expects you to forecast your taxable income on a quarterly basis and submit a portion of your estimated tax liability. Form 1040-ES looks simple enough on the surface, but what we don't have room to show are the three worksheet pages you'll use to derive the amount you enter into the Dollars and Cents fields. You don't send the Form 1040-ES worksheet pages to the IRS, only the payment coupon if you mail a check. You'll likely find it easiest to pay online, as we discuss later in this chapter.

Be sure to keep the worksheet as documentation for the IRS, but also as a lead-in to paying estimated taxes to your state. You're off the hook here if your state doesn't have an income tax. Georgia waives the requirement to file estimated taxes if the tax return is filed by March 1 (instead of April 15), and your state might have a similar option. Most states tend to follow federal tax payment deadlines, but check your specific requirements so you don't incur unexpected penalties. Many states offer online payment options, but these are separate from any federal tax payment options.

Depending on your income level, you might be required to conform to the safe harbor rules established by the IRS. For tax year 2014, if your taxable income was $150,000 or more (or $75,000 for married filing separate returns), you are expected to pay estimated payments amounting to the smaller of 90 percent of your current tax year liability, or 110 percent of the previous year's actual tax liability. You'll receive a refund for overpayments if your actual tax liability falls below your estimated payments, but if you're subject to the safe harbor regulation and do not comply, the IRS will assess an underpayment penalty.

Estimated tax payments are due in four installments throughout the year, as shown in the next table. As with all the tax due dates we mention in this book, if an estimated tax date falls on a weekend or holiday, the deadline is extended to the next business day.

Due Dates for Estimated Tax Payments

Installment	Due Date
1	April 15
2	June 15
3	September 15
4	January 15

Notice that unlike the payroll tax returns we discuss in Chapter 18, the second and third estimated tax payments do not follow a calendar quarter-end, but instead fall a month earlier. So it won't be just your imagination each summer when you think, *Wait, didn't I just make an estimated payment two months ago?*

When remitting estimated tax payments, you can either mail a paper version of Form 1040-ES, register as an individual to pay online via the Electronic Federal Tax Payment System (EFTPS) website at eftps.gov, or use directpay.irs.gov. The EFTPS site is free to use, as is the DirectPay site if you transfer funds from your bank account, but fees apply if you opt to use a credit card.

 **ACCOUNTING HACK**

Although the IRS expects four estimated installments each year, there's nothing stopping you from making monthly estimated payments instead. Monthly payments might fit into your household budget easier, and you can raise and lower the monthly amounts throughout the year and get more certainty about where your taxable income level may fall. If you receive W-2 income from a business that's in excess of your expected tax liability, you can pay your estimated taxes through withholding instead. The IRS considers paycheck withholding to be distributed evenly throughout the year. So if you fund your tax liability through paycheck withholding, you don't have to file Form 1040-ES. The safe harbor rules apply no matter what method you choose.

Owners and partners of C corporations and LLCs who opt to file tax returns as C corporations must also remit estimated taxes by way of Form 1120-W. The due dates are the same as for personal taxpayers.

Corporations that overpay their estimated tax liability can request a refund before filing their corporate tax return by using Form 4466, Corporation Application for Quick Refund of Overpayment of Estimated Tax. Conversely, underpayment penalties for corporations must be computed by using Form 2220, Underpayment of Estimated Tax by Corporations.

Business State Income Tax Returns

Businesses with operations in more than one state may be required to file a state income tax return in each state they do business. The states that levy income taxes on businesses each have their own forms you're required to file.

Supporting Tax Forms

Your ownership stake in a business may result in a number of supporting forms that document the amounts of profit or loss that flows to your individual income tax return. You might issue some of these directly from your business, or in the case of Form 1099, you might receive these forms from businesses that pay you for services during the year.

Form W-2

As discussed in Chapter 18, you must issue a Form W-2 to each employee in your business who receives a paycheck. Sole proprietorships are the exception to this rule, as you the owner already report the income or loss of the business on your personal tax return. You'll only need to pay yourself a salary that would appear on Form W-2 if you have an ownership stake in a S or C corporation, or a limited liability company (LLC) that has elected to be treated as a corporation.

Partnerships and LLCs that are recognized as partnerships report the owner's share of income or loss on Schedule K-1 instead of Form W-2.

You'll receive a Form W-2 from each business that pays you a salary or wages, no matter if you have an ownership stake or not.

Schedule K-1

This tax form is a subset of Form 1065 filed by partnerships and Form 1120S filed by S corporations. Each partner or S corporation owner receives this form, which documents their share of income and loss generated by the business.

Your personal tax return, Form 1040, has provisions for you to record amounts from Schedule K-1. Each partnership or S corporation you have a stake in will issue Schedule K-1 to you.

Form 1099

There are more than a dozen iterations of Form 1099, but the version you'll most likely encounter as a business owner is Form 1099-MISC. Other businesses that issue payment to you—often for work as an independent contractor, for example—are required to document accumulated payments of $600 or more in a given year.

This catch-all form is intended to provide the IRS documentation of numerous types of payments, but you'll most frequently receive a 1099-MISC for these two situations:

Rent: If you own property you rent to another business, the business is required to issue a Form 1099-MISC to you for each calendar year. The rent amount paid to you is reported in box 1 of the form.

 **RED FLAG**

> You might need to issue a 1099-MISC to yourself if your business rents property from you. Some business owners own real estate personally and rent it to their business. Or maybe you rent a portion of your house or an outbuilding on your property to your business. Rent your business pays to you is an expense to the business but taxable income to you personally.

Nonemployee services: This catch-all category covers almost anything you do for another business that results in a payment to you. Generally Form 1099 isn't required to be issued for payments to S and C corporations, but you still might receive 1099s from some of your customers. Sole proprietorships and partnerships are required to receive a 1099 for each year any compensation is paid.

Personal Income Tax Returns

At this point in your life, you're probably well versed with the annual rite of filing an income tax return. As we've noted in this chapter, having an ownership stake in a business can result in more complexity in the spring of each year, or the fall if you opt to extend your filing deadlines.

Federal Income Tax Return

Taxpayers in the United States pay income taxes based on a sliding scale. The lowest-income earners pay 10 percent of income in tax, subject to certain standard deductions and exemptions. Other tax brackets as of this writing are 15 percent, 25 percent, 28 percent, 33 percent, 35 percent, and 39.6 percent. The dollar amounts associated with these percentages vary based on whether one is filing as a single individual, married couple, or head of household.

In the past, before you owned a business, filing your tax return might have taken only a few minutes. As discussed, many taxpayers are able to take advantage of the simplified Form 1040EZ or Form 1040A.

As a business owner, that's changed now. Business income of any amount typically requires you to use the full Form 1040, U.S. Individual Income Tax Return, often referred to as the Long Form. You'll include all sources of income on your tax return as before, along with some additional information that might be new to you:

- W-2 income from your business or any other jobs you've held during the year.

- Schedule C if you have income from a sole proprietorship or a single-owner LLC. (We discussed this form in detail earlier in the chapter.)

- Schedule E if you own rental property, including renting any type of real estate to your business.

- Shareholder's Basis Worksheet if you have income from an S corporation or partnership. The amounts from the Schedule K-1s you receive appear on this form.

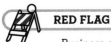 **RED FLAG**

Business owners are sometimes caught off guard by two unexpected taxes. Sole proprietors, partnership owners, and LLC owners who elect to be taxed like partnerships must pay self-employment tax of 15.6 percent of their business income. Employees and employers share the burden of FICA and Medicare taxes, with each paying a total of 7.65 percent. Business owners are considered both employer and employee, and must pay both halves of the tax. In addition, dividends distributed to owners of C corporations may be taxed as capital gains at rates up to 20 percent, depending on the taxpayer's tax bracket. Your estimated tax payments take into account your entire tax liability for a tax year, including but not limited to income, self-employment, and capital gains taxes.

State Income Tax Return

Most but not all states levy a state income tax. Your state income tax return typically is far less detailed than your federal tax return. States often require you to file a copy of your federal tax return with your state return.

ACCOUNTING HACK

You typically have up to 3 years after the scheduled filing date to amend any income tax returns you file. For personal returns, you'll file Form 1040X, partnerships use Form 1065X, and corporations use Form 1120X. Amended returns can be used to correct accounting errors that materially misstates your income or to add expenses or deductions that may lower your tax bill.

Getting Help Versus Filing on Your Own

As a U.S. citizen, it's your responsibility to pay your share of taxes to federal, state, and local government agencies.

Hiring a Professional

As you've learned in this book, being involved in a business entails an almost bewildering amount of taxes, returns, and deadlines. You can outsource the payment and processing, as noted in Chapter 12, and you can, and likely should, outsource the filing of any business and personal tax returns to a tax professional. Many tasks are best performed by an expert, and taxes are no exception. The U.S. Tax Code is filled with ambiguities that present both risks and opportunities.

Maybe you've seen a news report wherein a reporter asks 20 different tax experts to prepare the same income tax return and gets back many different results. It might seem hopeless if even tax professionals can't agree on the amount of taxes due, but still, a tax adviser can often save you from yourself.

For instance, many taxpayers avoid legal and rightful deductions in fear of triggering an audit from the IRS. Others set off on a path of handling certain expenses and deductions in a way that becomes set in stone for them, not realizing that along the way they're overpaying taxes.

Filing on Your Own

With that said, you have multiple options if you want to file on your own. The IRS will mail paper forms to you at no charge if you call 800-TAX-FORM (800-829-3676) or order online at irs.gov/Forms-&-Pubs/Order-Products. If you opt to fill out your tax return by hand, do yourself a favor and triple-check all calculations to ward off unwanted correspondence with the IRS a few months after you file your return.

You have many choices in tax software, both cloud-based and desktop-based. H&R Block (hrblock.com), TaxACT (taxact.com), and TurboTax (turbotax.com) all offer cloud-based services that include electronic filing of your tax returns. H&R Block and TurboTax also offer desktop versions of their products. In all cases, pricing varies based on the complexity of your tax returns, and you might have to pay separate fees for federal and state returns.

Consumer-based services such as this, as opposed to professional tools tax advisers use, walk you through the process and sometimes include "deduction finders" and other aids to help you file correctly while not unnecessarily leaving money on the table.

Because we devote two chapters of the book to spreadsheets (Chapters 21 and 22), we'd be remiss if we didn't mention the Excel-based version of Form 1040 (excel1040.com). Glenn Reeves has faithfully re-created this venerable tax form every tax year since 1996 and includes every schedule sole proprietorship owners need.

 RED FLAG

The IRS doesn't allow taxpayers to file returns directly online, so you'll have to go through a tax professional or use an online service if you want to file electronically. But take precautions. Ensure the service you use is a brand-name one. And when using cloud-based services, be sure the website address contains the prefix *https://* instead of just *http://*. The *s* signifies a secure and encrypted connection. Never enter any tax return information in a site without the *s*. Your web browser might indicate secure sites, such as with a lock symbol.

In addition, the IRS will provide you with all the forms and instructions you need through its irs.gov website. Using your computer search engine, you can query various tax issues and read summaries from many tax professionals who will share their experiences and opinions with you.

Be aware, however, that if you hire a professional to help you with the preparation of your income tax return, you get the opportunity to have that professional represent you in the case should your tax return get audited. This is one of the greatest benefits of hiring a tax professional—the peace of mind of not having to deal with questions and correspondence from the taxing authorities.

Tax Return Tips

Many things can position your tax return as one that will be examined. Here are some basic rules to watch out for that, if followed, help keep you above the radar of the tax examiners:

Calculate your return correctly: Mathematical mistakes are a leading cause of tax audits. If you use software to complete your tax returns, the software will ensure everything adds up correctly.

Report *all* your income: Whether you're filing an individual tax return or a business return, the people and businesses who pay you money are often taking a deduction for the money they pay you and reporting that amount to the IRS, and the IRS is cross-checking to ensure all those deductions are resulting in income reported elsewhere—like on your return.

Don't cheat: Not only is cheating wrong, but the penalties for intentionally falsifying tax documents are much steeper than those for making honest mistakes.

File all required tax returns: Nonfilers are more likely to raise the attention of the taxing authorities than those who diligently meet every filing deadline.

Be lucky: What does luck have to do with it? Each year tax authorities randomly decide to audit tax returns. Even if you're doing everything right, you still might have a tax examination in your future. Don't panic. As long as you saved your documentation and did your best at following the tax rules, you have no reason to be afraid of a tax audit.

The Least You Need to Know

- Every business generates taxable income (or a loss), so every business must file federal and state tax returns.
- Where the income (or loss) from a business is reported depends on the type of business entity, the type of ownership of the business, and the level of business income.
- The information from your business tax returns flows to your personal tax returns via supporting forms.
- If you make a mistake on your tax return or discover unreported income or expenses, you have at least 3 years from the original filing date to amend your return.
- You have several ways to file your taxes, including using tax software or a tax professional.

Recordkeeping Rule Book

As you've seen throughout this book, a wide variety of parties have an interest in your business. This goes far beyond a direct financial stake in your business. Federal, state, and local governments all have an indirect financial interest in your business through the taxes and fees you pay. Lenders, merchant account providers, insurance companies, and even vendors who extend you credit also have an indirect financial interest.

Each of these parties often retains the right to require you to produce copies of various records related to your business for a surprisingly long time. Further, there's often no rhyme or reason, and you might need to keep records to remain in compliance with state or local regulations for a much longer period of time than the federal government requires. Litigation, such as divorce proceedings or a civil suit filed by a disgruntled customer, vendor, or employee, also could result in situations where you're compelled to produce documentation.

In this chapter, we discuss the types of records you should plan to retain, and we offer general guidelines on how long you should keep each type of record.

In This Chapter

- Storing copies of electronic accounting records
- Holding on to employee records
- Saving your tax returns
- Maintaining other business records

Keep in mind that this is a "trust but verify" situation; it's impossible for us to give specific guidance that covers every situation. However, we can give you an overview of the range of records you might need to retain, along with an understanding of the expectations the aforementioned stakeholders may have.

Maintaining Your Accounting Records

As you've seen in Chapters 12, 18, and 19, businesses can be subjected to a dizzying array of taxes. Each tax return you file can be audited for varying periods of time.

Your best source of documentation is generally your accounting software, so it's important to keep backup copies of your records. When you're unable to produce documentation supporting a return you've filed, governmental entities may *impute* values for the return and assess interest and penalties.

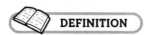 **DEFINITION**

In financial circles, the term **impute** means to replace missing values with a sometimes arbitrary value. If you can't verify your revenues were a certain value reported on your return, and the tax auditor feels a higher number is more appropriate, you'll have a tough time fighting the assertion.

In Chapter 15, we discuss the importance of backing up your data so you can restore your information or protect your records from a disaster-recovery standpoint. You also want to back up your records periodically so you can respond to requests from any of the stakeholders we mentioned at the start of this chapter. Although you'll want frequent backups of your live accounting data, you might only keep one backup per year for archival purposes. Given the nature of technology, having a duplicate backup from a given accounting year is always a good precaution.

As we discuss in Chapter 3, you might decide at some point to migrate from one accounting program to another. If you move between desktop-based accounting programs, be sure to keep copies of your accounting software installation discs or the program download. A backup of your data won't do you any good in the future if you don't also have the corresponding software you can use to access the data.

ACCOUNTING HACK

Recently, Internal Revenue Service (IRS) auditors have demanded a backup of accounting records from your accounting software as part of an examination. Potentially, this can expose far more information to their scrutiny than just the period in question. For cloud-based accounting programs, you'll have to provide a user ID and password if you're audited, which means you might not be able to limit the records the tax authorities can examine. Some desktop-based programs, such as QuickBooks, let you produce a copy of your accounting records for a specific period. In QuickBooks, choose File, Utilities, and Condense. You'll see an option to create a period-specific version of your data you can share with the auditor.

Keeping Employee Records

The significance of maintaining payroll and personnel records transcends many of the other concepts we cover in this book. Not only must you maintain documentation to support the payroll taxes you've paid (see Chapter 12), but there are also age, wage, and other statutory requirements you must be able to prove you've complied with.

Federal Requirements

IRS Publication 583 states that you must keep all employment tax records for a minimum of 4 years after the employment tax was due or paid. The caveat here is the clock starts based on the later of these two events.

Let's say your payroll taxes were due to be paid January 15, 2019, but because of an oversight, you actually paid them on July 24, 2019. In this case, you'll need to hold on to those records until at least July 24, 2023. If you'd paid the taxes on time, you might be able to fire up the shredder on January 15, 2023.

Keep in mind that these are the federal regulations, and as you'll see, your state or local municipality may have additional recordkeeping requirements.

Unfortunately, the IRS isn't the only federal agency that has an interest in your employee records. The Equal Employment Opportunity Commission requires that employers keep all personnel and employee records for 1 year—for both active and terminated employees. However, the Age Discrimination in Employment Act and Federal Labor Standards Act both extend this time period to at least 3 years.

State Requirements

As an employer, you not only have to keep track of the federal recordkeeping requirements discussed in the preceding section, but you also must comply with myriad state requirements.

Unfortunately, these are too vast and varied for us to cover in this book, but we can provide an example for one state. The Georgia Department of Labor mandates that employee records must be maintained for up to 7 years. This means Georgia companies must keep any documentation related to their state unemployment tax returns for as many as 3 or 4 years longer than the federal requirements. That's just for SUTA returns; the Georgia Department of Revenue, to which businesses remit state income tax, could have a different time frame still.

Regulatory approaches vary widely from state to state. This means agency names can also vary. For instance, Hawaii's Department of Taxation is the equivalent of California's Franchise Tax Board, which corresponds to the Department of Revenue many other states have. As you've read in Chapter 12, every state levies an unemployment tax, typically administered by a Department of Labor, but the agency name could vary. If your state doesn't offer a centralized online resource for resources, try contacting your governor's office or a tax professional.

BOTTOM LINE

The American Institute of CPAs maintains a list of all state taxing departments of revenue. You can find it at aicpa.org/Research/ExternalLinks/Pages/TaxesStatesDepartmentsofRevenue.aspx.

Local Requirements

Roughly 13 percent of cities and counties around the country levy income taxes. These represent yet another documentation time table you must keep in mind.

To determine your local requirements, do an internet search with your local jurisdiction and "employer resources." You also can contact your city councilperson, county commissioner, or mayor's office, as appropriate, for specific guidance. Governmental agencies at all levels have a vested interest in enabling you to be compliant. A local tax professional can help you navigate the federal, state, and local regulatory terrain as well.

Other Stakeholders

Governmental agencies aren't the only stakeholders that can require you to provide documentation related to your employees. Assuming your business is subject to workers' compensation, your insurance carrier can have its own set of requirements with regard to how far back they can look.

Keep in mind that workers' compensation fraud or even the suspicion of it can reset all clocks.

RED FLAG

The recordkeeping requirements we discuss here all assume you've paid your employees and payroll taxes on time and correctly. The clock never stops in situations where taxpayers maliciously or accidentally fail to file returns, withhold employee paychecks, or file fraudulent tax returns. As noted, if you can't prove your situation, the government will be more than happy to make up numbers that suit its purposes and penalize you accordingly—and in some cases bring criminal charges.

Dealing with Other Records

If you keep every record related to every aspect of your business, particularly on paper, you'll soon be overrun. In this section, we suggest some ways to triage what records you should absolutely keep, which you should consider keeping, and those you can shred.

Records to Keep Permanently

Plan on finding space to keep the following records indefinitely:

- Any documents that relate to the formation and ownership of a business
- Minutes from meetings of the board of directors, shareholders, and/or partners
- Intellectual property, such as trademarks, copyrights, and patents
- Annual income tax returns along with supporting documentation such as end-of-year financial statements
- Canceled checks or other documentation for payment of income taxes
- Depreciation schedules
- Any documentation related to audits from any governmental agencies, as well as insurers such as workers' compensation carriers
- Correspondence or documentation related to important legal matters
- Accountant's audit reports
- Property appraisals
- Stock certificates (Hold for as long as you own the stock.)

- Mortgages, deeds, bills of sale, and vehicle titles for all assets owned

- Accident reports and insurance claims

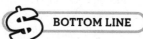 **BOTTOM LINE**

Keep any notarized records in paper form with an electronic backup.

Records to Hold Temporarily

As you've noted from the employee records section of this chapter, the term *temporary* can cover a wide span of time. When it comes to saving records for several years but not forever, you'll find that most records need to be saved for at least 3 years and in some cases up to 7.

Here's a list of common documents that should be saved for at least 3 years; you'll see notations for documents that should be saved for 7 years:

- Income tax returns and supporting documentation (Although this appears in the permanent list, it's included here as well because it's so important. It's imperative that you keep income tax returns and supporting documentation for a minimum of 3 years from the date filed or the date due, whichever is later.)

- Bank reconciliations

- Personnel records of current employees (7 years is recommended)

- Personnel records of terminated employees (at least 3 years but longer if there are any pending insurance claims)

- Payroll and related tax records (4 years is recommended)

- Expired insurance policies

- Sales records including invoices sent to customers (7 years is recommended)

- Invoices received from vendors (7 years is recommended)

- Purchase orders

If you use accounting software, it's possible you won't have paper documents for items like invoices and purchase orders, so the electronic version will have to do. For anything else on this list, particularly any documents that contain signatures, the original should be retained.

In addition, you should be archiving meaningful correspondence and emails that relate to your business. Your decision on how long to keep those letters and messages depends on the information they contain.

ACCOUNTING HACK

You don't necessarily need to keep permanent copies on paper of all these items. Most modern accounting programs allow you to attach one or more documents to a given transaction. If you use a document scanner or a scanning app, you can easily convert paper documents to electronic formats and embed them in your accounting software. Do be sure, though, that you understand where your accounting software stores the documents. Cloud-based accounting software uploads the documents automatically, while some desktop-based accounting programs may simply link to a document location on your hard drive. Document links become invalid if you delete a linked document or replace your computer.

On-Demand Records

A benefit to so much of our lives being online these days is that you can look up certain records on demand. You should easily be able to request copies of the following types of records should the need arise:

- Bank statements

- Credit card statements

- Federal income tax returns

The Least You Need to Know

- Always keep duplicate backups of your accounting data from the end of each year.
- Federal guidelines for retaining records may be much shorter than state or local requirements.
- Legal and ownership records must generally be kept permanently, while other business records should be kept for up to 7 years.
- You might not need to keep copies of records you can easily request from your financial institutions.

Data Analysis and Forecasting

Even the highest-end Swiss Army Knife doesn't contain every tool in the world. Likewise, entry-level accounting software does cover a wide array of business tasks, but even businesses using enterprise-scale accounting software still supplement its capabilities from time to time with spreadsheets, databases, analytics, and other tools to perform additional business analysis activities.

This final part looks at software you might choose in addition to your accounting system. We also go over the types of analysis, reporting, and other activities you might want to perform. We begin with an introduction of why spreadsheets are a good choice and walk you through a spreadsheet example to show you how quickly you can build a useful business tool such as an amortization schedule. Next, you learn how to use a spreadsheet not only for budgeting, forecasting, and trend analysis, but also for getting a sanity check on the numbers your accounting system is reporting. Finally, we explore the relatively new universe of apps, some of which might supplement the features of your accounting system, and others that make you more productive and effective.

Working with Spreadsheets

Back before computers became such an integral part of our daily lives, accounting records were maintained in paper ledgers, and any supporting work had to be done on additional pieces of paper. Calculations were made either in one's head or by using a calculator. Such efforts were time-consuming and fraught with risk for errors.

Thankfully, today's spreadsheet software can make many accounting-related tasks easier. However, spreadsheets also can be time-consuming and fraught with risk for errors if they're used improperly.

In this chapter, we share some techniques that can help you use spreadsheets more effectively. In the next chapter, we show you how to access ready-made tools that save you time and reduce your risk of mistakes.

In This Chapter

- Spreadsheet programs to supplement your accounting software
- Getting started with spreadsheets
- Using basic Excel functions and tools
- Creating a sample loan amortization table

Spreadsheet Options

Your accounting software can handle the lion's share of your recordkeeping. However, you may need to perform some outside calculations, maintain supporting schedules, or analyze your accounting data. For those tasks, spreadsheet software is exactly the right tool for the job.

The grandfather of all spreadsheets is a program called VisiCalc, which first appeared in the 1980s. VisiCalc's spreadsheet files emulated the classic accountant's ledger paper with columns and rows of information and enabled users to type data on-screen and build reusable calculations known as formulas. VisiCalc was soon overtaken in popularity by Lotus 1-2-3, which later was supplanted by Microsoft Excel.

Presently, Microsoft Excel is the most widely used spreadsheet program. You can use it on a surprising number of devices, including Apple and Windows-based computers, numerous tablets and smartphones, as well as any device that has internet access and can get to the online version of Microsoft Excel, Excel Online.

You'll need to purchase a software license or subscription if you want to use the full version of Excel on your Windows or Apple-based computer. However, Windows 10 offers Office Apps, which are scaled-down versions of Microsoft Excel, Word, and other traditional desktop applications available at no charge.

Depending on which platform you're using, you might find that some features or techniques differ or are unavailable from our coverage here. Microsoft has recently embarked on a unification of its software interfaces across all devices. For example, the menus in Excel for Mac 2011 bear only passing resemblance to those in Excel 2010 and Excel 2013. However, the upcoming 2016 versions of Excel for both Windows and Mac will share very similar menu structures.

In any case, you're certainly not limited to using Microsoft Excel as your spreadsheet application. Other choices abound, including these:

Google Sheets: This browser-based spreadsheet works in the cloud and enables you to access your spreadsheets anywhere you can get online. Browser-based spreadsheets currently offer far less functionality than desktop-based programs, but they're free. Plus, the relative simplicity of features can make it easier for beginners to get up and running with spreadsheets. You can access Google Sheets at google.com/sheets.

Numbers: This Apple product comes free with some Apple devices. It offers similar functionality to Excel for basic spreadsheets but doesn't offer nearly as much. If your Apple computer or device doesn't include Numbers, you can purchase it from the App Store for $19.99, as of this writing.

LibreOffice: This open-source software is a free competitor to Microsoft's Office suite. LibreOffice can be used to open and edit most spreadsheets created in Microsoft Excel. This free download is available from libreoffice.org.

Gnumeric Portable: The program files for this spreadsheet app are small enough to fit on a flash drive, which means you can use the program on any computer without installing it directly. Download it free from portableapps.com/apps/office/gnumeric_portable.

Introduction to Spreadsheets

Spreadsheets are a specific type of document also referred to as workbooks. Actually, a workbook is the file that contains spreadsheets, and it can be made of just one or many spreadsheets. Spreadsheets are often referred to as worksheets, but for simplicity, we'll stick with spreadsheets throughout.

Spreadsheet Basics

Spreadsheets are based on a grid system with numbered rows and lettered columns inside a frame. The column letters and row numbers serve as coordinates for specific locations within the spreadsheet, much like you might use to find a location on a map. Each box within the grid is known as a cell. The first cell in the top-left corner of a spreadsheet is cell A1, where A represents the first column, and 1 represents the first row.

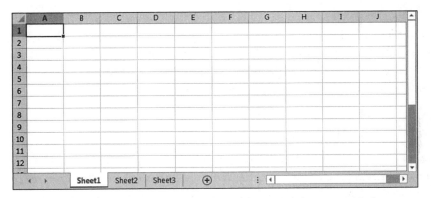

In a spreadsheet, numbers and letters identify rows and columns, respectively.

Depending on the spreadsheet program and file type you're using, a single spreadsheet may have more than 16,000 columns, roughly 1 million rows, and approximately 1.7 billion cells. Most users barely scratch the surface of what's possible with spreadsheets.

To add data to a spreadsheet, simply click in a cell and start typing. Don't worry if what you type is wider than the cell itself. You can widen the column or allow the cell contents to spill over into adjacent cells.

RED FLAG

A common mistake new spreadsheet users make is to forget to press the Enter key after adding data to or editing data within a cell. Doing so can leave your spreadsheet program in a state where most commands are disabled. In this situation, you might mistakenly think the software is frozen. When you press Enter, the command functionality is restored.

Text that's too wide for a column will simply overlap into adjacent cells as needed. If you type the word *Accounting* in cell A1 of your spreadsheet, for example, it'll typically overlap slightly into cell B1. If you type *101* in cell B1, suddenly cell A1 might only show *Accountin* and you'll no longer see the *g* at the end. Fortunately, you can widen any column in the spreadsheet.

A simple approach is to position your mouse in the spreadsheet frame to the right of the column you want to widen and then drag while holding down your left mouse button. In this case, positioning your mouse on the spreadsheet frame between columns A and B and dragging slightly to the right as you hold down your left mouse button widens column A enough to show the entire word *Accounting*. You might be able to just double-click the right edge of column A's heading to automatically widen the column as much as necessary.

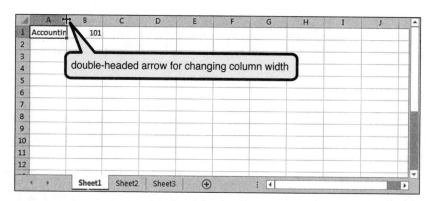

To widen a column to the width of the longest cell entry, double-click when your cursor changes to a double-headed arrow.

Spreadsheets exhibit a different behavior when a column isn't wide enough to display an entire number. In some cases, you'll see a series of pound signs (#) in the affected cells. They vanish when you make the column wide enough.

Let's put together a simple exercise in Excel 2013 that will enable you to get a feel for spreadsheets. Our example spreadsheet helps you develop an amortization table to determine the cost of borrowing money for your business. This allows you to determine monthly payment and total interest cost to finance a car, another piece of equipment, or any other business need.

BOTTOM LINE

In reality, you'll probably never actually need to build an amortization spreadsheet like this because ready-made templates abound. But following through the steps gives you some general exposure to what's possible with spreadsheets. Many other templates can help you create other types of financial and business spreadsheets.

Making Basic Cell Entries

The exact commands may vary in different spreadsheets, but you should be able to re-create these steps in any of the aforementioned spreadsheet programs.

First, start a new, blank spreadsheet. This often appears automatically when you launch your spreadsheet program or app, but you might have to choose New or Blank Workbook.

This amortization schedule is first going to require that you store some assumptions needed to calculate the monthly payment. As noted, spreadsheets are broken down into cells, and just like houses, every cell has an address. The first cell in the upper-left corner is cell A1. In this cell, type *Interest*. When you press the Enter key, the next cell below, A2, is activated. The active cell in a spreadsheet always has a bold border around it.

Next type *Term* in cell A2, *Loan* in cell A3, and *Payment* in cell A4.

You now need to input some numbers into your spreadsheet, specifically an interest rate in cell B1. The interest rate for this example is 5.25 percent. You can enter this number in two ways: *.0525* or *5.25%*. If you choose the former, 0.0525 will appear in the spreadsheet. Spreadsheets automatically add leading zeros to decimal-based numbers such as an interest rate, but there's no other formatting such as dollar signs or commas. This can make numbers hard to read, but you can add various types of formatting to remedy this.

In this case, if you click cell B1 and then click the Percent Style button (with the percent sign %) on the Home tab, the number appears as 5%. You'll then need to click the Increase Decimal button twice to display the full interest rate, as shown in the following screenshot.

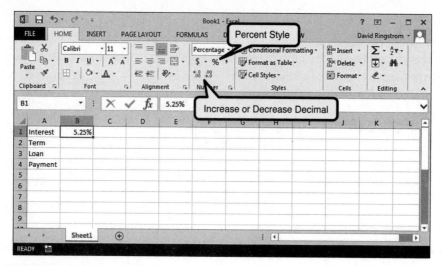

Excel offers one-click access to the Percent Style, but you might have to expand the number of decimals.

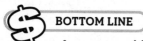

BOTTOM LINE

In many spreadsheet programs, you can save time and make numbers easier to read by typing the formatting when you enter the number. For instance, instead of typing .0525, enter 5.25% in a cell. For dollar amounts, type $30,000. If you typed 30000, it can be tough to distinguish at a glance if you entered three hundred thousand, thirty thousand, or three thousand. When you click the Accounting Number Format ($) button on the Home tab, Excel adds the dollar signs but also adds two decimal places you may have to remove using the Decrease Decimal button.

To continue with our example, enter *48* in cell B2 and *$30,000* in cell B3. For the moment, leave cell B4 blank. Instead, move down to row 6 and type the following words in cells A6 through E6:

> *Period*
>
> *Date*
>
> *Interest*
>
> *Principal*
>
> *Balance*

Enter the number *1* in cell A7.

At this point, cell A8 should be selected. That's where we'll enter our first *formula*.

DEFINITION

In a spreadsheet, a **formula** performs a calculation. You can always distinguish a formula for other types of inputs by the equal sign (=) that sits at the start of the formula.

Entering Formulas and Filling Entries

In cell A8, type *=A7+1*. This formula tells Excel to add 1 to whatever value is in cell A7. Because A7 contains the value 1, when you press Enter, the number 2 should appear in cell A8.

When typing cell addresses, you don't need to worry about capitalization because =a7+1 and =A7+1 mean the same thing to Excel. In fact, you'll notice that the spreadsheet software automatically capitalizes column letters when you press Enter.

At this point, you need to create a series of numbers from 1 to 48. However, you don't need to type the formula that appears in cell A8 46 more times. Instead, you can use a feature that lets you replicate the formula by simply dragging with your mouse. To do so, click on cell A8 and notice the little square in the lower-right corner. This is the Fill Handle. If you position your mouse over the handle and drag down while holding down your left mouse button, Excel copies the formula for you. Drag down and stop at row 54. When you release your mouse button, you should see a series of numbers from 1 to 48.

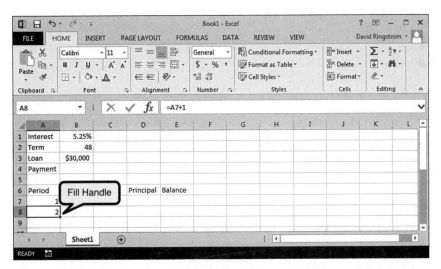

Excel's Fill Handle serves multiple purposes, including allowing you to copy data and formulas down a column or across a row.

Next, you'll create a series of dates. In this case, you won't use a formula, but instead create a series of numbers. In cell B7, enter *1/1/2019* to indicate the loan will commence as of January 1, 2019.

 RED FLAG

Be careful not to include an equal sign when entering dates like you do when entering formulas. If you enter =1/1/2019, Excel will interpret that as a formula that should divide 1 by 1 by 2019, for a result of 0.000495. Or you might find that 1/1/2019 appears as the number 43466. Many spreadsheets use a convention where, behind the scenes, dates are represented by the number of days since January 1, 1900. January 1, 2019 falls 43,466 days after the turn of the previous century.

Next, enter *2/1/2019* in cell B8. You'll now use a shortcut to complete the series of dates. Drag over cells B7 and B8 with your mouse to select both cells. Double-click on the Fill Handle, and Excel will populate the entire column of dates down to row 54. Alternatively, you could drag the fill handle as you did previously, but double-clicking is faster and easier.

To use this trick, you do have to select two cells to seed the series. If you only select one cell and double-click, you'd copy *2/1/19* all the way down the column.

Widen column B slightly if you find that certain cells are filled with # symbols.

Inserting a Function

Let's move on to working with spreadsheet functions. As you've seen, spreadsheets allow you to carry out calculations in cells. Some calculations are simple, as in division, multiplication, addition, and subtraction. Other calculations can't be carried out with simple arithmetic, such as a loan payment. Or if they could be carried out by hand, it would involve many cells and inputs. You can use functions in a spreadsheet formula to perform complicated calculations in a single cell.

Most spreadsheet programs have hundreds of functions available, so it can be daunting to determine if there's an easier way to perform a calculation. We'll walk you through each step.

First, click the cell where you want the formula—B4 in this case. Next, click the Formulas tab at the top of Excel and then click the Insert Function (fx) button in the Function Library group to display the Insert Function dialog box, shown next. Type what you'd like to do in the Search for a function: field, such as *loan payment*. Click Go, and the Select a function: list will show potential spreadsheet functions. In this case, the PMT function appears first on the list, and that's what you need to calculate your loan payment. Click OK to use this function.

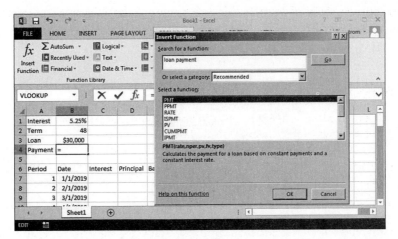

The Insert Function dialog box helps you determine if a function is available for a particular type of calculation.

At this point, a Function Arguments dialog box appears, which breaks down the input requirements for the function. Along the left side, you'll see Rate, Nper, and PV in bold, while Fv and Type are not bolded. Required inputs are bolded; optional ones are not.

Excel can calculate the monthly payment for your loan if you instruct it where the inputs are:

- **Rate:** This is the interest rate in cell B1, which must be divided by 12 to arrive at the monthly rate, so enter *B1/12*.

- **Nper:** This is the length of the loan, otherwise knows as the term, which appears in cell B2, so enter *B2*.

- **Pv:** This is how much you want to borrow, or the loan amount in cell B3, so enter *B3*.

RED FLAG

Banks calculate loan interest on a monthly basis when applying the interest to your payments, but state the interest on an annual basis, so always be sure to convert annual interest rates to monthly amounts in spreadsheet formulas. In this case, enter =B1/12 in the Rate field to convert the annual interest rate of 5.25% (which appears in cell B1) to a monthly amount. If you forget to divide by 12, Excel will compute the loan as incurring 5.25% interest per month, or 63% per year, which means your loan payment will appear to be outrageous.

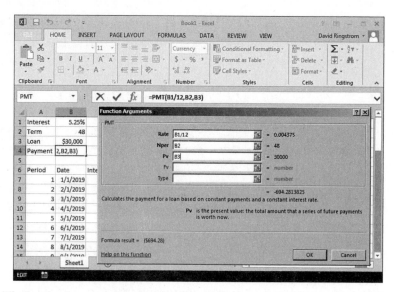

The Function Arguments dialog box identifies required versus optional inputs when crafting formulas that involve spreadsheet functions.

Once you've filled in the function arguments, the formula result returns -694.2813825. This is because Microsoft Excel calculates values to as many as 15 decimal places (only 7 decimal places were required for this calculation). However, in your spreadsheet, you can format the number to only show 2 decimal places. Click OK to place the formula in cell B4.

Now, ($694.28) should appear in cell B4. The parentheses indicate this is a negative number. Excel's PMT function returns a negative value because it considers the loan payment to be an outflow. Leaving this number as a negative value complicates some of the other formulas you need to add to the spreadsheet, so let's change it to a positive value. To do so, double-click on cell B4, which enables you to edit the formula. Add a minus sign (-) just after the equal sign so the formula reads =-B1/12, and press Enter.

Finishing the Amortization Table Formulas

You're now ready to build the rest of the amortization table. Click on cell C7, and enter this formula:

=B3*B1/12

In plain English, this means multiply $30,000 from cell B3 by 5.25% (the interest rate in cell B1) and divide the result by 12.

Your formula should return $131.25, which means $131.25 of your first month's payment of $694.28 goes to the bank as interest.

Next, enter this formula in cell D7:

=B$4-C7

Your formula should return $563.03. You'll notice this formula includes a dollar sign, which has special significance to Excel. If you refer to the formulas in cells A8 to A54, you'll see that as you copied the formula down, Excel changed each row number automatically. That's the natural process, and that's what you want for these formulas. In this case, you always need to refer to cell B4, so adding dollar signs instructs Excel not to change row 4 to a 5 if you were to copy the formula down a row. In spreadsheet parlance, this is known as an *absolute reference.*

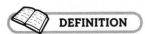 **DEFINITION**

> Most spreadsheet formulas involve relative references, which mean column letters and row numbers increment automatically as you copy a formula down a column or across a row. An **absolute reference** instructs Excel not to change the column letter and/or row number when you copy the formula. Place dollar signs as needed in formulas to prevent column letter and row number changes.

This brings you to cell E7, where you'll calculate the ending balance as of each month:

=B3-D7

The formula should return $29,436.97, which is the amount you'll still owe on the loan after the first month's payment. You're now ready to add the second row of formulas, after which you'll be able to copy the formulas down the rest of the column.

Enter this formula in cell C8:

=E7*B$1/12

The formula should return $128.79. This amount is slightly less than the interest for the first month because you've paid down the loan slightly. For the first month, you based this calculation on the initial loan balance of $30,000, but going forward, interest will be based on the ending balance for the previous month. A dollar sign in the formula instructs Excel to always refer to row 1, where the interest rate is, as you'll be copying this formula down the rest of the column.

In that regard, you don't need to actually write a formula in cell D8. You can use the Fill Handle to drag the formula in cell D7 into cell D8.

For cell E8, you'll enter this formula:

=E7-D8

There are no dollar signs in this formula because you want to refer to the ending balance for the previous month, as well as the amount you paid down in the current month. If you want to check your work, cell D8 should return $565.49 and cell E8 should return $28,871.47.

At this point, you're ready to populate the rest of the amortization table, but you don't need to write any more formulas to do so. Simply select cells C8 through E8 with your mouse, and double-click the Fill Handle in cell E8. Excel will copy the formulas down through row 54, stopping just before it encounters a blank cell in column B. Cell E54 should return 0, because at that point, the loan will be fully repaid.

If this isn't the case for you, check each of your formulas by double-clicking on the respective cells. Most likely, you'll find you omitted or misplaced a dollar sign to create an absolute reference back to one of the assumption cells.

Freezing Rows On-Screen

As we noted earlier, spreadsheets can house astronomical amounts of data, but it's easy to get lost even in the small spreadsheet you just created. When you scroll down to row 54, you could lose sight of the column headings you added in row 6. However, you don't have to sift aimlessly through columns of numbers; you can freeze certain rows on-screen.

To freeze the rows containing your titles, scroll your spreadsheet up until you get to row 1. You can use the scroll bar on the right-hand side of the screen, or press Ctrl+Home on your keyboard. Next, click on cell A7 in preparation for freezing rows 1 through 6 on-screen. Click the View tab at the top of Excel, choose Freeze Panes in the Window group, and choose Freeze Panes again. Now, when you scroll down either with the scroll bar or by pressing the down arrow or Page Down keys, rows 1 through 6 always remain on your screen. You can use the same steps to unfreeze the rows. You'll see the Freeze Panes command has changed to Unfreeze Panes.

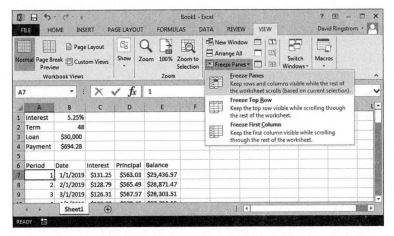

You can use the Freeze Panes command to prevent rows with titles from scrolling off screen.

You'll add one more type of formula to your amortization schedule and print the data. Select cells C55 and D55 with your mouse. Click the Home tab, and click the AutoSum button (Σ) in the Editing group. This adds the SUM spreadsheet function to both cells, and that shows the total interest and principal you'll pay over the course of the loan. You'll likely need to widen columns C and D slightly to show the totals of $3,325.51 and $30,000.00 respectively.

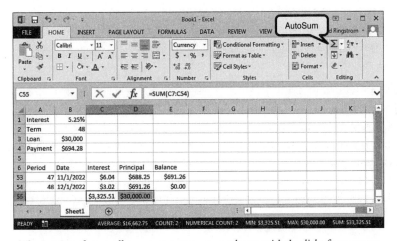

The AutoSum feature allows you to sum rows or columns with the click of your mouse.

Printing

Earlier, you froze rows 1 through 6 on the screen, but you'll need to take a different approach to freeze these rows on your printout. To do so, click on the Page Layout tab in Excel's ribbon, and click the Print Titles button in the Page Setup group. Enter *1:6* in the Rows to Repeat at Top text box, and click the Print or Print Preview button to print your amortization schedule or click OK to close the dialog box without printing.

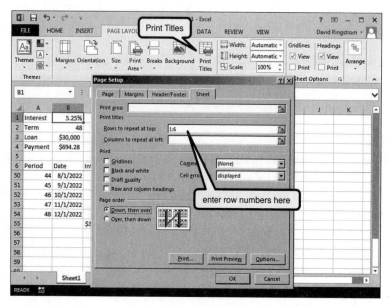

You can easily set certain rows to appear at the top of each page of your printouts.

In this chapter, we were only able to scratch the surface of what's possible with spreadsheets, but now you should have a good idea of how to get started using Excel. In the next chapter, we look at some other ways you can use spreadsheets. If this is all new terrain for you, we recommend you refer to *Idiot's Guides: Microsoft Excel 2013* by Michael Miller.

The Least You Need to Know

- Microsoft Excel is the most popular spreadsheet program, but other options are available, some of them free.

- Spreadsheets are electronic versions of accountant's ledger paper that are capable of carrying out calculations.

- An amortization schedule is just one of many ways you can use spreadsheets to calculate numbers related to your business.

More Spreadsheet Tools and Techniques

No matter what accounting software you choose, you're always going to bump into limitations when it comes to analyzing data or tracking additional information your accounting software can't manage. For instance, in Chapter 14, we discuss a supporting schedule for prepaid expenses. Your accounting software requires you to lump all prepaid expenses into a single bucket, but you'll want to maintain a listing of the amortization rate of each expense if you have more than one prepaid expense at a given time. Spreadsheets give you an easy way to supplement weaknesses such as this in your accounting software.

You also might find it helpful to create a budget for your business. Most accounting software programs have a budget feature, but these are often limited to carrying forward actual amounts from prior years. Within a spreadsheet, you can develop calculations that allow you to do much more targeted forecasting than just simply raising last year's office supply expense account by 5 percent.

In This Chapter

- Using spreadsheet templates
- Building a budget template
- Developing a shadow accounting system
- Filtering and analyzing data
- Creating supporting schedules

Over the years, we've seen people use spreadsheets as their accounting software. This is very risky because at some point, your transactions will overwhelm your spreadsheet. However, we will propose using a spreadsheet to create a shadow accounting system you reconcile to your accounting software. Doing so allows you to forecast cash flow and ensure that key transactions don't get lost amidst the numbers in your accounting software.

We close the chapter with examples of ways you can analyze data from your accounting software, such as by creating charts and filtering lists of data.

Spreadsheet Templates

In Chapter 21, we walked you through an exercise of building an amortization schedule from scratch. Although the exercise was a useful vehicle for giving you some exposure to how spreadsheets work, we're happy to report that you won't need to build such a schedule ever again.

Spreadsheet templates are prebuilt forms you can use and sometimes adapt to your own purposes. You'll find it easiest to locate templates in Microsoft Excel, but even cloud-based spreadsheets such as Google Sheets have templates you can use.

Accessing Templates

In Microsoft Excel, you can access templates in two ways. The first is to choose File, New, and search for the template you want, as shown in the following figure. In this case, you'd enter "loan amortization" in the search field and press Enter. Double-click on the template that appears, and you have a ready-to-use amortization schedule.

A second way is to right-click on any tab within an existing spreadsheet and choose Insert. Click the Spreadsheet Solutions tab in Microsoft Excel to choose from templates such as a billing statement, expense report, loan amortization schedule, and more. The benefit of this method is that the template will be inserted in your current workbook instead of as a standalone workbook.

 **ACCOUNTING HACK**

Spreadsheets don't have to be all about accounting. In Microsoft Excel, you can use the search term "NCAA" to locate a bracket template to use when college basketball's tournament time rolls around in March. You also can search for other sports, recipes, and movies.

Types of Templates

Spreadsheet templates can give you a jump-start on a number of aspects of your business.

Business plan templates, for example, can help you organize your thoughts on a new business you're contemplating starting. You also might need to present a business plan to a bank or other lender if you need to borrow money. Marketing budget templates can help you forecast how to best allocate funds to promote your business. Employee shift schedule templates can give you a framework for scheduling employees. Buy versus lease templates have built-in calculations that can help you determine whether you'd be better served buying or leasing equipment or vehicles for your business. And breakeven analysis templates can help you determine the minimum price needed to cover your costs. Once you know this amount, you then can use other calculations to determine the *markup* you should add to your products to deliver an adequate *gross profit*.

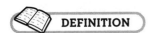 **DEFINITION**

The **markup** on a product is the difference, usually shown as a percentage, between its selling price and its cost. The selling price of a $100 item with a 40 percent markup is $140 ($100 × 140 percent). In every case, you'll add 100 percent to the desired markup percentage and then multiply by the unit cost. The words *markup* and *gross profit* are sometimes used interchangeably. **Gross profit** is the selling price for an item less the selling costs. On your profit and loss report, you might see the gross profit for your entire business instead of just a single product.

There are a dizzying number of spreadsheet templates available. If you're using Microsoft Excel, you can search within the software itself. Or do an internet search for the name of your spreadsheet program and a specific term, such as *Google Sheets budget template*. Most of the results will be free to use, but some may require a nominal fee.

Developing the Foundation of a Budget

Budgeting is a key part of a successful business. By using budgeting tools to predict, compare, and analyze your business performance, you can have a clear picture of where you're going and how you're going to get there.

With most software programs, the easiest way to start a budget for the coming year is to start with all the income and expenses from the current year. You then can apply a percentage increase or decrease to individual accounts, or even across the board to all accounts if you think everything will increase or decrease at the same pace. More likely, you'll probably examine each account individually and decide, based on your experience and knowledge of your business, how you expect those accounts to perform in the coming year.

For example, you might expect income to increase by 10 percent, salaries to increase similarly, but other expenses like rent and utilities and office supplies to remain the same from the current year to the next. That kind of analysis helps you nail down your budget numbers.

Once you have the budget in place, it's important to rely on it regularly for information about your business. At least quarterly, you should compare your budget to how you're actually doing and see if you're on target to meet the budget for the rest of the year.

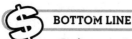

BOTTOM LINE

Budgets aren't written in stone (unless you're a government office), so it's okay to make adjustments during the year. The idea is for the budget to be a conduit toward success, not an albatross that dogs you when things don't go as expected.

Business budgets can take many forms, and everyone approaches budgeting from a different angle. Here, we show you an easy way to get a jump-start on creating a budget for your business. Assuming you want to create a budget for an entire year, a customized report from your accounting software can get you started quickly.

The exact steps you'll carry out will vary based on your accounting software, but we'll demonstrate the techniques in both Xero and QuickBooks to give you a good idea what to do in your program. In short, we'll generate a 12-month income statement in Xero and again in QuickBooks, export the reports to Excel, and convert the reports to budgets. Along the way, we'll explain some nuances you need to know to avoid frustration with this seemingly simple task. You'll likely discover other uses for a 12-month income statement as well.

Exporting from Xero

To export a 12-month report in Xero, choose Reports, Compare Periods, and make these selections:

- **Date:** Set this to the last month of your calendar year, or actually the end of the 12-month period you want to analyze.

- **Period:** Set this field to 1 month.

- **Compare With:** Set this field to Previous 11 Periods.

Click Update to see the report.

When you have the report arranged on-screen, you'll export the report to your accounting software. From the Export button in the lower-right hand corner of your report, you can make one of three choices:

Excel: This enables you to create an Excel 97 to 2003–compatible workbook almost any modern spreadsheet can open.

PDF: This creates a file you must open with Adobe Acrobat Reader (acrobat.com/reader) or a competing PDF viewer. PDF files are not suitable for spreadsheet analysis.

Google Docs: This choice enables you to post the report to your Google Docs account, within which you can use the Google Sheets application as we discussed in Chapter 21.

When exporting reports from a cloud-based software such as Xero or QuickBooks Online, you're prompted to save the file onto your computer if you choose the Excel format. You must then double-click on the resulting download icon to open the file in your spreadsheet program. Conversely, when you export a report from a desktop-based accounting software, you'll find that the report generally opens automatically in your spreadsheet program.

 RED FLAG

As of this writing, when you export Excel files from Xero, the files end in .xls. Be careful when opening such files in Excel 2007 and later because certain features in these versions of Excel are incompatible with .xls spreadsheets. You also won't be able to insert templates into .xls workbooks. To resolve this issue, convert the files to .xlsx using the Convert command either on the main menu or in the Info section of the File menu. This updates the file and restores full functionality. QuickBooks Online recently added the .xlsx format as an export choice, but your accounting software might still use the old .xls format.

Exporting from QuickBooks Desktop

To export a 12-month report in the desktop versions of QuickBooks, choose Reports, Company & Financial, and Profit & Loss Standard. You'll then carry out two steps using the drop-down lists across the top to create a 12-month report:

- **Dates:** Change this to Last Fiscal Year or use the From and To fields to specify a given date range.

- **Show Columns:** Change this from Total Only to Month.

At this point, a 12-month report will appear on-screen. Next, click the Excel button, choose Create New Worksheet, and click Export. Your report will automatically open in Excel.

In most cases, the exported report contains formulas that will recalculate automatically if you change any of the numbers in your report. This can give you a helpful jump-start on any analysis you need to perform. The trade-off is that the report format might not lend itself to some of the features you want to use in your spreadsheet program.

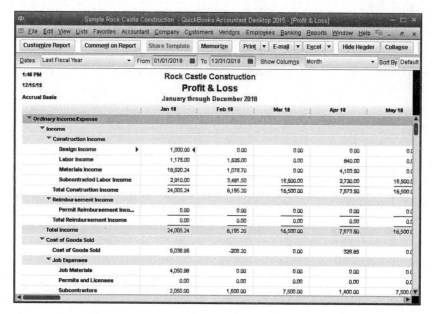

Most accounting programs enable you to export on-screen reports to an Excel spreadsheet format.

RED FLAG

Some accounting programs apply a special Text format to certain columns of exported reports. Because of this, if you insert formulas in or adjacent to a column with Text format, you'll often see the formula itself in the cell instead of the result, as you'd expect. The solution is to change the number format before you add any formulas. In Excel, click on the affected column and choose General from the list in the Number section of the Home tab. CSV files only contain text and numbers—without formatting—so you won't experience this problem with those exports.

Building Your Budget

At this point, you should have a 12-month income statement available in Excel. Assuming you have some familiarity with functions in Excel, you can use this format as the basis for projecting revenue and expenses for an upcoming calendar or fiscal year. Edit the values in various cells as needed to adjust the budget to reflect your assumptions and projections for the next year. As noted, not every accounting software export includes formulas in the total rows, so you might need to build new formulas for the budget total rows.

	A	B	C	D	E	F	G
1		18-Jan	18-Feb	18-Mar	18-Apr	18-May	18-Jun
2	Ordinary Income/Expense						
3	Income						
4	Construction Income						
5	Design Income	1,000.00	-	-	-	-	-
6	Labor Income	1,175.00	1,635.00	-	840.00	-	-
7	Materials Income	18,920.24	1,078.70	-	4,103.50	-	-
8	Subcontracted Labor Income	2,910.00	3,481.50	16,500.00	2,730.00	16,500.00	11,605.00
9	Total Construction Income	24,005.24	6,195.20	16,500.00	7,673.50	16,500.00	11,605.00
10	Reimbursement Income						
11	Permit Reimbursement Income	-	-	-	-	-	-
12	Total Reimbursement Income	-	-	-	-	-	-
13	Total Income	24,005.24	6,195.20	16,500.00	7,673.50	16,500.00	11,605.00
14	Cost of Goods Sold						
15	Cost of Goods Sold	5,038.95	(208.20)	-	329.85	-	-
16	Job Expenses						
17	Job Materials	4,050.98	-	-	-	-	-

12month

Exporting a 12-month income statement from your accounting software into a spreadsheet gives you a jump-start on developing a budget or performing other types of forecasting and analysis.

You might be able to pull in templates, such as the breakeven analysis we discussed earlier, or other tools to help you use intricate calculations that allow you much more control over your forecast rather than just increasing last year's numbers by, say, 5 percent.

Once you get your budget developed, you can either manually type the results back into your accounting software or, depending on the program you're using and your spreadsheet skills, convert your budget into a format you can import into your accounting software.

Maintaining a Shadow Accounting System

Accounting in general is oriented to be a historical record of your business. However, as a business owner, you also must look to the future—to forecast your short-term cash flow needs, for example. Your accounting software might offer a forecasting feature, but cash flow forecasts don't generally lend themselves to one-size-fits all solutions. You might find it helpful to use a spreadsheet program instead to develop a shadow accounting system.

In effect, this will be a very simplified version of your accounting records you can use to forecast cash flow and ensure you don't miss handling an expected transaction. Everyone has different requirements, so the solution we suggest here might not be an ideal fit for your business. But hopefully it will spark ideas that might work for you.

Another benefit to creating a shadow accounting system is that your numbers are broken down into an understandable format you can keep reconciled with your books. This gives you another way to summarize revenues and expenses and forecast upcoming cash requirements. We have two primary sections in the spreadsheet: Cash Inflows and Cash Outflows.

The first column of our shadow accounting system is a listing of customers who presently have outstanding invoices. Adjacent columns cover time periods that make sense for your business, which might be daily, weekly, semimonthly, or monthly. Our example assumes we're able to arrange paying most of our bills on the fifteenth and the last day of the month.

Forecasting Inflows

You'll notice in the following example that the spreadsheet leads off with Beginning Cash. The ultimate goal of this spreadsheet is to be able to accurately forecast cash flows. Cash flow forecasts involve both known amounts and unknown amounts, which we address as follows:

- The Customer rows represent unpaid invoices from your customers and when you expect to receive payment.

- The Projected Revenue row represents the amount of revenue you expect to collect during that time period.

- The Total Cash Available row enables you to see your forecasted ending cash balance for that period of time.

	A	B	C	D	E	F	G	H	I
1		1/15/2019	1/31/2019	2/15/2019	2/28/2019	3/15/2019	3/31/2019		
2	Beginning Cash	3,250.47	4,620.47	5,670.47	7,070.47	6,720.47	8,120.47		
3	Customer1		800.00						
4	Customer2	4,000.00							
5	Customer3		2,500.00						
6	Customer4	970.00							
7	Customer5		3,100.00						
8	Projected Revenue			5,000.00	5,000.00	5,000.00	5,000.00		
9	Total Cash Available	8,220.47	11,020.47	10,670.47	12,070.47	11,720.47	13,120.47		
10	Vendor1		(875.00)		(875.00)		(875.00)		
11	Vendor2	(2,250.00)		(2,250.00)		(2,250.00)			
12	Vendor3		(3,000.00)		(3,000.00)		(3,000.00)		
13	Vendor4	(1,350.00)		(1,350.00)		(1,350.00)			
14	Vendor5		(1,475.00)		(1,475.00)		(1,475.00)		
15	Ending Cash	4,620.47	5,670.47	7,070.47	6,720.47	8,120.47	7,770.47		
16									
17									

Cash Flow Forecast

Here is the beginning of our shadow accounting system that can forecast cash balances.

Forecasting Outflows

The Vendor rows shown in the preceding example assume your business typically has recurring bills for the same set of vendors. The amounts shown can either be actual or forecasted amounts you need to pay each vendor during that time period.

The Ending Cash balance should match your accounting software for periods that have already elapsed, and it will show your projected Ending Cash balance for future periods.

Depending on your spreadsheet skills, you may be able to make portions of the forecasting spreadsheet update automatically by exporting reports from your accounting software, but there's also value in taking the time to manually key in the amounts. Doing so forces you to reflect on the realities of your business. Glancing at on-screen reports doesn't always force the necessary deep thinking required to successfully plan for your business' short-term needs.

Analyzing Accounting Data

As you gain familiarity with your accounting software, you might find yourself frustrated by the limited ways you can analyze your data. Or you may tire of repetitively changing parameters on reports just so you can get a different view of your data.

This is another area where exporting reports to a spreadsheet can be rather beneficial.

Filtering Data

Even accountants can get overwhelmed easily by looking at too much data at once. The Filter feature available in many spreadsheet programs gives you an easy way to temporarily collapse a list of data down to just the rows you need to see at a given time.

To filter your data, first select any cell within a list of data and then choose Filter from the Data menu in Excel or Google Sheets. When you do, each column in your list will get a little arrow from which you can select the rows you'd like to see on-screen.

You can filter on as many columns as you want, which enables you to hone in on exactly the data you need to see. This is helpful in locating transactions you might struggle to find in your general ledger, such as those we discuss in Chapter 7. Filtering also enables you to isolate transactions by customer name, vendor name, account, or amount.

The following example shows the Filter arrows in place on a Vendor Summary report exported from QuickBooks Online. By clicking the arrow in cell B6 and then choosing Number Filters, we can display a submenu of options for filtering ranges of numbers. For instance, this can help you quickly identify expenses above a specific threshold.

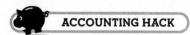

ACCOUNTING HACK

A hidden benefit of the Filter feature in a spreadsheet is that the drop-down list at the top of each column shows you one of each item in a list. It's far easier to turn on the filter feature and take a quick look to see if what you're trying to find is there or not than page down through a report hoping what you're looking for will catch your eye.

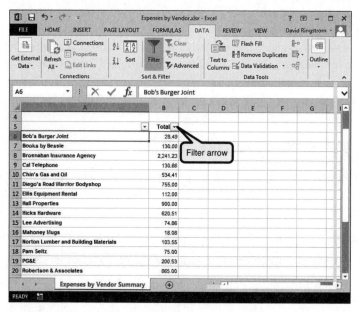

The Filter feature available within many spreadsheets enables you to collapse a list to just items that meet certain criteria.

Quick Analysis

Microsoft Excel in particular offers so many analytical features most spreadsheet users are unaware of. Recognizing that most users can't easily get their head around features like Conditional Formatting, Charts, PivotTables, and so on, Excel 2013 and later versions offer a Quick Analysis feature.

For example, if you export your Profit and Loss report to Excel as described earlier, you can select, say, the Revenue section and click the Quick Analysis button that appears below your selection. From there, hovering over any command previews various analytical features in Excel.

As shown in the following screenshot, positioning your mouse over the Data Bars command adds bars to the numbers you've selected. The larger the number, the larger the bar; the smaller the number, the smaller the bar. Hover over any Quick Analysis feature to preview the effect a given analytical feature adds to your spreadsheet, or click on the command to apply the setting.

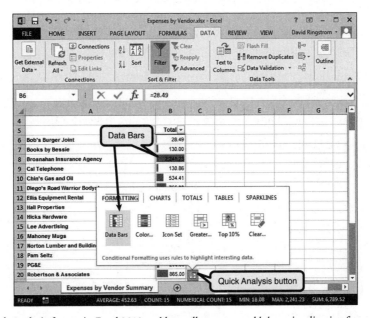

The Quick Analysis feature in Excel 2013 and later allows you to add data visualization features to your accounting reports.

Recommended Charts

The Quick Analysis feature in Excel 2013 and later offers a couple choices of charts, but you also can click the More command on the Charts tab to display the Recommended Charts feature. This allows you to quickly visualize what your data would look like in a variety of charts.

Excel offers dozens of different types of charts, and it can often be daunting to determine which type of chart works best to tell the story for a given set of data. A preview of each chart, based on the data you selected, appears on-screen when you hover over each of the recommended chart options. Just click on a given chart to add it to your spreadsheet. A Recommended Charts command also appears on the Insert menu of Excel 2013 and later.

Recommended PivotTables

If you've explored Excel much, you've probably heard of PivotTables but, like many users, assume they're an advanced feature beyond your reach. In reality, PivotTables are easy to use as long as your data is in the expected format, which is a list within a spreadsheet that has a title at the top of each column.

For example, in the desktop versions of QuickBooks, an ideal report for using PivotTables is the Transaction Detail by Account. Here's how to run this report:

1. Choose Reports, Accountant & Taxes, and Transaction Detail by Account.

2. When the report appears on-screen, change the Total By drop-down list at the top of the report to Total Only and then export the spreadsheet to Excel.

3. Delete any blank rows from the report. QuickBooks Desktop in particular adds a blank row beneath column headings.

4. Select any cell within your list, and click Recommended PivotTables on the Insert tab to view different summaries of your accounting data.

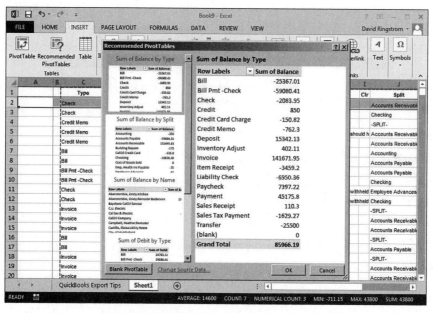

The Recommended PivotTables feature in Excel 2013 and later provides instant summaries of list-based reports.

BOTTOM LINE

You can also use the features we describe throughout this chapter in Excel 2010 and earlier, but the newest versions of Excel offer more enhancements. *The Complete Idiot's Guide to Microsoft Excel 2010 2-in-1* by Richard Rost is a useful reference for anyone using Excel 2007 or 2010. Features such as charts, PivotTables, and conditional formatting can feel intimidating at first, but they're often some of the easiest features to use because Excel performs the number-crunching and presentation for you, often with just a few mouse clicks.

Maintaining Supporting Schedules

In Chapter 14, we discussed how your accounting software won't always be able to store the amount of detail you need to monitor a given account balance. For instance, we talked about prepaid insurance, where you pay for an entire year at once but must move $\frac{1}{12}$ of the amount to an expense account each month.

If you only have one prepayment amount you're *amortizing* in this fashion, your accounting software will have the supporting detail. But if you have two or more prepaid expenses, particularly those that are amortizing over different rates, you'll be hard-pressed to keep track of where the different prepaid balances stand.

In this case, you could create a supporting schedule in a spreadsheet to help you keep track.

	A	B	C	D	E	F	G	H	I
1	Prepayments	Car Insurance	Business Insurance	Ending Balance					
2	Jan 2019			-					
3	Feb 2019			-					
4	Mar 2019	2,500.00		2,500.00					
5	Apr 2019	(500.00)		2,000.00					
6	May 2019	(500.00)	1,250.00	2,750.00					
7	Jun 2019	(500.00)	(250.00)	2,000.00					
8	Jul 2019	(500.00)	(250.00)	1,250.00					
9	Aug 2019	(500.00)	(250.00)	500.00					
10	Sep 2019		(250.00)	250.00					
11	Oct 2019		(250.00)	-					
12	Nov 2019			-					
13	Dec 2019			-					
14									
15									
16									

Sheet1 ⊕

Supporting schedules, such as this one that tracks prepaid expenses, can provide detail your accounting software cannot.

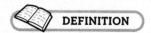 **DEFINITION**

Amortizing (or *amortization*) is the process of decreasing a balance over a period of time. When you amortize a prepaid expense, you reduce the prepaid amount month by month until the prepayment is extinguished. In a similar fashion, you amortize loans such as a car payment or mortgage by paying down a portion of it each month.

The Least You Need to Know

- Before you start creating spreadsheets from scratch, check the Excel template library. Chances are good that what you need is already there.

- Budgeting gives you a map for the year ahead, keeps you focused, and allows you to compare actual performance with the expectations you had when you began the year.

- Using a shadow accounting system provides you with a simple way to maintain a forecast of cash flow so you don't have to wonder whether or not you're going to have the ability to meet future commitments.

- Supporting schedules help you store activity related to account balances that your accounting software can't store.

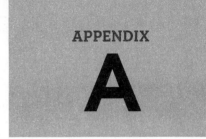

Glossary

absolute reference   An instruction that tells a spreadsheet program not to change the column letter and/or row number when you copy a formula.

account balance   The amount being carried on your books as an asset, liability, equity, revenue, or expense. Account balances that affect your income statement are reset to 0 at the start of each year.

accounting   A system of recording financial transactions that can be thought of as a way of keeping score within your business.

accounting ledger   A traditional paper accounting book with at least four columns: date, description, and two amount columns.

accounting method   The method of revenue and expense recognition for a business.

accounts   An accounting system category that stores the value of things a business owns or owes as well as monies earned or spent.

accrual basis accounting   An accounting method in which a business reports revenue as soon as it's earned and expenses as soon as they're incurred.

accumulated amortization   The amount of an intangible asset such as goodwill or intellectual property that's been expensed. *See also* book value.

accumulated depreciation   The amount of an asset's cost that has been expensed over time. *See also* book value.

adjusting journal entry   A correction process whereby account balances in your books are changed, or adjusted, so they reflect the correct amounts as of a given point in time.

amortization   The process of decreasing a balance over a period of time.

amortization schedule   A calendar that details how each loan payment you make is allocated between principle and interest, as well as reflecting the timetable over which the loan will be repaid and the loan balance at the end of each month during the loan.

Assets   The section of a balance sheet that contains the book balances of accounts that reflect what your business owns, or is owed, as well as physical and intangible items your business owns.

audit   A financial examination of a business's books and records that may be carried out by a governmental agency to test the veracity of a tax return or by a certified public accounting firm to verify the business's financial statement integrity.

Audit Trail report   A feature within most accounting software that records the date, time, username, and details of all new and changed transactions in the books for later review purposes.

automated clearing house (ACH)   An electronic network most banks participate in and use to perform electronic transactions called ACH withdrawals or deposits.

available balance   The amount in a bank account that's available for immediate withdrawal.

balance sheet   A financial statement that reflects what a business owns and is owed, owes to others, and the owners' net equity as of a point in time, typically the end of a month or year.

beginning account balance   Within your General Ledger, the balance for this account as of the end of the previous accounting period. *See also* account balance.

benefits   Compensation given to employees in addition to their agreed upon pay, which may include health insurance, life insurance, paid time off, and other motivational offerings.

book balance   The amount paid for an asset less accumulated depreciation.

book value   A theoretical figure within the financial statements that shows what the owners would get if the company was liquidated or an asset was sold as of the financial statement date. Often an appraisal is required to establish the fair market value of a company or asset. Book value is also the net amount of an asset less any accumulated depreciation or amortization.

books   Accountant's jargon for a set of accounting records.

bootstrap   To use one's own financial resources to start a business instead of borrowing.

business day   In the context of payroll tax deposits and reports, this typically means Monday through Friday, with the exception of state or federal holidays. If a tax deadline falls on a Saturday, Sunday, or holiday, the deadline is extended to the next business day.

business plan   A document that states a businesses' financial (and other) expectations and goals.

business structure   The legal structure or organization for a business. Some entail more complexity and expense to establish than others.

C corporation   A business structure that's taxed separately from its owners. Owners of the corporation are referred to as shareholders, and profits are distributed in the form of dividends that are subject to tax again on personal tax returns as capital gains.

cash basis accounting   An accounting method in which a business only reports revenue when deposited in the bank and expenses that have been paid by cash or check.

cash flow   The net amount of money a business takes in after covering expenses and liabilities.

chart of accounts   A list of all the accounts a business has. It's used for categorizing the money-related aspects of a business.

check transaction   A document (for a transaction) that records a payment made by checking account check.

cleared transaction   A transaction marked to indicate it matches both on the bank statement and in the books. *See also* reconciliation.

cloud-based software   Software housed on remote servers so users can access it online.

collateral   Business or personal assets pledged as security as repayment for a loan.

collected balance   Deposits to an account that have fully cleared the banking system.

compound interest   Interest charged on unpaid interest amounts as well as the principle due. *See also* simple interest.

contra-asset account   An account that offsets a corresponding asset account. Both Accumulated Depreciation and Accumulated Amortization are contra-asset accounts. *See also* book value.

cost of goods sold (COGS)   The accumulated price of inventory items that have been sold to customers. *See also* costing method.

costing method   A technique used in accounting software to determine the amount that should be recorded as an expense when a business sells an inventory item it keeps on hand for sale.

credit card transaction   A transaction that records a sale paid for by credit card or a purchase your business has paid for via credit card.

credits   Amounts recorded in the right amount column for a transaction in an account; depending on the context, may increase or decrease the value of an account.

Current Assets   The section of a balance sheet that represents liquid assets including cash as well as items that can be turned into cash quickly, such as accounts receivable and inventory.

current balance   In the context of a reconciliation, the amount the bank reports as your current cash on hand you should reconcile your books to.

Current Liabilities   The section of a balance sheet that represents amounts a business must pay within the next 12 months. Also referred to as short-term liabilities.

debits   Amounts recorded in the left amount column for a transaction in an account; depending on the context, may increase or decrease the value of an account.

debt service   Relates to repayment of a loan over time. Payments may include interest, principle, or both.

distribution   Profit from a business that's shared with owners above and beyond paychecks. Typically, distributions are not subject to self-employment taxes.

double-entry accounting system   An accounting system that requires that the sum of all debits and the sum of all credits balance within a given transaction.

employee   A person who works for wages or salary. Depending on the business structure, owners might need to be classified as employees.

employer ID number (EIN)   Also referred to as a federal ID number; this unique number identifies an individual tax-paying business, which is required when the business has employees.

ending account balance   Within your General Ledger, the ending balance of an account as of an accounting period. The ending balance is the beginning balance plus or minus any activity for a given period. *See also* account balance; beginning account balance.

Equity   The section of a balance sheet that theoretically reflects what would be distributed to stakeholders of a business should the business close, the assets be liquidated, and all liabilities paid off. *See also* book value; fair market value.

estimate   A document (or a transaction) similar to an invoice that might reference accounts. It provides a potential price for a product or service and doesn't increase or decrease any accounts in the books. Sometimes referred to as a quote; a proposal or bid for a job wherein you set out how much you think work will cost based on particular circumstances.

exempt employee   A salaried worker who isn't eligible for overtime pay; typically managers or directors within a company.

expenses   Costs incurred in operating the business; often referred to as overhead.

fair market value   The amount an unrelated third party would willingly pay to purchase an asset or a business as a whole. *See also* book value.

FICA   Another name for the collective Social Security and Medicare tax withheld from employee paychecks. Often referred to as the FICA tax, this acronym stands for Federal Insurance Contributions Act, the legislation that authorized the tax.

fiduciary   An individual or entity entrusted with a legal or financial responsibility on another's behalf.

formula   A means of performing a calculation in a spreadsheet.

full-time employee   Typically a salaried employee; can also be hourly employees who work 40 hours per week. In certain contexts, part-time workers who work 30 or more hours per week are also considered full-time.

FUTA   Federal Unemployment Tax; a tax all employers must pay on behalf of every employee.

General Ledger   A comprehensive report that records every transaction affecting a company's accounting records.

general partner   Within a partnership, a partner who is fully authorized to make decisions on behalf of other partners. General partners typically oversee the operations of a partnership and bear full liability for its actions.

gross profit   The revenue from a business less the cost of goods sold; also referred to as the gross margin or gross income.

impute   To replace missing values with a sometimes arbitrary replacement value.

income   Total sales from the income statement, less cost of goods sold. *See also* net income.

income statement   A summary of revenues and expenses for a specific time period; also called P & L or Profit and Loss.

independent contractor   A person who provides goods or services to others based on written or verbal agreements. Independent contractors who work for a single entity run the risk of being classified as employees by the Internal Revenue Service, which can result in penalties to the entities paying the independent contractor.

insolvency   When a person or business is unable to pay its financial obligations. A temporary situation during which a business needs more time to raise cash is referred to as technical insolvency. Permanent insolvency is resolved by filing for bankruptcy.

intangible asset   An asset that can't be seen or felt but has value to a business. Examples include patents, trademarks, franchises, and goodwill.

interest   The portion of loan payment that compensates the lender for their risk and the use of their money.

internal control   Procedures and precautions implemented to secure your accounting records, the assets of your business, and any fiduciary responsibilities to your employees and customers.

inventory   Physical goods a business keeps on hand for sale to its customers. In the context of an accounting program, inventory has a broader meaning that includes all products and services offered by a business, which may or may not be physical goods kept on hand.

invoice   A document (for a transaction) that records a sale for which the customer will make payment in the future.

leverage   With regard to finance, the ratio of the company's debt to the value of its equity. The higher the leverage, the more it appears the business is using debt to finance its operations.

Liabilities   The section of a balance sheet that reflects what your business owes to others. When used in singular form, an amount your business owes to others.

limited liability company (LLC)   A business structure that's a hybrid of a partnership and a corporation that can protect the owners' personal assets. The LLC files a tax return each year to report its operations, with income or loss usually passing through to owners, known as members, for reporting on their personal income tax returns. However, LLCs can also elect to file and pay taxes like a C corporation.

limited partner   Within a partnership, a partner who has less or no authority to make decisions on behalf of other partners; sometimes referred to as a silent partner. Limited partners primarily provide investment capital to the partnership without taking an active role and have liability to the extent of their capital contributions.

liquidity   A measurement of the amount of cash on hand, as well as assets that are easily converted to cash. Liquid assets include the balance in a business bank account, near-term accounts receivable, stock and bond investments, certificates of deposit, and in certain cases, inventory.

loan guarantee   A promise to repay a loan should a borrower fail to do so. Guarantees can cover all or a portion of a loan. Sometimes called co-signing. *See also* loan guarantor.

loan guarantor   A person or entity who agrees to repay all or part of a loan should a borrower fail to do so. Often referred to as a co-signer. *See also* loan guarantee.

markup   The difference between a product's selling price and its cost. Also called gross profit.

matching principle   An accounting principle that says a business should strive to match revenues and expenses in the same accounting period when possible.

net income   The profit or loss from a business after all expenses have been accounted for in a given period; often referred to as the bottom line of an income statement.

nonposting transaction   A transaction that doesn't post in the General Ledger. Estimates, sales orders, and purchase orders are nonposting transactions.

North American Industry Classification System (NAICS)   A numbered list of business activities governmental departments can use to track and compare economic activity.

officer   A high-ranking employee authorized to transact business and make decisions on behalf of a company. Officers often, but not always, have an ownership stake in a firm.

partnership   A business structure that's a relationship between two or more individuals. Each person contributes money, assets, or talent to the venture and shares in the income or loss.

payroll tax   A tax owed to federal, state, and local governments that's borne by employees and employers. Employers withhold the employees' share from paychecks and remit and report the collective taxes to the corresponding governmental agencies. *See also* withholding.

principle   The portion of a loan payment that reduces the remaining balance of a loan.

prior year adjustment   A journal entry to correct an error, such as an error in depreciation recorded, from the prior accounting year.

reconciliation   A process that ensures your books agree with what your bank or financial institution shows as your current balance.

remit   To send money, usually payroll tax money, to the appropriate governmental agency.

restore   To replace accounting data from a backup, typically to recover from an error of some sort or computer failure.

Retained Earnings   The section of a balance sheet that reflects the accumulated net income a business has generated from inception to date, less any dividends or distributions that have been paid out to owners or shareholders.

retirement plan   A plan that helps an individual save for retirement years after employment. Retirement plans can be a formal benefit offered by an employer, or individuals can establish their own independent retirement accounts.

risk management   A discipline that focuses on identifying risks and mitigating their potential impact on an organization.

S corporation   One of the simplest business structures for an incorporated business; it protects the owners from legal liability relating to the business and offers them tax benefits. S corporations pay no income tax; income or loss is reported on the owners' personal income tax returns.

sales order   Similar to an estimate, a sales order represents a confirmed customer purchase your business will eventually deliver.

sales receipt   A document that records a sale a customer has paid for on the spot.

short term   From an accounting perspective, refers to 12 months or fewer.

shrinkage   Events that reduce inventory for sale, such as breakage, theft, and so on.

simple interest   Interest charged only on the original amount due. *See also* compound interest.

social engineering   Takes many forms, but commonly hackers or others intent on ill will toward your company pose as someone reputable to gather passwords or information they can use to determine passwords or access to protected spaces or data.

sole proprietorship   A business structure in which the owner is the business and is personally and legally liable for every obligation of the business and for any damage caused by the business. The business can have employees, but the owner doesn't have partners or co-owners.

statement of cash flows   A financial statement that reports cash inflows and outflows for a month or year by type.

succession planning   The process of grooming existing employees for future promotions to leadership and other key positions, as well as using insurance and other tools to minimize the financial ramifications of an unexpected change in succession.

supporting schedule   A report that provides supporting detail to amounts reflected on a company's financial statements.

SUTA   State Unemployment Tax; all employers must pay this tax on behalf of every employee in all 50 states.

T account   A device you can use for visualizing how to record an accounting transaction, with debits on the left and credits on the right.

tax ID number   A business's EIN, or an owner's Social Security Number for a sole proprietorship. *See also* employer ID number (EIN).

tax year   The period of time that represents a company's annual accounting period. It's most often the calendar year, but businesses can request an alternate tax year.

tax-exempt organization   Often referred to as a nonprofit; a business structure in which the money a business earns generally isn't subject to income tax. The most common form is 501(c)(3), but the IRS can approve many other specialized types.

transaction   An entry in an accounting system or books reflecting financial activity.

Trial Balance report   A report that provides a concise listing of every account balance on your books as of a given point in time.

usury   Interest rates that are generally exorbitant or excessive.

withholding   A mechanism by which employers may have to set aside a prescribed amount of each employee's check for federal income tax withholding. *See also* payroll tax.

withholding allowance   A withholding option that gives an employee a measure of control over the amount of state and federal income taxes withheld from each paycheck.

workers' compensation   A form of insurance that provides a safety net for workers who are injured on the job.

Key Business Forms

Throughout the book, we've discussed a number of forms you need to get your business started. These are the most common forms business owners use. They might not all apply to you, but here are some easy resources for finding what forms you do need.

IRS tax resources for small businesses are available via its Small Business and Self-Employed Tax Center, irs.gov/businesses/small. You can access many of the forms and full instructions at irs.gov/Businesses/Small-Businesses-&-Self-Employed/Forms-and-Instructions-Filing-and-Paying-Business-Taxes or search for forms and publications at apps.irs.gov/app/picklist/list/formsPublications.html.

The forms listed here are federal forms. Your state, city, county, or even township has more paperwork for you to complete. Contact your state and local government revenue departments for information about running your business within your state and local jurisdiction. Here are some of the forms you should be on the lookout for:

- Business license application (for new businesses)
- Business license renewal
- Annual franchise tax form
- Corporation registration form
- Annual corporation renewal form
- State and local income tax withholding remittances
- State and local income tax withholding returns (monthly, quarterly, and annually)
- State unemployment forms

Form or Publication Number	Description
I-9	Employment Eligibility Verification
SS-4	Application for Employer Identification Number
W-2	Wage and Tax Statement
W-2C	Corrected Wage and Tax Statement
W-3	Transmittal of Wage and Tax Statements
W-3C	Transmittal of Corrected Wage and Tax Statements
W-4	Employee's Withholding Allowance Certificate
940	Employer's Annual Federal Unemployment (FUTA) Tax Return
941	Employer's Quarterly Federal Tax Return
1040-ES	Estimated Tax Worksheet and Estimated Tax Payment Vouchers
1065	U.S. Return of Partnership Income
1065 (Schedule K-1)	Partner's Share of Income, Deductions, Credits, etc.
1099-MISC	Miscellaneous Income
1120	U.S. Corporation Income Tax Return
1244	Employee's Daily Record of Tips and Report to Employer (includes Form 4070: Employee's Report of Tips to Employer and Form 4070A: Employee's Daily Record of Tips)
5500	Annual Return/Report of Employee Benefit Plan
8027	Employer's Annual Information Return of Tip Income and Allocated Tips

Index

C

income tax withholdings
  federal, 150-151
  local, 151
  Medicare, 152-153
  Social Security, 151-152
  state, 151
independent contractors versus
  employees, 116-118
inland marine insurance, 133
insolvency, 26
insurance
  benefit tax deductions, 135-136
  health, 133
  liability, 128-132
  life, 134-135
  property, 132-133
  recording costs and reimburse-
    ments, 136-137
  temporary disability insurance
    tax, 156
intangible assets, 48
interest
  compound, 165
  simple, 165
  usury interest rates, 165
internal control security precautions
  antivirus software, 188
  backing up records, 189-193
  destroying records, 195
  disaster recovery plans, 196
  fraud protection, 193-194
  identity theft management, 193
  password protection, 188
Internal Revenue Service. *See* IRS
interruption insurance (business),
  132-133
inventory
  COGS (cost of goods sold), 65
  costing methods, 64
  inventory turnover financial
    ratios, 207-208
  Inventory Valuation reports,
    70, 216
  item types and setup, 59-63

month-end closing tasks,
  215-216
recording purchases, 85
reporting, 70-72
reviewing balance sheets, 183
shrinkage, 59
tracking and valuing, 58
valuation methods, 63-67
Investing Activities section (cash
  flow statements), 178-179
invoices
  progress billing, 82
  recording sales transactions,
    77-78
  transaction examples, 14
IRS (Internal Revenue Service),
  financial statement reviews, 198
Items Sold to Customers report,
  71
item types (inventory), 59-63

J-K

journal entries (general ledgers)
  adjustments, 92-96
  finding misplaced transac-
    tions, 97-98
  noncash transactions, 98-99
  nonposting transactions, 99
  one-sided journal entry, 95
  prior year adjustments, 97
  recording transactions, 12
  when not to use, 100

Keogh retirement plans, 141

L

labor laws, 120-121
last in, first out inventory
  valuation method. *See* LIFO
  inventory valuation method

lenders, financial statement
  reviews
  cash flow concerns, 200
  collateral, 199-200
  consistency, 199
  depreciated assets, 201
  discretionary expenses,
    201-202
  financial ratios, 201
  risk management concerns,
    200-201
leverage, 204
liabilities, 4-7
  accounts, 48-50
  balance sheets, 174
    current, 176, 184-185
    long-term, 176, 185
  payroll, monthly closing, 217
liability insurance
  automobile, 131
  cyber risk, 131
  D&O coverage, 130
  general, 130
  personal umbrella policies,
    131-132
  product liability, 130
  professional, 130
  workers' compensation, 128
LibreOffice, 258
licenses
  business license tax, 232
  businesses, 27
  zoning, 27
life insurance, 134-135
LIFO (last in, first out) inventory
  valuation method, 66
limited liability companies. *See*
  LLCs
lingering balances, correcting,
  220
liquidity, 200
LLCs (limited liability companies)
  business structures, 21-22
  filing taxes, 238

Keogh plans, 141
remitting contributions, 142
SEP, 141
SIMPLE IRAs, 140
vested, 140
Revel Systems POS software, 43
revenue accounts, 51
risk management, 200-201

S

S corporations
business structures, 21
filing taxes, 237
Sage 50, 37-39
salaried employees, labor laws,
121
sales
orders, 16, 81
POS (point of sale) software,
42-43
receipts, 15
recording transactions, 74-78
Sales by Item report, 71
Sales Tax Payable account, 49
tax, 230-231
Savings Incentive Match Plan
for Employees Individual
Retirement Account. *See*
SIMPLE IRAs
Schedule C, 238
Schedule K-1, 242
security concerns, 188-196
SEP (Simple Employee Pension),
141
service items (inventory), 62
shadow accounting systems,
277-278
shrinkage, inventory, 59
sick leave, employee benefits, 147
Simple Employee Pension. *See*
SEP
simple interest, 165

SIMPLE (Savings Incentive
Match Plan for Employees)
IRAs (Individual Retirement
Account), 140
Simple Start, QuickBooks
Online, 39
social engineering, 192
Social Security taxes, 151-152
software
antivirus, 188
changing, 43-44
cloud-based, 32-42
backing up data, 192-193
FreshBooks, 41-42
QuickBooks Online, 39-40
Xero, 41
desktop, 32-34
backing up data, 190-191
QuickBooks Enterprise,
36-37
QuickBooks Premier, 36
QuickBooks Pro, 35
Quicken, 34-35
Sage 50, 37-39
month-end closing tasks,
212-214
payroll processing, 123-125
POS (point of sale), 42-43
spreadsheets. *See* spreadsheets
updating, 189
user help, 44
sole proprietorships
business structures, 19
filing taxes, 236-237
special-use items (inventory), 63
specific identification inventory
valuation method, 66-67
spreadsheets, 259-261
amortization table formulas,
266-268
analyzing data, 279-283
basic cell entries, 261-263
budgets, 273-277
entering formulas, 263-264

freezing rows, 268-269
Gnumeric Portable, 259
Google Sheets, 258
inserting functions, 264-266
LibreOffice, 258
Microsoft Excel, 258
Numbers, 258
printing, 270
shadow accounting systems,
277-279
supporting schedules, 283-284
templates, 272-273
stakeholders, employee records
management, 250-251
startup capital, 24
statements
Customer Statements, 162-164
financial statements. *See*
financial statements
state requirements
employee records, 250
hiring employees, 119
state taxes
filing, 241
income tax withholdings, 151
liability accounts, 49
paying, 227
personal income tax returns,
244
reporting, 229-230
State Unemployment Tax Act.
See SUTA
stock items (inventory), 59
structure types (businesses)
C corporations, 22, 23
comparisons, 18
LLCs (limited liability
companies), 21-22
partnerships, 20
S corporations, 21
sole proprietorship, 19
tax-exempt organizations,
23-24
succession planning, 135